ADVANCE PRAISE FOR

THE MISSIONARY

"*The Missionary* is a revelation—a perspective on our culture that no one knew we needed; that of the brave gleaming door-knockers trying to save us from ourselves. And Elder Hudson is the perfect dichotomous guide: a super-smart, very funny kid who's been taught how to think, trained how to act, and yet somehow finds a way to narrate his mission with brilliant, blazing honesty. And then—in ultimately failing as a Mormon, and telling his true story, Hudson succeeds at so much more: he becomes a great writer—one who renders a path towards our very best selves."

SHAUGHNESSY BISHOP-STALL,
bestselling author of *Hungover*

"As a fellow former youth evangelist, I felt *The Missionary* in my bones. Many of us are expected to embody spiritual perfection while being guided by leaders more invested in appearances than in our well-being. It's no wonder Greg Hudson turned to comic-book heroes for a better model of world-building. With wit, clarity, and tenderness, he reconstructs that search in this beautiful memoir. Readers of all stripes will recognize themselves in Hudson's story, in the tongue-in-cheek way he navigates life's many paradoxes. Hands down, he's one of the funniest voices in the religious coming-of-age genre."

DANIEL ALLEN COX, author of
I Felt the End Before It Came

"As a reader of a determinedly irreligious bent, I admit to hesitating before opening *The Missionary*, which I knew to be written by a door-knocking disciple of Joseph Smith. But as the chapters flew past, as I delighted at the candor, warmth, humor, and humility of Greg Hudson's recollections, I came to the final page feeling terribly glad to have read something so outside my comfort zone."

CRAIG DAVIDSON, bestselling author of *Cataract City* and *Precious Cargo*

"When I picked up this book I worried it might be just another one of those standard hilarious but poignant Mormon coming of age memoirs. Okay, that's not what I thought at all. Instead, I discovered that this is among the most uncommon, unusual, and unrestrained memoirs I've ever read. And I could not stop turning the pages. Hudson transported me to a different yet somehow familiar world where his honest, powerful, and conflicted story made me laugh and think, again and again, often at the same time. Greg Hudson is a rare and true storyteller."

TERRY FALLIS, two-time winner of the Stephen Leacock Medal for Humour

"I'll admit books about Mormons aren't usually the first I reach for. But a Mormon in Canada? Now you've got my attention. Greg Hudson's *The Missionary* is so hilarious, sad, and beautiful that I almost wished I had gone door-to-door with him."

DAVE HILL, comedian, musician and author of *Parking the Moose*

"If you have ever thought of superheroes, souls, or sex . . . this book is for you."

JON SCIESZKA, bestselling author and inaugural US National Ambassador for Young People's Literature

"Reminiscent of the writings of Tobias Wolf, this coming-of-age memoir within the Mormon church, with its particular teachings and endless rules, showcases Hudson's fine storytelling and impeccable timing for comedy. Readers will be moved by minimalistic prose that is both lyrical and precise, in addition to memorable characterizations that delight, entertain, and evoke authentic feeling. The true test of a successful memoir is whether it reads and turns pages like a novel. In *The Missionary*, Greg Hudson delivers a beguiling personal account, crafting a poignant history of his faith, the irreconcilable tensions from his religious upbringing, and finally, a stirring delivery of his own metamorphosis and spiritual reckoning. Hudson has masterfully captured the candid joys and frustrations imposed by guilt, shame, adolescence, memory, sin, and morality. An extraordinary and witty debut."

LINDSAY WONG, bestselling author of
The Woo-Woo and *Villain Hitting*
for Vicious Little Nobodies

THE MISSIONARY

THE MISSIONARY

A MEMOIR OF SUPERHEROES, SIN & SAVING SOULS FOR THE MORMON CHURCH

GREG HUDSON

VIKING

VIKING
an imprint of Penguin Canada, a division of Penguin Random House Canada Limited

Canada • USA • UK • Ireland • Australia • New Zealand • India • South Africa • China

First published 2026

Viking, an imprint of Penguin Canada
A division of Penguin Random House Canada
320 Front Street West, Suite 1400
Toronto, Ontario, M5V 3B6, Canada
penguinrandomhouse.ca

The authorized representative in the EU for product safety and compliance is Penguin Random House Ireland, Morrison Chambers, 32 Nassau Street, Dublin D02 YH68, Ireland, https://eu-contact.penguin.ie

Library and Archives Canada Cataloguing in Publication

Title: The missionary : superheroes, sin, and saving souls for the Mormon Church / Greg Hudson.
Names: Hudson, Greg (Journalist), author.
Identifiers: Canadiana (print) 20250331438 | Canadiana (ebook) 20250332841 | ISBN 9780735245266 (softcover) | ISBN 9780735245273 (EPUB)
Subjects: LCSH: Hudson, Greg (Journalist)—Childhood and youth. | LCSH: Latter Day Saint missionaries—Canada—Biography. | LCSH: Church of Jesus Christ of Latter-day Saints—Missions—Ontario. | LCGFT: Autobiographies.
Classification: LCC BX8695.H83 A3 2026 | DDC 289.3092—dc23

Book design by Kate Sinclair
Typeset by Daniella Zanchetta and Six Red Marbles
Cover design by Kate Sinclair
Cover images: (door) © hwanchul, (mail slot) © dpproductions / Getty

Printed in Canada

10 9 8 7 6 5 4 3 2 1

Penguin
Random House
VIKING CANADA

Of all these words, these are my favourite:

for Hannah

INTRODUCTION

THE FIRST DOOR I knocked on belonged to a witch, not that I could exactly tell that by looking at her. Witches can be pretty sneaky that way.

I had landed in Toronto the day before, on October 30, 2002, and been paired with my first companion, Elder McDaniels. The next day, we drove three hours south to Sarnia, in Southwestern Ontario, to have dinner with a woman from the congregation, which is called a ward in Mormon parlance. She lived in a community of townhouses where everyone's front lawn also served as a parking lot. It was dark by the time we had finished dinner and given our little devotional as payment. Elder McDaniels shared a spiritual thought based on some scriptures about faith from the Book of Mormon. I had nodded along, excited to be there.

There had been two kids hanging out near our Chevrolet Cavalier, which was the only car missionaries in the Canada Toronto West Mission drove. It was the only car missionaries back home in Alberta drove, too. Apparently, Chevrolet gave the Church a good deal. I had chatted the kids up. I guessed they were about twelve years old. I tried to impress them with my knowledge of Eminem lyrics. Growing up, I had thought Mormon missionaries were so cool. They were like superheroes, complete with secret identities we weren't supposed to know. To help them stay focused on their missions, missionaries never went by their first names. Naturally, as a kid, whenever the missionaries would visit my family, I tried my darnedest to find out what they were: by stealing their scriptures, or taking their wallets, anything that bore their first names. We only called them Elder, like that was their rank in Heavenly Father's army.

The kids I rapped with weren't Mormon, but I wanted them to think missionaries were cool, too.

I hadn't rapped anything inappropriate to them—the verse I dropped only had one or two bad words I had to skip—but after I had finished performing and was sitting in the car's passenger seat, Elder McDaniels gently reminded me to have quiet dignity.

"It was good that you talked with them, Elder," he said. "Just remember who you are, and whose name is on your chest."

"Elder Hudson" was printed on the badge on my chest. This was the name by which I would be known for the next two years. My first name would be waiting for me back home in Calgary. On my mission I would be known exclusively as Elder Hudson. But that wasn't the name Elder McDaniels was talking about. Below "Elder Hudson" was the name of the church we represented: the Church of Jesus Christ of Latter-day Saints.

The small missionary handbook we kept with us at all times, nestled in our breast pocket behind our name tag, reminded us of our purpose: "As an ambassador of the Lord Jesus Christ, learn and obey all mission rules and strive to represent the Savior properly. Keep your thoughts, words, and actions in harmony with the message of the gospel . . . Conducting yourself with quiet dignity will open doors for teaching the gospel."

I worried I'd have a problem with quiet dignity. Carrying myself like a monk didn't come naturally. Nor was it the way I was raised. But it was one of my goals to cultivate it over the next two years.

The next day was my first full day as a missionary.

We were tracting near a relatively busy street. That is to say, we were knocking on doors, hoping to find someone who would let us in, hear our message, and ultimately join the Mormon Church. So far Elder McDaniels had generously done all of the talking. But I knew it would soon be my turn to stand at a door and knock.

Further down the street, I saw two boys walking toward us. They looked to be about ten years old. I wondered if Elder McDaniels would want to stop and talk to them, too. Not so much to teach them, but to introduce them to the Mormon brand and give them a good impression of missionaries so that one day, when they were older, maybe they'd let a couple of Mormons into their home to hear what they had to say. But I knew that if we did stop the approaching kids, I wouldn't bust out any more Slim Shady, or any raps for that matter.

"Go ahead, Elder, next door is yours," Elder McDaniels said. He stepped aside so that I could walk first up the short path to the front door. My first door. It might have been a lack of faith on my part, but I wasn't expecting to be let in. Not that it would be a problem if we were. I was prepared, since I had memorized the first discussion a couple of weeks prior, in the Missionary Training Center in Provo, Utah. The first discussion was the introductory lesson we taught the first time we met with someone. It quickly covered our belief in God and Jesus, then introduced Joseph Smith and the Book of Mormon, along with the possibility that ours was the only true church on earth. At the end of the lesson, we'd leave them with a Book of Mormon and commit them to read and pray about it. There were six discussions in total that we had to teach people before they could be baptized.

If we were let in the house, I assumed Elder McDaniels would take the lead. Still, it was comforting to know I wouldn't be entirely useless if the opportunity to teach a lesson presented itself. This was the one upside of going to an English-speaking mission. My sister, Gillian, who was sent to Russia on her mission a few years before I went on mine, wouldn't have been able to do much more than smile on her first day in the field.

Actually, I felt like I had been preparing for this moment for a very long time. I had been waiting to go on a mission my entire life, and was well-equipped for this part of it specifically. Before I was shipped to Ontario I worked for a summer at a restaurant. I had become a natural at approaching strangers and getting them to like me. Granted, the circumstances were a little different: the restaurantgoers were typically happy to see me since I was their means of obtaining food. But if the people of Sarnia understood the importance of our message, they'd be happy to see me now, too. Eternal salvation was infinitely more satisfying than chicken wings.

I knocked on the door. It was black, with an autumnal wreath encircling the peephole. A woman opened it. She was tall and blonde and her smile didn't fade when she saw that two Mormon missionaries were standing on her porch. I put on my best boyish grin, which seemed to put people at ease.

"Hi, I'm Greg Hudson," I said, out of habit. I would make a very bad spy. "I mean, er, I'm Elder Hudson. And this is my friend, Elder McDaniels. We're in your neighbourhood to share a message about Jesus Christ and His Church. Would you have a few moments to talk?"

"I'm Wiccan," she said, as if that would deter us. I knew that Wiccan was another name for being a witch. Wiccans had come to my world religion class in high school. They were as harmless as old hippies. But if she thought being a Wiccan would dissuade us from trying to share the gospel with her, she was mistaken. One's religion wasn't unchangeable. That's why we were there.

"That's okay. We're Mormon," I said. "Would you have a few minutes to hear a true message about Jesus Christ?"

She politely declined and shut the door softly.

"She turned me into a newt," Elder McDaniels whispered to me in a British accent as we walked back to the sidewalk. "I got better . . ."

It hadn't taken long for Elder McDaniels and me to realize we shared a lot of the same film references. I recognized he was quoting *Monty Python and the Holy Grail.* I contributed a few lines from the same scene and we chuckled. Quoting movies wouldn't exactly help our spiritual work progress—it wouldn't help us teach with the Spirit. But I could forgive a little lack of focus every now and then. It's not like we would go out and rent the movie or anything. That would be against the rules. As missionaries, we could only watch, read, or listen to things put out by the Church.

By the time we got back to the sidewalk, the two kids I had seen earlier were past us, up the street. They had missed their opportunity to speak with two of the Lord's missionaries. Poor them. From a distance, they made some noise as if they were going to shout something at us. I'd soon learn that people loved shouting things at us, mostly from passing cars. Usually it was some variation of "Satan Rules!" I assumed this was meant to shock and offend us.

Elder McDaniels and I looked back at them. Once the two boys saw we were looking, they faced each other, screamed like the kid from *Home Alone*, and ran off as if they had just seen a pair of g-g-g-ghosts. Their timing was perfect.

"Do you think they rehearsed that?" I asked.

"You have to admire the planning," Elder McDaniels said as they kept running, getting smaller and smaller.

So little kids made fun of us, and witches possibly cursed us. Mostly, that day and nearly every day after for two years, we had doors slammed in our faces. It was a small price to pay to serve the Lord and His Church.

I owe my existence to the Church of Jesus Christ of Latter-day Saints.

I suppose anyone whose parents met at college could say the same thing about Mom and Dad's alma mater. But I'm talking about something deeper than that.

I come from pioneer stock, as it's called. My Mormon roots go back to the mid-1800s, the very early days of the Church of Jesus Christ of Latter-day Saints. Benjamin Franklin Johnson, my great-great-great grandfather on my mother's side, was personal friends with Joseph Smith, the founder of the Church. According to *My Life's Review*, Johnson's autobiography, because of his faithfulness to Smith, the Prophet blessed him such that the hairs on his head would never turn grey. And as family folklore goes, they didn't. That blessing dribbled down through the generations, too, leaving a line of people without much salt in their pepper.

Like a lot of men in the early Mormon Church, Benjamin Franklin Johnson was a polygamist. As such, he has a lot of descendants. Had he married just one wife, I think the odds of me being born would have dropped dramatically.

My dad's side of the family goes back more than a century in the Church too. My great-great-great-grandfather George Coleman came to Canada from England in 1836. He bounced around the Northeast, settling in New York, where he was baptized. He wasn't personal friends with the Prophet, but he marched in the Mormon Battalion, "the only religious unit in United States military history in federal service, recruited solely from one religious body and having a religious title as the unit designation," which isn't nearly as cool.

Fast-forward a few generations and you get to Andy and Esther, my parents. They met through the Church in the early 1970s, when they were university students in Calgary. They courted at Church activities, of which there were many. Dances, firesides, potluck dinners, and classes at the Institute of Religion, a chapel-like building just off campus where Mormon university students took extracurricular classes. My dad asked my mom to marry him after just eleven dates. They both felt that Heavenly Father had answered their prayers. They got married in Cardston, Alberta—a small Mormon town near the Montana border—when my mom was nearly twenty and my dad was twenty-four. They moved to Kingston, Ontario, to attend Queen's University, and had my oldest sister, Erin, while my dad was still in law school. After graduating, they moved back to Calgary, where they had Gillian and my brother Sam. My sister Mary and I were born in Edmonton, after my family moved there for my dad's work.

My parents' lives, and our lives, revolved around the Church. Participation in the Church, including three-hour services on Sunday, weekly youth activities, service projects, home visits, and various meetings, was always a given. It was non-negotiable, except we never tried to negotiate out of anything. We never wanted to.

My family wasn't just Mormon. We were very good at being Mormon.

I read my scriptures every night before bed. I memorized the Scripture Mastery verses I was supposed to memorize. I answered the teachers' questions in Sunday School and participated in class. I never swore. Obviously I didn't drink alcohol, coffee, or tea, since they were specifically verboten by the Church, thanks to a revelation given to Joseph Smith.* But I also avoided caffeinated soft drinks, even though they weren't officially against Church rules. Were they not basically carbonated coffee? I listened to and obeyed my parents. In high school, I went to seminary before school started every morning, and

* The revelations given to Joseph Smith are collected in a book called the Doctrine and Covenants. For the curious, the dietary strictures, known collectively as the Word of Wisdom, are found in section 89 of Doctrine and Covenants.

LDS Young Men's activities at least once a week. And I'd always help put away chairs when Church activities were over. When I made money, either through allowance or a part-time job busing tables, I paid a full tithe: ten percent of my gross income went to the Church, even though technically my allowance had already been tithed. But tithing wasn't about money so much as it was about faith. I said my prayers, morning and night. I did my best to stand as a witness of God at all times and in all things and in all places. I wasn't perfect, of course. The Church of Jesus Christ of Latter-day Saints is a high-demand religion, and we were brought up to meet that demand. There was not an aspect of our lives that was untouched by the Church.

In this, we were not unique. From what I gather, mine was a fairly typical Mormon upbringing. My family was devout but we were far from fundamentalists. I had a normal childhood, I think. But my family was Mormon. And we cared deeply about the Church.

Naturally, I still had other interests. Other obsessions. My family called them my jags. When I was three years old, I cared only for cowboys. Then, thanks to the Tim Burton movie, when I was six, I got on my Batman jag. Later, comic books more generally took over my attention. Batman, yes, but also Steel,* Green Lantern, Superman. I quit comics cold turkey when I hit thirteen. In high school, I started on my Robbie Williams jag. I rode that one until my twenties. My parents supported my pop culture obsessions, or kept up with them at least. My jags came and went, but my devotion to my religion, my yearning to be righteous and obedient, was constant.

---

* Steel was like a Black Iron Man, who wore a red cape and an S on his chest in homage to Superman.

But I'm getting ahead of myself, talking about the Church as if it were familiar to everyone. What's the Church of Jesus Christ of Latter-day Saints all about?

The story of the Mormon Church started when Joseph Smith was fourteen. He was confused by the many religions all claiming to be correct while disagreeing with each other. This was happening in Upstate New York, at a time when that area was experiencing a boom in religious fervour. There was no shortage of churches, preachers, and prophets to listen to. Surely, young Joseph thought, one religion must be the correct one.

Joseph turned to the Bible. He found a verse in the book of James in the New Testament. "If any of you lack wisdom, let him ask of God, who giveth to all men liberally, and upbraideth not, and it shall be given him."* Inspired, Joseph decided he'd put that scripture to the test. He would ask God which church was right. After all, if anyone would know, it would be the Big Guy.

Joseph retired to the woods near his home. The simple farm boy knelt down and prayed. What happened next was miraculous. God the Father and Jesus Christ appeared to him (as two separate and distinct beings) in a pillar of light. God introduced his Son, and then let Jesus do the talking. Once the mortal got his bearings, Joseph asked the Saviour his question. Jesus told Joseph that actually there wasn't any church or religion on the earth at that time that was right. They were all wrong. But fear not: young Joseph was told that when he was older, he would restore Christ's legitimate church to the earth.

Some time later, when Joseph was around seventeen, he received an angelic visitor in his bedroom who told him about

* James 1:5.

an ancient history etched into gold plates that happened to be buried nearby. When he was old enough—I want to say twenty-one? Twenty-two?—the angel, whose name was Moroni (*More-own-eye*), led him to where the metal tome was buried. Per the angel's instruction, Joseph wouldn't let anyone else see these gold plates, not even his wife, Emma.* But with a friend, a schoolteacher named Oliver Cowdery, working as a scribe, Joseph began translating the mysterious etchings on the plates. He would sit behind a curtain and dictate to Cowdery, who wrote down what Smith said.

What Joseph ultimately translated was the Book of Mormon. It was the history of the people who lived in America in ancient times. The record was edited and compiled by a man named Mormon (hence the name) around AD 400. It told the story of an Israelite family leaving Jerusalem around 600 BC and sailing across the ocean to the promised land (America). There, the family split into two tribes, the righteous Nephites (*Knee-fights*) and the wicked Lamanites (*Lay-men-ites*), who were cursed to have dark skin because of their wickedness. The Book of Mormon is concerned mainly with the Nephites. When they are righteous, they prosper. But when they are wicked, they are punished, usually via a war with the Lamanites. The climax of the Book of Mormon is when Jesus Christ, fresh from his residency in the Holy Land, comes to visit the Nephites and Lamanites in America. While he was there, he played the hits, which is why you'll find a lot of Matthew quoted in that section of the Book of Mormon.

* He would later allow three men to hold the gold plates and sign an affidavit stating that they had done so. He also let eight other witnesses see the plates under a cloth.

But it's all downhill for the Nephites after that. By the end of the book, the Nephites have fallen into decadence and corruption. As punishment, they are completely wiped out by the Lamanites in one last giant battle. According to the Book of Mormon, the surviving Lamanites go on to be the primary ancestors of Indigenous people in North America. That's how they got there!

Naturally there's a lot of doctrine in the Book of Mormon, too, but narratively speaking that's the gist.

What the Church doesn't brag about—though it really should—is how singular the Book of Mormon truly is. By that I don't mean it takes the Book of Mormon for granted. No, it's "the most correct of any book on earth, and the keystone of [the Mormon] religion." Mormons stake their entire faith on it. If the Book of Mormon isn't true, then Joseph Smith wasn't a prophet, and if Joseph Smith wasn't a prophet, why the heck aren't we drinking some cappuccinos? No, they know their book is special.

But they don't talk about how unique it is. For instance, it represents the only known time in history a people used metal plates as paper. It's the only record of Christ coming to America, which, considering he came down glowing from the sky, you'd think more people might have noticed and written about. A fresco or something. And it's the only historical document that shows horses and chariots and steel all existed in the Americas before Columbus. It's truly one of a kind.

What the Mormon Church is, then, is a reboot of the church Christ started in the Bible. The structure of the Church is similar to the one alluded to in the Bible, with twelve apostles at the top. But any church can cop an org chart. The real difference between the Church of Jesus Christ of Latter-day Saints and every other religion is that, along with the divine organization of the Church, Joseph Smith also restored the priesthood. The priesthood is the power and permission to act in God's name. No other church has that. Your rabbi, imam, minister, priest, or guru might think they have the authority to speak or act in God's name, but they don't. Think of them like spiritual vigilantes, whereas the Mormon Church has God's badge. Some churches might say authority comes from the Bible, or from faith, or schooling. Nope. It doesn't. Authority comes from God's priesthood, which He shares with worthy Latter-day Saint men on earth. And only men.

What does that mean? That means no other church has the authority to baptize someone, say. Obviously, other churches perform baptisms, but unbeknownst to them, they don't count. They might as well be taking a bath, or a very small shower.

It's through the priesthood—I, and many other young men, liked to think of it kind of like the Force in *Star Wars*—that the Church of Jesus Christ of Latter-day Saints has the power to bind families together, forever. Whereas a regular marriage ends at death—"till death do us part" is the famous phrase—when two worthy Mormons get married in a Mormon temple they are *sealed* together for time and all eternity. That's the phrase the Church uses. Sealed for time and all eternity. That is a long time.

Classic Mormon joke: a recently married young man is giving a talk (or a sermon) in his church one Sunday. "My wife and I have only been married for a month," he says by way of introduction, "but already I understand what time and all eternity feels like."

And just as Joseph Smith was a prophet, the Mormon Church is led by a prophet today, who is also known as the President of the Church. He leads the Church, with two counselors, and Twelve Apostles. The leaders of the Church, called

General Authorities, look like old businessmen. The vast majority of them are as white as Utah snow.

The prophet today doesn't get paid for his work.[*] This is because the Church of Jesus Christ of Latter-day Saints has a lay clergy. Everything is done by the members, who are each given "callings," for free. Callings are basically part-time jobs. For instance, a man might be called to be a bishop, which is like a pastor. That man would keep his day job, but most of his spare time would be devoted to his congregation, his ward. And, like jobs, some callings are more prestigious than others. That being said, callings aren't something one is supposed to aspire to. That would be to assume one is worthy of the important calling, and that would be prideful or, worse, power-hungry.

That should be enough history to feel a little grounded. Now when someone like myself talks about Mormonism, you'll know a little of what they are talking about.

Don't worry. I'm not going to try to convert you.

Before we begin you should know how it all began.

Before I was born, before you were born, we lived with Heavenly Father[**] as spirits, shadows of our future selves.

---

* Since Joseph Smith, who was given the job personally by God, all following presidents/prophets of the Church are chosen in a very orderly fashion. Namely, after the current president dies, the most senior apostle becomes the new president. No need for voting or politicking. It's the very definition of hierarchical.

** The preferred term for God among Mormons. So much so that when I was a child, I thought it was blasphemous to call Him anything else, including God.

That's Mormon doctrine, but it's alluded to in the Bible. All the way back in the Old Testament, the Lord told Jeremiah, "Before I formed you in the belly, I knew you. Before thou cameth forth out of the womb, I sanctified thee and ordained you a prophet unto the nations."

Now, would it make sense if Jeremiah, who did his prophesying between 626 and 586 BC, were the only person God knew before birth?

It would not.

It's fair then to assume that my story (and your story, and everyone else's) didn't start when we were born. That's because we lived as spirits with our Heavenly Father in a place that we unromantically call our premortal life. We were essentially ghosts. We had spirit bodies that looked how we look now.

Heavenly Father has revealed only a little about our premortal life. We don't know how our premortal selves organized their society or how they spent their time, or if time existed at all before the universe was created. But we do know about the event that had the greatest effect on our current existence: the War in Heaven. It's referred to in the Bible—in Revelations 12 and Isaiah 14, for example—so a lot of religions know *something* went down in heaven before life on earth began. But thanks to Joseph Smith, Mormons know a few more details.

What happened was this:

God brought his spirit children together and told us of His great plan: we would all go to earth—which either had just been formed or was about to be—to get physical bodies. Those bodies would be necessary for us to be tested on earth, to see whether we would recognize and follow Father's commandments. It wouldn't be an easy test—we wouldn't remember our prebirth existence and so we'd be starting from scratch.

We would need faith. Believing without seeing and acting on that belief would be the only way that we would gain the experience necessary to, one day, become like our Father in Heaven. Which is to say, perfect. And what child doesn't want to grow up to be like their parents?

According to Heavenly Father's plan, it is the purpose of life to be tested, so that we can one day, if we live by all of His commandments, be gods like our Heavenly Father is God. It's not something that's discussed all that openly, but that's the end goal of our existence: to graduate humanity and become gods.

That's how our Heavenly Father became our Heavenly Father, after all.

This plan was presented to us all by our oldest spirit brother and Heavenly Father's most beloved son, Jesus—then known as Jehovah. He would eventually go down to earth and provide both a flawless example for us to follow and a means for us to be forgiven for the times we broke Heavenly Father's rules.

But at this massive general conference of spirits in the premortal world, another one of our older brothers, Satan, got up and presented a slightly different plan.

The contours of Satan's plan were the same: we'd go to earth and get bodies, but instead of our being tested, Satan would withhold free will. We'd do as we were commanded because we'd have no other choice. In this way, Satan could guarantee that every one of us would return home to Heavenly Father. And the bonus? There would be no need for anyone to suffer for sins, since sinning wouldn't exist.

Satan had one condition. He wanted God's glory.

Jehovah, on the other hand, was deferential to Heavenly Father. One brother was proud, the other humble. One wanted to usurp God's position, the other to sustain it. Two opposing views, both intractable. Jehovah's way would be difficult and potentially damning, while the other promised a life of ease, free from the burden of free will, and guaranteed a return ticket to God's presence. The fate of mankind's existence—and God's—hung in the balance. And thus began the War in Heaven.

Feel free to imagine it however you want, since no prophet has really elaborated on what the War in Heaven consisted of. Did we ride on spirit horses, carrying spirit shields and spirit swords, looking like something from a Renaissance painting? Was territory gained and lost? As a kid, of course I pictured an epic Tolkienesque battle; the technology of the preexistence never reached much past the Middle Ages. But it was likely more of a war of words, like a particularly nasty election. None of us had bodies. What does a war even mean to ghosts?

In the end, God's plan won and Satan was kicked out of . . . wherever we were, along with a third of our spirit brothers and sisters, who sadly would never get physical bodies. But we can confidently say that we—including you, yes, you!—did follow God's plan because we were ultimately born and we have free will.

We also know that whatever condition you were born into on earth wasn't random, but rather was a direct result of how righteous and obedient you had been in the premortal life.

I must have been very righteous in my premortal life since I was born able-bodied, in a free country (Canada), and into a loving Mormon family. Some might say I was born with a handful of privileges, but church doctrine is clear: I earned my station in life before I was formed in the belly. And so did you! If you were born into hardship, you really only have your premortal self to blame.

Through my understandings of Church teachings, I believed growing up that families were predetermined before they actually came to earth. No family was a mistake. In fact, we knew the challenges that we were going to have upon coming to this earth. As spirits, we each accepted our circumstances and our roles on earth. Whether we'd be born to an abusive father, or be addicted to opioids, or not make it into Harvard, or die in childbirth. Whatever our situation in life, whatever trials and tribulations we may experience, we knew back in the premortal life that they were coming.

Our life on earth is a continuation of our premortal life. We are blessed if we're righteous, and not blessed if we're wicked, though both the rewards and the punishments will mostly be doled out after we die.

When our lives are over, our spirits are sent to a kind of purgatory, where we'll wait for the final judgement. For the righteous, this waiting period will take place in some kind of paradise, while the wicked will be sent to await judgement in a spirit prison. But don't feel too bad for the spirit prisoners. This liminal existence allows those who didn't hear or accept the gospel in life to accept it as spirits. Heavenly Father gives all His children as many chances as He can.

When the final judgement comes, all of God's children will be assigned what's called a degree of glory. Unbeknownst to most Christian faiths, there are three possible destinations. The celestial kingdom is where the righteous Mormons will go to live with their Heavenly Father again, while the wicked will be sent off to the telestial kingdom. The telestial kingdom is still a kingdom though. It's still better than earth. The good, but not great, will find themselves in the terrestrial kingdom—the middle child of the degrees of glory. Mormons do believe in a kind of hell, called outer darkness, but it's a place reserved for those who reject Christ. It's actually pretty difficult to be damned in outer darkness. You have to basically see the Saviour and be like, "Nah, I want to keep sinning, thanks."

This narrative, this journey from premortal existence to the degrees of glory, is called the plan of salvation. Remember that. It's the meaning and purpose of life. Now you know.

I AM A CHILD OF GOD

(1991–1994)

OUR FAMILY HAD a pew. Always. The second pew from the front was ours. It might as well have been assigned to my parents before the world was. Even if we were going to church in a different city, or attending a different ward, we'd try to sit in our row.

The second pew made sense strategically. My parents needed space enough for five kids ranging in age from seven (me) to sixteen (my sister Erin). The chapel always filled up from the back. The chances of finding the space needed to seat the Hudsons increased the closer to the front we ventured. As with a movie theatre, there was always space in the front row, but then you're in the front row and could practically see up the bishop's nose. Also, the front row with kids would be impossible. They need to be penned in by another pew.

Being close to the front came in handy at those surprise moments when the organist didn't show up, or the chorister fell ill. My mom was right there to step in and serve as needed. I assumed every mom knew how to play the piano and read music. But my mom was just good at noticing when she needed to help out.

I appreciated the consistency of our pew position. It was a part of who the Hudsons were. The Hudsons of the Second Pew. It was tradition, and therefore sacred.

But there were dark times, too. Even in our own ward, where everyone knew to whom the pew belonged, sometimes we got to church late and discovered some strange family sitting in our pew. Visitors. On these Sundays I would beg my mother to ask the usurpers if they'd mind moving to one of the other empty pews. I was certain if she explained properly that the second pew was ours that no one would be offended. The visitor family probably had their own regular pew at their regular church, of course they'd understand. They'd be apologetic as they gathered their things and moved several rows back.

But of course she never would. We'd find another empty pew. I'd sit through sacrament meeting uncomfortable and hard done by, exiled in our own home.

Mormon temples are easily identifiable. They are typically grand, neo-Gothic structures made out of white stone, and most of them have a golden angel perched on their steeple, forever blowing his trumpet. They look like buildings from a utopian future. But Mormon *churches* aren't like that. There are no special crosses or telling architectural quirks. There are no crosses at all, actually. Mormons believe in Jesus, but they eschew crosses. Likely because crosses represent regular Christianity, and since regular Christianity is viewed as corrupt and wrong, they want to differentiate themselves from it. Apart from the sign outside claiming the building for the Church of Jesus Christ of Latter-day Saints, the aggressive banality of its architecture is probably a Mormon church's most recognizable feature.

Our ward, along with two others, which together covered the southeast corner of Edmonton, met in a stake centre across a traffic circle from Bonnie Doon Mall. A stake is made up of a group of wards, the way a diocese is made up of a group of parishes. As such, stake centres are bigger than regular meeting-houses, but not any different in appearance. The Bonnie Doon Stake Centre was made of faded orange brick that looked almost beige. There was a chapel and a gymnasium, with a small overflow area in between the two. The hallways leading away from the chapel were filled on either side by Sunday School classrooms and administrative offices. At the other end of the building was the Relief Society room, which was the centre of the women's activity. It was where I would hang off my mother's arms, encouraging her to stop talking so we could go home at the end of church.

Church service lasted three hours on Sunday. One hour for sacrament meeting, one hour of Sunday School—where all the adults attended a class called Gospel Doctrine, which either went through a book of scripture week by week or took up teachings from modern-day prophets—then one final hour of priesthood class for the men and Relief Society for the women. Priesthood and Relief Society were usually taught the same doctrine, but tailored to the gender of the audience. In preparation for that, teenagers went to boys' and girls' classes, too. The boys would begin preparing to be missionaries, and the girls would prepare for their future missions as wives and mothers. Waiting for my mom to finish talking to the other women after Relief Society often added another hour to the whole thing.

Every Mormon church I'd ever been to always smelled as though it had been bathed in disinfectant and chlorine bleach. They smelled neither minty nor citrusy nor floral—instead it was a bit like how new carpet smelled, but less harsh.

Every church building had the same art on the walls, too. Paintings of a handsome, broad-shouldered, American-looking Saviour in different scenes from scripture, portraits of Joseph Smith, and dramatic moments in Church history. Each lobby had one floral loveseat and two plush chairs. In our church building, the carpets and cushions on the pews matched the orange tone of the bricks, but were a bit darker. Almost rusty. Halfway up the walls in the hallways and in the chapel was burlap, which made the walls scratchy.

On what I assumed would be a typical Sunday, I sat in our pew before sacrament meeting started. Organ music was playing as members milled about and got settled in their pews. I only knew a handful of hymns, but I recognized this one: "I Am a Child of God." Mom would sometimes sing it to me when I had trouble falling asleep, or was feeling sad at bedtime, which wasn't infrequent.

The organ stopped as the bishop approached the pulpit to begin the meeting. There was an opening hymn, an opening prayer, then announcements about upcoming ward events, and new callings that had been extended. The bishop welcomed us and informed us what song we'd be singing and who would be saying the invocation.

After the opening prayer, the bishop came back to the pulpit. "We'll now prepare to take the sacrament by singing hymn number 193, 'I Stand All Amazed,' after which the sacrament will be blessed and passed by the priesthood." He smiled and nodded at the organist.

I did not understand "I Stand All Amazed."

From what I could discern, "I Stand All Amazed" was sung from the point of view of an actual villain. Mostly because of the chorus, which was the only part I knew. As with most hymns, my mom whispered the words to me seconds before they were to be sung. But I knew the chorus.

Oh, it is wonderful that He should care for me
Enough to die for me!
Oh, it is wonderful, wonderful to me!

My seven-year-old brain wondered who this was that thought it was wonderful that Jesus was killed? I imagined a comic book villain preening in his lair, his sycophantic henchmen giggling along. His plan was coming to fruition, all the pieces were falling into place. And now, how wonderful it was. He stifled a laugh. *That He should care for me enough to die for me!* Maniacal laughter.

My brother Sam was among the young men who passed the bread and water of the sacrament to the congregation. To one side of the dais there was a table covered in a white cloth. You could make out the shapes of the trays underneath. The smaller ones were for the bread. As the sacrament hymn was being sung, two sixteen-year-old boys, who were called priests, tore slices of

Wonder Bread into pieces. When the song was over, one of the priests knelt down behind the table and spoke the sacramental prayer into a small microphone. If he stumbled he would have to repeat the prayer until he got it just right.

Erin's boyfriend, Evan, was one of the priests. He wasn't technically in our ward. He was in the ward that met just after ours in the same building, but wards that met in the same building were relatively porous. We were in 4th Ward.

Evan blessed the bread, then he and the other priest gave each twelve-year-old deacon who had approached the table, including Sam, a white plastic tray piled with torn bread. The children spread through the chapel in a pre-arranged pattern and passed the bread along the pews. When Sam came to our pew, I tried to make him laugh. He never did. He took his priesthood duties very seriously. And I wasn't that great at making him laugh at the best of times. Sam was the funny one in the family. Usually when I tried to make him laugh, I'd end up giggling too hard to speak.

"Think about Jesus," my mother whispered, and put her arm around me. That was my cue to settle down.

Once the congregation had partaken of the bread, the process was repeated almost verbatim with big trays of clear plastic thimbles filled with water.

Bishop Doohan was big. All adults were big, but Bishop Doohan seemed especially so. He played basketball. He could sink a hook shot from half court. His kids played basketball, too. But not just basketball. There were four kids in their family—Chris, Michelle, Ava, and Stuart, two girls and two boys. Chris was close in age to my sisters Erin and Gill, Michelle was Sam's age, Ava was a year older than my sister Mary, and Stu was a year younger than me. All four excelled at many sports, but basketball was their game.

Our family played basketball, and dabbled in volleyball, too. We played sports, but we were not a sports family. Our dad wasn't a sports dad. He watched playoff games if they were on, but professional sports didn't interest him. He did not pick a team for all of us to follow.

Could a family be a good Mormon family if they didn't play, watch, or care about basketball? Basketball wasn't a tenet of the Mormon Church . . . or was it? Why else were there basketball courts in every church building? Unlike hockey or football, which required special equipment, basketball was simple and inexpensive, so even families with lots of children could play it. Basketball might not be ordained of God, but Heavenly Father was obviously a fan.

At the same time, could a person be smart if they only cared about balls and baskets and sticks and pucks? More importantly, could you be both righteous and competitive? Competitiveness always seemed a bit mean and self-centred. It was a drive to be better than others. Competitive people only cared about winning, at the expense of other people's feelings. I didn't care for that.

After the sacrament, before turning the service over to the ward members who had been asked to speak that week, Bishop Doohan had a special announcement to make. The podium rose to meet him as he walked the few steps from his seat to the pulpit. Like every man at church, he was a wearing a business suit and white shirt. Young boys could get away with wearing non-white shirts to church until they became deacons; then the dress code applied to them, too. The suit was optional, but the white shirt and tie weren't. Bishop Doohan was an accountant in his regular life, but I didn't really know what that meant. He was Mary's community league basketball coach though, and he'd probably be mine when I started playing the next year.

The bishop reported that the renovations to the Cardston Alberta Temple were almost complete. Cardston was a small Alberta town near the Montana border that was founded and mostly populated by Mormons. The First Presidency—the top tier of the Church's leadership, consisting of the prophet and his two counselors—would be coming from Salt Lake City for the rededication ceremony and the exciting news was that all members in the province who were eight and older were invited to attend the event.

My eighth birthday was six months away, in July. The temple dedication was happening in April. My mom watched me hear the news and do the arithmetic in my head.

I wouldn't be allowed to go. My whole family would go to the temple together. But not me. I was born two months too late.

"Does that mean everyone who isn't eight can't go?" I asked my mom. "What about if you're almost eight?"

"I'm sorry, sweetheart," she said.

"But why?" What was so magical about being eight? What would I understand then that I wouldn't understand now?

"I think they want to make sure it's reverent, so no crying babies."

"I'm not a baby, though. I can be reverent." We sang songs about what it meant to be reverent in Primary, the Church's children's program.

"I know you can. But not every kid is as mature as you. You'll still be able to go through the open house. You'll see the temple. And the dedication will be boring. You wouldn't be able to bring in any toys or anything."

Nothing she was saying made me feel any better.

"It's because everyone can go through the open house, but they only want members to be at the dedication. Only people who've been baptized," Sam whispered to me.

I was suddenly overcome by the injustice of my birthdate and swept away by a sea of sobs. It wasn't a tantrum, it was the kind of grief that called for torn garments. So began a crying jag like a weather system, with swells and squalls. But all in a whisper, lest I disrupt sacrament meeting.

Halfway through sacrament meeting, I was still crying. The bishop's messenger, a deacon who sat near the bishop in case he needed to discreetly deliver a note to someone, passed a note to our pew that was handed down to me. It was a small piece of paper, torn from the service program and folded in half. The words "Be happy" were written above a crudely drawn smiley face.

Naturally, the unprompted attention from Bishop Doohan, who was all the way up on the stand, made me cry even more. He didn't know why I was sad, but he still saw me. I was special enough to get a note from the bishop. But it didn't change the temple situation.

I was acting like a baby, but I couldn't help it. I knew my mom was right. That it would just be boring talks, and then a really long prayer. If I were to go, I would be bored. But it still felt unfair.

From my very first days in Primary, I had always been taught that I wanted very much to go to the temple because that was where families went to be sealed together forever, so they wouldn't be separated after death. The specifics of how that was done, like much else that went on inside its walls, were a mystery. People didn't talk about those acts because they were sacred. Too special to be explained, taboo to ask about. I accepted this explanation. Being able to see a temple dedicated would be as close to knowing temple stuff as I would get before I was nineteen and going on my mission, which was the usual impetus for going to the temple.

There wasn't a time in my life that I could remember when I didn't know I was going to go on a mission when I turned nineteen, to, according to the Primary song, preach and teach and work like missionaries do. Preparing for a mission was basically the purpose of every boy's and young man's life. Going was a commandment, but also a privilege. That's why you had to always live worthily, lest you be barred from serving a mission because of sin. Then where would you be? Ashamed and a disappointment to your parents, that's where.

I thought missionaries were superheroes; with their white shirts, ties, and name tags, they even had special costumes and secret identities. They were automatic big brothers that would come over to our house for dinner once a month. They knew everything. If you caught a glimpse of the scriptures they carried everywhere, you'd see why: every page seemed to be covered in notes, with verses highlighted in different colours and arrows pointing to other verses.

I wanted to be like that. Going to the temple dedication seemed like it would give me a spiritual head start. The fact that I wasn't going to be allowed to go seemed to be incontrovertible proof for a theory that I had been toying with, also for as long as I could remember: that to be the youngest in a family is to be ignored and probably unloved. I might have expected this cruel neglect from my siblings or even my parents. But Heavenly Father, too?

I hoped that somehow my visible heartbreak would convince Bishop Doohan to make an exception for me, even though I knew it wasn't actually his decision. But surely he'd see and report it up the chain of command to the stake president, who would repeat the story to the prophet: so great was my despair that it would be a sin to keep me from the dedication ceremony of the temple. For clearly, he'd tell the stake president, no child desired it as desperately as I did.

I hoped for a lot of things that I knew would never happen.

My dad baptized me soon after I turned eight.

We got to the church and my dad and I changed into pure white outfits. He had white slacks, a white shirt, white tie, and white belt. He wore the same outfit when he and my mom went to the temple whenever they happened to be in Cardston. They fit him comfortably. I wore a short-sleeved white jumpsuit that had a tiny torso and long pants that I had to roll up. I thought I looked a little like a small psychiatric patient, whereas my dad looked like a heavenly accountant.

No one had informed me that I wasn't the only person getting baptized that day. Sitting in the front row were a girl from a nearby ward and a man who was converting. The convert was flanked by eager missionaries, one of whom was wearing white clothes like my dad. The convert himself wore an adult version of the jumpsuit I was wearing. My dad and I took our seats between the missionary in white and the other girl's father.

I felt a little silly doing something so important looking so foolish, and in front of so many people. I felt like I was wearing hand-me-downs and everyone could tell. I still felt excited though. I had learned and sung songs about baptism for as long as I could remember.

The first part of the ceremony was held in the Relief Society room. Like sacrament meeting, it started with an opening hymn and prayer. Then there was a short talk about baptism before we walked down the hall to the room where the baptismal font was hidden behind regular closet doors. The baptismal font looked like a cross between a shower and a bathtub. It was tiled, about the size of a truck bed, and deep enough for the water to rise just above my dad's waist. There was a mirror on the ceiling above the font, angled so that everyone in the room would be able to witness me getting dunked, while also making sure that I was, at least for a moment, entirely submerged. The cleansing waters of baptism only worked if the person being baptized was fully immersed.

While we waited for the seats to fill up behind us, my dad told me that in Utah they held baptisms once a month, and the kids who had just turned eight would all be baptized on the same day. Maybe he could sense my disappointment that I had to share my special day.

I took my baptism very seriously. Because even though it was a foregone conclusion that I would be baptized at eight, it was still an important decision. Other than being born, which I didn't have much choice about, getting baptized was the first thing I would do that had eternal consequences: "Except a man be born of water and of the Spirit, he cannot enter into the kingdom of God." I was doing the water part now, and I'd do the Spirit part right after, when my dad and a few uncles would encircle me, each put one hand on my head, confirm me as a member of the Church, and give me the gift of the Holy Ghost.

I hoped I would feel the Spirit. When adults talked about their baptisms, they often talked about how they felt coming out of the water: warm, loved, embraced by Heavenly Father. I had seen people feel the Spirit in church. They cried as they spoke from the pulpit. I wouldn't mind crying. I was curious about the burning in my bosom I was told I might feel. I didn't think I had ever felt that, but wasn't it about time I did? I wanted a real spiritual experience. One that I could share whenever I bore my testimony at church.

I wanted to be reverent. I repeated to myself the fourth article of faith,* which I had memorized: "We believe that the first principles and ordinances of the Gospel are: first, Faith in the Lord Jesus Christ; second, Repentance; third, baptism by immersion for the remission of sins; fourth, Laying on of hands for the gift of the Holy Ghost."

Baptism by immersion for the remission of sins.

That part confused me a little. I knew why I was supposed to get baptized—it was how I officially joined the Church—but I didn't understand why the rush to get baptized when I turned eight. The Church believed that before that, children were innocent—not accountable for their moral decisions.

---

* In response to a reporter asking him about his new religion's beliefs, Joseph Smith wrote thirteen Articles of Faith. Because they were written by the Prophet, they carried the weight of scripture.

Sin became a real thing on your eighth birthday. That meant if you got baptized right when you turned eight, you hadn't had much time to sin. Why get remission of your sins when you had so few of them? Didn't it make more sense to be baptized when you were an adult, after you racked up some legitimate wrongs? It's not that I wanted to sin, but I knew it was inevitable. No one was perfect. And you only got this absolute clean slate once. It just seemed like a waste to do it as an eight-year-old.

After I was baptized, I would technically be perfect, spiritually speaking, but I was careful not to think that, because even if it were true, thinking about it—basically bragging to myself about it—would ruin it. I'd stop being perfect the second I thought about how I was perfect.

"Kind of," Sam said when I described my dilemma at the dinner table, filling our plates with food after we got home and I dried off. "You're sinless after you get baptized, but you're not perfect exactly."

"Yeah, I am," I said, then felt ashamed I had admitted that.

"You're not wicked or anything," Sam said. "But let's say you wanted to stay 'perfect' for as long as you could after you get baptized, so you lock yourself in your room and never come out. All you do all day is read scriptures, let's say."

"Sounds fun," I said.

"You can watch Church videos, too," Sam said.

"Okay."

"Are you perfect?"

I didn't say anything. Sam was probably right. I just had to wait until he explained why.

"Well, you might not be doing anything wrong, but you're not doing anything right, either," Sam said. "I mean, you're reading your scriptures, but you aren't helping anyone, or loving thy neighbour. 'Faith without works is dead.' Do you know that scripture?"

"Uh huh," I said. I was pretty sure I had heard it before, but I hoped Sam didn't ask me more about it.

"It's like that."

"Okay," I said, but I didn't understand.

"See, there are sins of commission, and sins of omission," Sam started.

My sister Gill broke in: "Commission is stuff that you do that you shouldn't, and omission is stuff that you don't do, but should. Punching Sam, that's a sin of commission. Not praying, that's a sin of omission." Gill was good at ensuring I understood things.

"Jesus commanded us to be perfect," Sam said. "And you're only perfect if you do what's right. You had your sins forgiven, but now have to actually do the commandments."

"It's called enduring to the end," Gill said. I had definitely heard that phrase before.

Perfect or not, I still suspected I wasn't getting the most bang for my baptismal buck.

Before I had any interest in comic books, I was a big fan of Batman. This was mainly a result of the 1989 movie *Batman*, which consequently made me into a pretty big Michael Keaton fan. I also liked the old Batman show from the 1960s, which played nightly on YTV. Before that, I liked He-Man. And after Batman, it would be the Ninja Turtles. My interests weren't obscure. I liked heroes. The good guys. But even though I liked them, I never could draw them.

I wasn't a strong artist. And at the age of eight or nine, I started to notice. From kindergarten to the second grade, everyone seems equally bad at drawing. But by grade three, those that have talent are starting to show it. Normally my doodles involved flat airplanes shooting rounds of dashes at flat tanks shooting missiles that looked uncannily like small planes. I had more interest in people, but, though I tried, drawing people was difficult for me.

But while bored in school, I started drawing meaty legs without knowing what they would support: four brackets, two big ones facing each other on top for the thigh, and two smaller ones below the knee. I drew some lines down the middle of the thigh to denote muscles. On top of the legs, I made a slightly V-shaped torso and drew some arms in the same fashion as I drew the legs. Then I added an empty oval for the head, which I covered with some spiky hair.

I then coloured the legs to give my character some pants, or tights, as the case may be. For his top, I went minimal. Just a criss-cross of fabric over the chest, like bandoliers, or like what He-Man wore. Didn't one of the Ninja Turtles have a thing like that? Instead of worrying about drawing a face, something that I could not do, I coloured it all black, save for three white slashes for his mouth and eyes.

I had clearly drawn a muscle-bound man in a gimp mask and leather pants, with a leather harness across his chest. Luckily, I never showed this doodle to anyone who could tell me that. I kept my art to myself.

I gave him a staff. Then I made it a spear.

I wasn't satisfied with my guy holding a spear, though. It was obvious to me that I had drawn a superhero of sorts. But how could a superhero fight crime with a spear? The spearhead was diamond-shaped, so I cross-hatched inside the diamond until the spearhead looked vaguely crystalline. A few wavy swooshes emanated from the crystal, implying power, not odour.

I named him Magic Stick. Because his stick was magic. It shot energy beams mainly, and it also gave Magic Stick the power of flight. But it could also conjure objects, transport people and things, control the weather, and perform various other feats of sorcery.

Magic Stick would lead the handful of other heroes I invented. I was a little unclear as to the origin and nature of Magic Stick's powers, but I knew he was a leader. The leaders of hero teams weren't the coolest, or the funniest, in the team, but they were the best. Like Leonardo in the Teenage Mutant Ninja Turtles. Raphael was the cool one, but he wasn't as good as the leader. Sometimes leaders were a little stiff, but that was because they were so virtuous, like Jesus.

I came up with my next character at our cabin on Shuswap Lake in British Columbia.

I didn't like water skiing, which was a favoured Hudson family activity, and I didn't have the patience for lying in the sun, which was nearly as popular, so I had a lot of time to fill. Often that meant playing with the small army of action figures I brought with me from home. G.I. Joes mostly, but depending on my current obsession, it could also include Ninja Turtles, Batman, or Dick Tracy action figures. But G.I. Joes were the best, since they moved the most.

Other times, I was my own action figure, fighting invisible bad guys along the lakeshore or in the woods behind the cabin.

Our cabin had a big window next to the front door. Because it was always brighter outside than it was inside, we could always see our reflections very clearly in the glass. It made a terrific, unavoidable mirror.

One afternoon, I had just walked up the long flight of stairs that led from the lake to the cabin. Below, my siblings were on the dock, deciding in what order they would water-ski. I had called dibs on going seventh before going upstairs. I enjoyed being dragged around the lake on an inner tube, but water skiing was scary. Plus, I was the only one in the family still stuck on two skis—the others were slaloming, looking like the water skiers in the boat magazines. My siblings looked cool, slicing from one side of the wake to the other, casting walls of spray with every turn. It was impossible to look cool water-skiing on two skis. I had all the grace of a seaplane with a prop engine, bouncing along the surface of the water, unable to take flight, while Erin, Gill, Sam, and Mary were fighter jets in their slick wetsuits and streamlined life jackets. I wasn't big enough for one of the cool life jackets. I still had to wear the orange kind, with the big headrest flap that looked like an elephant ear and crotch strap for safety.

The large cabin windows were my friend: the light and shadow falling through the pine trees above were such that in my reflection I looked like I had muscles. I didn't normally have muscles. My prepubescent body possessed little muscle definition, but I wasn't skinny. This was partly due to the size of my bones, which my mother diagnosed as being big. I didn't look skinny in the window, but I didn't look fat, either. That was cool.

It was also cool how the double-pane windows superimposed one of my reflections on top of the other. They mostly lined up, but one of the reflections was slightly bigger, clearer.

As I made comic-book-battle-ready poses in dead seriousness, the two reflections made it look like I had an aura, or like I could see both my body and my spirit.

Brilliance.

The guy in the reflection would be called Spirit—not to be confused with any other superhero I wasn't aware of who shared that name. Also not to be confused with the Holy Spirit, the third, separate, and distinct member of the Godhead. This spirit would be like a ghost, the kind of spirit we all had hidden away somewhere behind our skin.

The reason Spirit looked the way he did, two reflections in one, was because he had a special suit. A body suit, if you will.

According to my understanding of metaphysics, spirits can't inhabit dead bodies. When the body is no longer functioning, it might as well be made out of wood. A spirit just passes through it. My character Spirit, though, had a special containment suit that, through supernatural technology, mimicked a living human body in such a way that he, a spirit, could inhabit it.

Spirit wasn't trapped in the suit though. Outside of it, he could do the things spirits do—fly, travel very fast, move through solid objects, possess the unsuspecting—but when he needed to interact more meaningfully with the physical world, he used the suit. Spirit was a crime-fighting ghost in an artificial human suit.

Despite the violence contained within them, and their general lack of godliness (if you don't count Thor), comics weren't considered bad by the Church or Heavenly Father. They weren't considered at all. And our family certainly wasn't strict about pop culture. The specific instruction from the Church was to avoid watching R-rated movies. But the Canadian movie-rating system was different, and no movies were rated R where we lived. There was 14A, which required those under fourteen to be accompanied by an adult, and there was 18A. There was some ambiguity because some R-rated movies in the States were 14A here. But we instinctually knew what we could watch and what we shouldn't. If the film had foul language, specifically the F-word, we didn't watch it. Likewise if it had any nudity. There were some parents who didn't allow their kids to watch *The Simpsons*, for fear those kids would wind up like Bart. But the Church never got into specifics. Comics didn't have bad language or sex, which were the two things that made a movie or TV show bad. Growing up, my mom bought me the odd comic when I needed to be distracted or rewarded, but I started reading and collecting them when I was nine years old.

We were allowed to shoot off fireworks at the cabin. We'd buy them at the Sea Store, a large houseboat that had been converted into a floating convenience store and Sea-Doo rental place. The Sea Store flew under the banner of various flags: the Jolly Roger, a cannabis leaf, the American flag, and the Maple Leaf, plus the flag of sunny British Columbia. It also sold candy, obscenely marked-up groceries, fishing tackle, pool noodles, and just-barely-out-of-date magazines. It had a wall of t-shirts for sale, and if they were any indication, houseboaters and other lake tourists were a horny bunch, obsessed with alcohol and breasts. The one t-shirt that I studied secretly whenever we were at the Sea Store showed cartoon frogs running through a gamut of sexual positions. You could tell one frog was a girl because she had lipstick and the mild suggestion of breasts.

According to the shirt, the frogs were doing the Shuswap Shuffle. But I knew it wasn't really a dance. They were doing it.

It! I knew about the basic components of sex, the where and the what of how babies were made. My mother had taken the opportunity to teach me about sex after I had asked about a tampon I found in her coat pocket when I was about five. I understood that the man lay on top of the woman and somehow his nevermind—which was my exclusive term for the penis—found its way into the woman. The logistics of it seemed improbable, but given how often two people woke up in bed together on TV and didn't remember if they had done it, it must happen very easily. I wasn't aware there were so many different ways to go about it though. The man frog was on top, underneath, even behind the lady frog. Some positions didn't even make sense. For instance, why was the man frog on top of the woman frog, but pointing in the opposite direction?

Regardless of position, the frogs were enjoying themselves.

I knew from how the shirt made me feel in my stomach—a little nervous and nauseated—that it wasn't a good shirt to look at. I didn't want my mom to have to talk to me about it, so I'd walk slowly back and forth in front of all the t-shirts, barely pausing at the Shuswap Shuffle.

We liked to have at least one night of fireworks, regardless of the occasion, but the fireworks we bought were unremarkable. It turned out that they were very expensive, so we mostly got Roman candles that shot ten tennis balls of colour each, with two or maybe three bigger ones to finish the night. Mostly these showstoppers would pop out Roman candles too, before spitting out a somewhat larger fireball that made a bigger bang.

The morning after our annual fireworks display, I walked along the rocky shore in front of the cabin and picked up the spent cardboard husks. They smelled the way I thought gunpowder probably smelled, like empty cap gun rounds.

I carried the small tubes around as if they were rifles or sticks of dynamite. Our family fireworks display always felt dangerous, with much running for cover after the fuses were lit. I worried because we always seemed to be closer than the instructions on the side of the box said we should be. The next morning, they were just charred cardboard.

But what if I could be even more dangerous with the fireworks? Ours was not a family that condoned guns. This was one of the ways my parents didn't fit in with mainstream Mormonism. Utah Mormonism. My parents weren't the kind of bleeding-heart liberal pacifists that outlawed pretend guns in the home. We could have as many toy guns as we wanted. But when I had asked for a .22 rifle the previous Christmas, I was rebuffed.

If I ever wanted to fight crime, which was something I spent a good amount of time thinking about, I would need a different kind of gun. There was probably a way to make a kind of holder for a Roman candle—like a caulking gun, is how I imagined it. And then if I added some kind of lighting mechanism using technology created by Bic, boom, I'd have a firework gun.

I didn't know how to make what I saw in my head real. Especially since it was probably more complicated than I was imagining. But I could pretend to be that kid, the crime-fighting inventor.

With that, Juvenile was born.

Juvenile was a weapons designer, but he was also a kid, in the same ambiguous age range as Batman's sidekick, Robin. A little older than me: twelve or thirteen, around my brother's age. Juvenile's entirely non-lethal arsenal would reflect his age and interests—exploding Nerf balls, high-powered glue guns, stink bombs—but his trademark sidearm would be his firework gun.

I didn't have the artistic talent necessary to give my growing stable of superheroes life outside of my own head, where I kept track of them like trading cards. As with Magic Stick, I could hint at them with a pen and paper, but I could barely draw a leg.

But back at home in Edmonton was our trampoline. I had superpowers on the trampoline.

Our trampoline was a narrow rectangle. Its only nod toward safety were the flat blue mats, each no thicker than a notebook, that covered the springs that pulled the canvas taut and gave the tramp its bounce. The biggest danger wasn't falling off, though that would have hurt. The biggest danger was landing on those springs when a mat had been knocked off and having a leg fall through and likely get pinched by a spring, too. We didn't have a fence in our backyard, so neighbourhood kids I didn't recognize sometimes asked to jump on the trampoline. No one ever broke anything.

Before the creation of my superheroes, the trampoline was mainly a setting for family play. For instance, Sam and I played a game of our own invention called the Head-Smashing Game. It was mostly Sam's idea. Older brothers have been coming up with similar games since Cain and Abel.

The goal of the Head-Smashing Game was for me to get from one end of the trampoline to the other. But in order to do so, I had to make it around my brother, who was bouncing in the centre, gaining height. He couldn't push me or plant himself in my way. His only means of preventing me from crossing was to jump as high as possible and then try to push my head into the canvas as he came down.

Such is the price younger brothers are happy to pay to spend time with their older brothers.

Note: we did not call this game Trampoline Tag, or even Get to the Other Side. Calling it the Head-Smashing Game gave away the secret: the smashing was the purpose of the game. And Sam, being a good foot taller than me and nearly six years stronger, was very good at it. As far as getting my head smashed, I was a natural.

I was never injured. Given the narrowness of the trampoline canvas, I rarely made it to the other end unsmashed. But Sam was pretty good at gauging how many losses I was willing to sustain in the Head-Smashing Game before giving up.

The back door of our house in Edmonton opened onto a small landing, about three steps high. Standing on its railing, I could jump onto the trampoline. When I was being a superhero, it became the ledge of a skyscraper, where Magic Stick could look down on the city and scan for trouble, like Batman. I'd leap from the building and pantomime fighting foes big and small. Mostly this involved bouncing on the trampoline while making comic-book poses. I'd blast energy beams from my invisible staff or, if I were pretending to be Spirit, I'd use a sword. I didn't play much as Juvenile. He could thwart a robbery, but a firework gun wasn't going to do squat against an alien monster or a killer robot. My heroes mostly fought a lot of henchmen in my imagination, and even they would give Juvenile trouble.

I needed a new weapons guy.

And thus Weapon came to be. As the name suggests, weapons were his thing. His alter ego, Thomas Pierce, was the head of Pierce Securities. He was kind of like Bruce Wayne or Tony Stark, only exactly the same. He didn't have superpowers, just money and a talent for making futuristic firearms: energy cannons, lasers, tractor beams. Never anything lethal.

For Mormons, and any group that cared about the Ten Commandments, killing was a serious sin. Nearly unforgivable, because there was no way to make restitution. My mom had told me that it could be forgiven if it were done in self-defence, or during war. As long as I was making heroes, they'd avoid killing. That was their code, like Batman. I wasn't pretending to be these superheroes so I could pretend to sin. Being a hero was no excuse to break rules. You'll recall that Jesus Christ, the greatest hero of them all, never broke any rules. It went without saying that Magic Stick, Spirit, Juvenile, and Weapon were all Mormon. They were my heroes. Of course they were members of the Church. Why would I invent heroes I couldn't look up to?

But why create my own heroes at all? Batman, Dick Tracy, the Teenage Mutant Ninja Turtles: as much as I loved their respective films, none of them were my IP. If I pretended to be one of them, it'd be like tracing instead of drawing. And while it's not like I was breaking new narrative ground for my heroes—though I did think that Weapon wearing business attire instead of a typical spandex suit was pretty original—if I played as someone else's character, I'd feel like I had to follow their rules, act out their stories. Any deviation from canon, even in play, was stealing. Cheating. No one could accuse me of stealing Magic Stick from anywhere.

Action figures, which were my main interest and hobby, were

a little different. I didn't have an obscene amount—not near as many as some of my friends—but I was satisfied. It was mostly G.I. Joes, but there were representatives from all of my areas of interest. In my mind, there were rules that governed how I played with them. Action figures couldn't deviate from their source material. Batman couldn't suddenly fly because I could wave my Batman action figure in the air, for example. And, as much as possible, action figures were supposed to stay in their own universes. Even though Dick Tracy figures were the same size and shape as Ninja Turtles, they couldn't interact. That just didn't make sense to me. Dick Tracy was from the 1940s.

Rules helped things make sense. They gave purpose to play and to life. Life was a test, after all, and every choice was a question: would you choose God's way or not? And if Heavenly Father hadn't revealed a preference, you did the best you could using the information you had. I didn't think my way of playing would actually have eternal consequences, not really, but it was proof I cared. I wanted to "choose the right." When I'd turned eight, I'd received a ring engraved with the letters "CTR" in Primary, and this is what they stood for. I wore it always.

My mom would sometimes sing the hymn "Choose the Right Way" sarcastically when she thought someone in the Church was being overly judgemental or prescriptive. The song claims there's a right way for people to live and be happy. She may have believed the Church was the one true church, but she didn't think that meant everyone had to live it in the exact same way. I didn't disagree with her, but I also believed a different, thematically similar hymn called "Choose the Right" when it said, "There's the right and the wrong to ev'ry question . . . Let God and heaven be your goal."

Every question. Every choice was an opportunity to choose the right or the wrong. I wanted to choose the right. If I didn't, I knew I'd disappoint my family and Heavenly Father. And I didn't want to disappoint anyone.

When I was in grade six, a number of kids from Hollyrood Elementary took the city bus after school. With so many kids my age around me, I felt safe on the bus, which was rare. Teenagers, especially mean-looking ones who smoked and used the F-word liberally, filled me with dread. They were like storm clouds that could turn into tornadoes without warning, and I was very scared of tornadoes. The main difference was that I didn't have to walk past real tornadoes every day, desperately hoping not to attract their attention.

Among the kids who took the city bus were my friends: Dylan, Adrian, Brayden, and sometimes Jonathan, who was hitting puberty well before the rest of us.

It was 1995 and Brayden and I were growing our hair out. Mine was nearly long enough to tuck behind my ears. And Dylan had recently started twisting his hair to look like braids, which was the coolest way a Black kid who liked alternative music could wear his hair. None of us had been interested in rap music since Vanilla Ice became uncool. I listened to the music my older siblings, mostly Sam, listened to, which was a mix of grunge, folk, and 60s rock, like Jefferson Airplane and Jimi Hendrix. I was still influenced by my parents, too: I liked Broadway musical cast recordings, which were what my mom and dad listened to the most.

Dylan and Adrian were reading a discarded newspaper in the seat in front of me.

Nerdy kids and immature babies sat up at the very front of the bus, where they could pester the driver the way nerds and babies do. The cooler you were, the further toward the back of the bus you sat. With no teenagers there to intimidate us, my friends and I were practically sitting at the very back.

The word "repent" was written in marker on the back of Adrian and Dylan's seat in the exact same cursive script I'd seen on a lot of other buses. Whenever I saw it, I wondered about the morality. Could there be such a thing as good vandalism? I always wondered, too, how the person wrote not only so legibly on the back of a bus seat but so consistently, all without ever being caught.

"Let's see, let's see. What was that band you were talking about again? The one that had the gay name?" Adrian asked, flipping through the entertainment section of the paper that some other passenger had left behind.

"The Tea Party," I said, though he could have also been asking about Feeding Like Butterflies, a local folk-rock band whose name didn't scream masculinity either. But I had a suspicion I knew the point Adrian was preparing to make, so I went with the band that was more likely to appear on the charts. The Tea Party at least had a couple of music videos.

"Right, the Tea Party. Huh. They aren't in the top 10. I'll keep looking. Do you see the Tea Party?" Adrian asked Dylan, who made a show of using his finger to scan the columns of the Canadian top 200 singles.

"I don't see them. Not even in the top 200," Dylan said. "Do you know how bad a band has to be to not make it into the top 200 in Canada?"

I had introduced a wedge into our group by standing firmly against punk music. The year before we had all liked the same stuff: Nirvana, Pearl Jam, the Red Hot Chili Peppers. Then Green Day's *Dookie* came out. It represented the logical next step in our musical development. It was a starting point for my friends; they moved on to harder, marginally more obscure punk bands like Pennywise and NOFX. I said that I didn't like them because I maintained that all punk rock sounded the same, and was therefore unoriginal and boring. Though if I were being honest, punk was just a little too fast and hard for my liking.

This had called my coolness into question. It didn't help that my favourite album at the time was the original cast recording of Andrew Lloyd Webber's *Sunset Boulevard*. Once, I tried to make the case that the album was actually cool because of how much swearing it contained, though the curse words never got worse than "ass." My friends had not been impressed. But now they were going after the music I listened to that I knew was cool. I knew the Tea Party was cool because my brother and his friends, all of whom had long hair and played guitar, liked the Tea Party. I also knew that being unknown by newspapers was, contrary to their thesis, actually a mark of coolness. But obscurity only feels cool when it's appreciated.

I could have just pretended that I liked the same music as the rest of my friends. But being a poser seemed worse than liking the wrong music. There was nothing more pitiful in our social circle than to be a poser.

"Cool story today," Brayden broke in. He didn't say it with sarcasm.

"Thanks," I said. In our English class, I had written a time-travel story about someone going to the future to stop the

Ku Klux Klan, which I envisioned as a criminal organization. I called it "Leap for Life" and drew a flaming cross on the cover. Our teacher had liked the message, so he had read it out loud to the class.

"But I thought Mormons didn't like Black people," Brayden said.

"Uh. No," I said, turning my head to look at Dylan.

"But you can't be Mormon if you're Black," Brayden said.

"Is that true?" Adrian asked.

"No, Black people can be Mormons. You're maybe thinking of how they couldn't hold the *priesthood*, but they could still be Mormon," I said, intentionally using a word that could easily be misunderstood. Mormons believed the priesthood, which was given to every worthy man, was the power and authority to act in God's name, and having it (or marrying someone with it) was essential to salvation. But it was easier if they imagined the Catholic priesthood. After all, if you weren't allowed to be a Catholic priest, it was no big loss. "And that was a long time ago."

"Like when Mormons had a bunch of wives," Brayden said.

"Yeah, like that. That was like more than a hundred years ago," I said. This was true about polygamy, but Black people weren't allowed to hold the priesthood in the Church of Jesus Christ of Latter-day Saints until 1978. It was a thing that didn't get mentioned much at church. When we did hear about it in Sunday School, it was usually used as an example of how the Church was guided by modern-day revelation. According to the Church, God spoke to the prophet at the time, Spencer W. Kimball, and let him know that after nearly 150 years of discrimination it was time to allow Black people to have equal religious rights.

I worried that the whole thing made the Church seem racist, which the Church couldn't be since it was God's true church, and God wasn't racist. There was a good explanation for the priesthood thing, I just didn't know what it was. Luckily, as far as my cognitive abilities went, anything that happened before I was born might as well have happened a hundred years ago. Times were different then.

"Why didn't they allow Black people to be priests?" Brayden asked.

"I don't really know," I answered honestly. "My mom said it was maybe because the Church was already persecuted or whatever, so they didn't want to rub anyone the wrong way by getting involved with civil rights."

"Why didn't people like Mormons?" Adrian said.

"The lots of wives thing," I responded. "And just because a lot of other Christian churches don't really like Mormons. That's why Mormons moved to Utah. They were kicked out of their homes in other states."

Persecution was embedded deep in the Mormon DNA. The persecution of early Latter-day Saints was taught to us so often that I was always surprised that people outside the Church didn't know about their plight. So reviled were the Mormons that the governor of Missouri signed an extermination order for them in 1838, effectively making it legal to kill Mormons in the state. That seemed up there with Nazi Germany, and yet non-members never talked about it.

"Hey, how can you like the Tea Party if Mormons aren't allowed to drink tea?" Dylan said, obviously proud of his sophistry.

"How do you like Green Day when your day isn't even

green?" Brayden said, answering for me. Then we all came up with band names that defied our identities. "How can you listen to the Presidents of the United States of America when you're from Canada?" And so on.

Capilano Mall—affectionately called Crapilano Mall—was our after-school playground. It lacked the size, stores, and popularity to entice larger packs of children, or teenagers for that matter, to its one lone hall. The mall had a Safeway at one end and a Walmart at the other. In between there were two discount department stores, SAAN and BiWay, a Love Stop, a music store, and the dreams of several storeowners in various stages of decay. Near the food court at the centre there was also an arcade.

We went to the mall arcade nearly every day to play *Mortal Kombat II*. If there was a group of teens crowded around the console, which was often the case, we mostly watched them fight each other. My friends and I preferred to keep play within our group, without an audience. But sometimes it couldn't be helped and we had to play against a stranger. Typically I'd stand next to a teenager twice my height and wait at the controls for the command to fight. Then I'd get annihilated handily. My turn would end with my avatar's spine getting torn out, or with being punched into a pit of spikes and dismembered torsos. It was predictable and humiliating.

But on this day I was in good spirits. I rested my quarter against the bottom of the screen, which was how you got in line to play. When my turn came, I stood next to a blond kid half made out of flannel and chose my fighter: Liu Kang, obviously.

I wasn't all that familiar with the lore behind the game's characters, but I knew Liu Kang was a good guy. He didn't look as dangerous or cool as some of the other characters, but that's how good guys were supposed to look. He looked like Bruce Lee; actually, he looked like the actor who played Bruce Lee in the film *Dragon: The Bruce Lee Story.* Plus, I had a pretty good grasp of his moves.

The match began and Liu Kang exploded from the ground and flew across the screen, kicking the blond kid's avatar, Sub-Zero, as if Kang were trying to ride his chest like a bicycle. I leapt away from my opponent and executed another flying kick. My leg hit him like a missile before he had the chance to block or duck. I did the same thing again. And again. I finished the round with a series of fireballs.

To kids our age, "cheap" was what you called someone who bested you without any creativity or skill. This was true in all aspects of life, not just *Mortal Kombat II.* If you posted up under the net in basketball because you were taller than everyone else and just scored baskets that way, that was cheap. Doing the same move over and over in a video game was cheap. I was being cheap. But for the first time, I had beaten a teenager. Round two went almost exactly the same way as the first round. I kept kicking his ninja avatar, then retreating, then kicking, then retreating. I knew I was being so cheap that I was practically cheating. But beating someone was thrilling. And the teenager didn't seem angry about losing. I giggled as the computer told me to "Finish Him." It was all I could do to mask the giddy tears that were pooling in my eyes, stinging.

The next kid in line knew how to block. He beat me back and forth across the screen then finished me off violently.

But for a very brief moment I was a champion.

By that time, my friends were already on their way to Walmart. There was a McDonald's right in the store and I liked to get a Happy Meal and make swamp water by mixing all of the pop flavours together at the self-serve fountain. After that, we walked through the store looking for easy ways to raise heck without breaking any laws. We weren't about to steal or damage property. Like always, we ended up in the toy section.

We walked down the aisle dedicated to *Lion King* merchandise and pressed buttons on all of the talking Mufasas so it became a cacophonous wall of James Earl Joneses promising his young son everything that the light touched. This was the height of my preteen rebellion. We never once got caught.

Leaving the toy section, Adrian did his usual bit with the teddy bear. He took the bear's arms and made it pantomime different activities while he narrated. "Today, I practised boxing. I washed the windows and ate dinner, and then . . . I felt myself up!" He always ended with the same line, and it killed every time. I smiled more than laughed. I wanted to be a good example, not go in for any of that dirty talk, but I didn't want to attract any attention by not reacting, either.

I got the joke. Adrian was making the toy masturbate. It looked like it was giving the Heimlich to its crotch and really going to town with it.

Generally, "whacking off" was the popular euphemism for what Adrian's bear was doing, and that seemed appropriate. "Spanking the monkey" was another phrase that I noticed getting thrown around in our class and in pop culture.

And in the Church, masturbation was sometimes called self-abuse.

Consequently, I thought masturbation involved batting your privates, like a cat attacking a dangling string. I suspected I was missing something.

The thing that was wrong about wasting time at the mall was exactly that: I was wasting time—and money—at the mall. This wasn't a sin, exactly, but it wasn't what good Mormon kids did. Sam didn't hang out at the mall when he was in elementary school. It wasn't something I wanted my parents to know about. And luckily, between my dad being called as the bishop in our ward and my mom taking care of my new baby sister, they didn't pay a ton of attention to where I went after school. What made it shameful was that all the money I spent consistently losing at *Mortal Kombat II* should have been earmarked for my eventual mission, which was only eight years away.

I was supposed to save $10,000 by the time I was nineteen, which was when I would receive my mission call. As far as I was concerned, $10,000 was an impossible figure. I always planned on reserving a chunk of the fifty dollars I was given for my allowance at the start of the month. But I never did. Instead, I squandered the money playing arcade games. My parents would be disappointed. Loitering at the mall after school was something bad kids did. And I didn't want to be a bad kid. Coming home in the dark confirmed and magnified my shame. I was basically a video game addict, stumbling home late.

I rang the bell on the bus to signal my desire to get off next and stood up to wait by the door. I realized my mistake instantly. There were teenagers at the back of this bus, and I was entirely alone. I waited by the door, dangling myself like a leg of lamb in front of a pride of miserable teens. I turned to face front, suddenly very curious where this bus was going to stop. But that was an even bigger mistake. Now the teenagers could see the back of my jacket. And the back was the worst part.

"Nice jacket!" someone called out to me. I knew he wasn't being genuine. The bus driver jumped to my defence.

"Hey, it's nicer than yours!" he called back to the teens. I got off the bus without saying a word.

I appreciated what the bus driver was trying to do, but his protection only made me seem more pathetic. And besides, the kids weren't wrong. I hated this jacket. I had wanted a Starter jacket, which every other boy at school seemed to have. They were pullovers that bore the colours and logos of professional sports teams. But Mom deemed them too expensive for their limited warmth. Instead, in time for spring, she got me an adult-size denim jacket emblazoned with the Toronto Blue Jays logo on the front and a nondescript scene of someone swinging a bat on the back. Not a specific player, mind you. Just a sort of faceless man in blue and white. The jacket looked out of date, and was too big for me. I thought it looked like an unlicensed knock-off of some better jacket. Only a bus driver would defend it.

Plus, I was a poser when I wore it. I had a firm rule: one should only wear a team's merchandise if one knew the names of at least two players on said team. I could wear my Utah Jazz cap because I knew Karl Malone and John Stockton. I might have wanted a Dallas Cowboys hat, but couldn't justify it, since I only knew of Emmitt Smith. And while I knew enough Chicago Bulls to safely wear their merchandise, I never would, because it was too easy to be a Bulls fan. They were already back-to-back champions, on their way to a three-peat. Liking the Bulls was cheap.

I hated walking home from the bus stop after dark. The quickest way was via a back alley that ran along a big property called Gold Bar Farm. This wasn't Gotham City, this was a darkened suburban alley, but in every street light I pictured myself like Bruce Wayne's parents, dead in a yellow spotlight.

I was excited for the coming of spring. I had been imagining a Magic Stick storyline that I was looking forward to playing out. Jumping on the trampoline was like writing for me. An idea for a story isn't a story until it's written down; likewise, I had to play through an idea on the trampoline to make it real. Otherwise it was just an idle daydream. In a plotline inspired by recent story arcs in Superman, Batman, Wonder Woman, and Green Lantern comics, Magic Stick was going to die and then be reborn with an updated look. I hadn't figured out who would kill him, but I had an image of what the new Magic Stick was going to look like. The biggest design change: he was going to lose the stick. Instead, the crystal would protrude from his forearms in glacier-like shards. He would lose the bandolier and the S&M mask. His skin would be porcelain white, almost glowing. Naturally, he'd have long hair, which would also be white.

Magic Stick was ripe for an upgrade. I had come up with several new superheroes since his invention. My new characters had better names: Midnight (a Batman type with a mystical helmet that flashed a blinding light that knocked out your average crook), Vengeance (a vigilante without superpowers consumed with revenge), and Sniperess (a female assassin), whose name I was especially proud of. To me, they sounded like they could be real comic book characters. I would probably have to change Magic Stick's name, especially if I were ditching his magic stick. Just calling him Magic seemed too vague. The only name I could think of was Saviour. But that might be a little too on the nose. A hero dies and is resurrected, but in a holier, purer form? That Magic Stick would be an allegory of Christ was unavoidable, but I wondered if it would be sacrilegious to use one of Christ's preferred names so cavalierly.

At the end of the alley, I walked down a hill with trees on both sides until I reached the grassy lane behind my street. I expected to see my family sitting at the kitchen table through the back window, but of course dinner wasn't ready yet. It felt so much later than it was. My mother was talking on the phone while flipping one of her thick homemade tortillas. My dad either hadn't gotten home yet or was already at the church for meetings. I could see that Mary was playing with our new baby sister, Anne, in the living room. No one had noticed that I was late.

Sunday dinner was the most important meal of the week.

With some slight variation for holidays, Sunday dinner consisted of roast beef, mashed potatoes and gravy, two vegetable dishes like carrots and beans, an often-neglected salad, and my mom's buns. The buns—not rolls, unless you were a missionary from America—were the best part. Not that the other stuff wasn't great, but my mother's bread was perfect.

Although my mom certainly did most of the heavy lifting, we all helped make Sunday dinner (and cleaned up after, unless I could successfully escape to the Super Nintendo downstairs without anyone noticing). In addition to setting the table and pouring everyone's water, I was responsible for making the barbecue sauce to accompany the roast beef. This sauce, which was an essential part of the dining experience, was made by putting a bunch of chili powder into a bowl of ketchup, and that was it. It was important to get the measurements right, with enough chili powder to darken the ketchup but not get it too dark or, heaven forbid, grainy.

My dad was always at the head of the table, and my mom was at his right. Although I was eleven, and getting too old to worry about such things, I always sat by my mom. Now that my little sister had been born, I knew my days at my mom's side were numbered.

The cast of Sunday dinner included the whole family: Erin, Gill, Sam, Mary, me, baby Anne, and our parents; our family friend Deanna and her mom, Peggy; and usually our neighbour Deb and her two young sons. This central cast was supported by rotating guest stars from church. Sometimes it was a young married couple who were new to the ward, and at least once a month the missionaries in the ward would come for supper, too.

Sunday dinner was also when we talked about church things as a family. We might have a little spiritual thought with family home evening,* but Sunday dinner was when we really got into it. During Sunday dinner we went around the table and reported on what we had learned that day in church.

"Sam, you get to go first," my dad said one Sunday evening, after everyone had filled their plates and I had shaped my mashed potatoes into a volcano. Sam was seated to my dad's left, which is the direction we always passed our food. My parents liked to tell people it was because of their liberal politics.

---

* All families were encouraged to set aside Monday night as family home evening. This was supposed to involve an activity, a gospel lesson, and refreshments.

"Wait, wait, wait," Deb said. "I want to know who these gentlemen are." She looked to the two young men in suits sitting at the end of the table.

"Oh, we're missionaries from the . . ." one of them began.

"I know you're missionaries. I've been around the Hudsons long enough to know what you are. But *who* are you?" Deb wasn't a member of the Church, a fact that excited every missionary that met her. To their chagrin, she had no interest in joining the Church, but she liked learning about it. She saw that we were a big family that liked one another and surmised that the Church had something to do with that.

"I'm sorry. Yes, Elders, who are you?" my dad said.

"I'm Elder Roylance," said Elder Roylance. He had strawberry-blond hair and soft features that burned crimson whenever he spoke. "I'm from Utah."

"Where in Utah?" Erin asked. She was sitting next to Sam.

"Centerville," he said. "I usually just tell people I'm from Salt Lake City though."

"And I'm Elder Smith," Elder Smith said. "I bet you that's a first, huh? A missionary named Elder Smith. But get this, I'm not from Utah." At that moment I decided I liked Elder Smith better than I liked Elder Roylance.

"Where you from?" Deb asked.

"Could someone pass the buns?" I asked.

"Las Vegas, Nevada," he said.

"Really? Are there lots of Mormons in Las Vegas?" Deb asked.

"Actually, yeah. There's quite a few," Elder Smith said.

"See, the Mormon pioneers moved from Missouri to Utah, then from there, groups of them settled in places in Idaho,

Alberta, Nevada, Arizona," my dad explained. "In fact, you know what I recently learned? You know the city Snowflake, Arizona?"

"Wasn't the last elder from there? Or it could have been the elder before him," Mary said.

"Please pass the buns," I repeated.

"It was the elder before me," Elder Roylance said. "Elder Fisher. I hear about him all the time."

"Elder Fisher was rad," Elder Smith said, almost to himself.

"I always thought it was a funny name for a city in Arizona, where there would never be a single snowflake," my dad continued. "And it turns out the first families to settle in the city were the Snows and the Flakes. And Snow, at least, is a famous family in the Church."

"Could someone please pass the buns," I said, no louder than the previous two times. I wanted the buns, but there was satisfaction in being ignored. It confirmed my status as the youngest. Gillian heard me and got me the buns. Gillian was good at hearing me.

"So, Sam," my mom said.

"My lesson was on service, I guess," Sam said. He was sixteen at the time, and had started growing his hair out long. It was nearly touching his shoulders, but he kept it in a tidy ponytail.

"And what did you learn about service?" Mom said.

"That it's good. Except we got on this huge tangent about Nazis and Mormons in Germany. But mostly, service is good, as long as it's not serving Nazis."

"Like military service?" Deb broke in.

My mom told her it was what most people would call charity.

"Doing nice stuff," my dad explained further. He had recently shaved his moustache, and it was still surprising to see his upper lip. My mom had made it clear that she wasn't a fan of the change. He had done it because bishops weren't supposed to have any facial hair.

"Is that what you're doing when I see you wrestling on the trampoline with that other young man?" Deb asked.

"What, Blake? I don't know if I'd call that service," Sam said.

"Oh, please," Erin said.

"Of course it is," my mom said. She explained to Deb that Blake was a young man in our ward who was around Sam's age, but because he had fetal alcohol syndrome he was a lot younger developmentally. The two great loves of Blake's life were the Book of Mormon and professional wrestling. He probably liked them for similar reasons: the melodrama, the clear good guys and bad guys, the monologues. He was born Cree and had been adopted by a retired white couple. He called himself a Lamanite.

When he wrestled Blake on the trampoline, Sam called himself Skull and Crossbones Jones, which I thought was a very cool name. They fought for the honour of carrying the world heavyweight title belt that Blake had fashioned out of construction paper and then had laminated. When Blake wrestled, he played to the crowd. He'd bug his eyes and flail when he got hit. Then he'd get energized from the invisible fans chanting his name. He choreographed fights on the fly. He let Sam know what moves were coming next.

"Calling it service makes it sound insincere. Like he's a service project. And that's not really it," Sam said.

"Who's got the belt now?" I asked.

"I'm the heavyweight champion at the moment, thanks for asking," Sam said. "But I did get a very threatening letter from him today, so it sounds like my days as champion might be numbered."

"Erin's next," my dad said.

My sister Erin had begun attending a young single adult (YSA) ward in the stake. As the name suggests, YSA wards are wards for adults aged eighteen to thirty who are unmarried. If you didn't meet the criteria, you were not welcome at a YSA ward. Except for the bishop. The bishops of YSA wards were older men who were married. Erin had also moved out of our house in the summer to live closer to the University of Alberta. She didn't always come home for Sunday dinner.

Erin's lesson from church was about the Atonement.

"But I did not know that at first," she said. "The teacher began by asking everyone what their favourite word was. And I'm sitting at the end of the row, so I go first. And at the time, I didn't know what my favourite word was. And so I said 'patio.'" She emphasized each syllable.

"That's a good word," Sam said. "Patio."

"I thought so! Pa-tio." Erin repeated it as if it were a rare delicacy in some foreign tongue. We all tested the word in our mouths, too. We said it in different accents: French, Italian, Japanese. "But then the next person went and her favourite word was 'forgiveness,' and the woman next to her chose 'love.' The teacher went around the entire room. Everyone added their favourite words and they were all gospel terms. Atonement, mercy, family. I mean, obviously that was the exercise! After everyone went the teacher came back to me and asked if I wanted to change my word."

"What did you say?" Gill asked.

"I said, 'Patio is a beautiful word, why would I want to change it.'"

When it was the missionaries' turn, Elder Smith answered for both of them. They had attended a class for visitors and new members called Gospel Essentials. Their lesson was on sacrifice.

"And what did you learn," my mom asked, looking at Elder Roylance.

"Sacrifice brings forth the blessings of heaven," the elder said, quoting a hymn. He looked like he was allergic to attention, and his skin was making him pay for what little he had just gotten: he started to blush.

"Greg, could you pass the buns, please?" Sam said.

"Airmail or Pony Express?" I asked. It was a question that needed to be asked at least once per meal. Sam answered that he would prefer the latter. I picked up the basket of buns and made it gallop in Sam's direction to the sound of the William Tell Overture.

"My lesson—drum roll please," my sister Mary said. We obliged. "Was on the law of chastity! I know, you're all terribly jealous."

"And what did you learn?" my mom asked, raising her eyebrows. After all, a lesson about the law of chastity was really just a lesson about sex. And, obviously, why it was bad before marriage.

"I learned that we are like blocks of wood. And when we break the law of chastity it's like someone hammers a nail into us."

"My word. That's awfully descriptive for church," Deb said.

"Yes. We're like blocks of wood with a nail in us, and repentance can take out the nail. But the wood will always have a hole where the nail had been," Mary said.

"Horrible, horrible analogy," my dad said.

"Why's that?" Deb asked.

"Well, because it's not true. It's meant to make people feel scared of sex and ashamed if they make a mistake. But the message of the gospel, as we believe it, is that of course repentance can fix the hole in the board. It's saying there are some sins that are too egregious for Jesus to fix," my dad explained.

"It doesn't do anyone any good to be made to feel like they are ruined," my mom said.

"I didn't say anything, but yeah, I thought the wooden block comparison was pretty dumb," Mary said.

"I didn't have a lesson today. We had a substitute and we watched *Johnny Lingo*," I said. The table became a cacophony of *Johnny Lingo* quotes. Naturally, Deb was confused. Erin explained that *Johnny Lingo* was a Church-made video about self-esteem from the 1970s. As with most Church movies, the production value was high, but that didn't make it any less goofy.

It takes place on an island somewhere in the South Pacific. The title character, Johnny Lingo, bargains with Moki for the hand of his daughter, Mahana. The time period is difficult to discern. Except for the one white man in the film, who seems to be a trader, everyone in the cast wears what appears to be traditional Polynesian attire.

Everyone on the island knows that Johnny Lingo is a shrewd trader, and thus they expect him to offer only one cow in exchange for Mahana. Johnny Lingo is also handsome, like a Samoan screen star with wavy black Bollywood hair. From what little we see of Mahana, she does not seem appealing. Still, when it comes time to settle on the dowry, Moki's opening gambit is to ask Johnny Lingo for three cows.

"Three cows? That is many," says Johnny Lingo, "but still not enough for Mahana." The gathered crowd gasps. Johnny then offers a stunned Moki eight cows! Moki, who is wearing an impossibly bad pageboy wig, accepts, and Johnny and Mahana go off on their honeymoon. When they return, we see that Mahana has blossomed into a beautiful and charming wife.

"Because someone thought she was an eight-cow woman, she became an eight-cow woman," Gill said.

"Okay, so I'm hearing that all a woman needs to have self-esteem is the approval of a man?" Deb said.

"That sounds about right!" My mom laughed. "It is a Mormon video, after all. Not the most feminist organization."

It wasn't unusual for Mom to complain about sexism in the Church. We knew she still believed in the Church. But we also knew that she thought a lot of men in the Church were dummies.

Deb and my mom kept talking about the Church and feminism while Erin and Gill cleared the table and Sam started taking orders for dessert. We had the choice of apple pie, blueberry pie, or banana cream pie, all homemade, with or without ice cream. I laid my head on my mother's lap and listened to her tell the story of what happened when my dad asked her father for permission to marry his daughter. Grandpa Wilcox firmly believed that a woman's life was over when she got married, and he didn't want my mom's life to be over just yet. He offered to give my dad some amount of money if he'd reconsider the proposal. My dad turned down the money.

Living according to gospel standards didn't make me unique among children my age. I called not drinking, smoking, or swearing being obedient, whereas most kids just called it being eleven. Prior to puberty, we are all Mormon. I wasn't ashamed of being Mormon because there was nothing to be ashamed about.

But I was ashamed of being a Boy Scout.

I hated Scouts.

Hated the paramilitary uniform.

Hated the condescending incentive of badges. Displaying them—on a red sash no less—seemed desperate. A sign of deep uncoolness. Scouts was a last resort for the socially awkward and unpopular, the kids who couldn't play sports or music, kids who had no affinity for science or technology and lacked the imagination for other nerdy pursuits. If you could do anything else, had literally any other interest, there was no reason to join Scouts. Unless your church made you.

As a result of some partnership probably dating from the early 1900s, the Church was connected to the Boy Scouts of America and therefore to Scouts Canada, too. The Church ran parts of its Young Men's program through Scouts, so going to weekly Scouts activities took on the weight of going to church. Attendance was mandatory—not because my parents would make me, but because it was a Church activity, and we attended all Church activities.

But Scouts wasn't the gospel, so I felt no guilt hating it. My parents didn't disagree. They hated Scouts, too. Aside from their natural (yet somewhat ironic) tendency to bristle at most instances of conformity, they both had their reasons.

My mom saw it as one example among many of the Church acting as though it was strictly an American church. It was pushing Americana and calling it the true church. And my mom was wary of American culture. She thought it was arrogant and proudly uninformed. My dad, on the other hand, didn't care for Scouts and the attendant camps because he had bad memories of them from his youth, of being in the tent with the other young men from his ward and listening to them tell dirty jokes all night that he only half understood.

And now, as a bishop, one of his major responsibilities was

overseeing the youth within the ward. He had to encourage kids to go to camp, including me.

But this year, it was to be no ordinary Scout camp. The summer of 1995 was the Scouts Canada ninth Alberta Jamboree. All the fun of pubescent boys, multiplied by however many Scout groups there were in the province, packed into one week in July.

No one was more excited about this camp than my Sunday School teacher, Brother Kemper. His enthusiasm for the Alberta Jamboree was so pure, so earnest, that it was nearly convincing. All the classic Scouting activities would be on offer: zip-lining, canoeing, rock climbing and rappelling, horseback riding, homesickness, and so much more! But most exciting for Brother Kemper was the badge trading with other troops. These weren't the badges you earned, but the troop badges that said where in the province you were from. They were meant to go on one of your shoulders. There was apparently a marketplace for them, along with scarves and woggles.

Brother Kemper was a grown-up nerd. He was lanky, had a tamed mop of blond hair, and wore large glasses that were at least a decade out of fashion. But he was arch, and I liked that. He taught the Sunday School class for ten- and eleven-year-old boys, called Blazers. There were only three of us in the class, me and a pair of brothers who were one year apart, Steven and Jason. Brother Kemper was not a Scout leader. But he really liked Scouting, and jamborees in particular, and so he was brought in as a Scout camp ringer.

The jamboree was set to take place in Kananaskis, near the town of Canmore, Alberta. The area, about an hour west of Calgary, was like New Jersey to Banff's Manhattan. The same mountains are right there, but you didn't have to pay national park rates. “We’ll be camping near a small mountain that, according to some vague Native lore, was really a giant who fell asleep a millennium ago,” he explained. “That’s why the camp’s theme is ‘Wake the Giant!’”

Brother Kemper opened the pamphlet he had in his hand to show us the jamboree theme in big block letters. He seemed as impressed with the marketing copy as we were.

And it came to pass that in July the time for the jamboree did come. And young men did pack their tents and pocket knives, yea their granola bars and hiking boots and jerky of all kinds. From the north and from the south they did gather together and did set up camp in a great and spacious field, surrounded by a great many trees and hills, yea, even the Rocky Mountains in the near distance.

Had I cried about having to go to the Alberta Jamboree? I had. I wasn’t anticipating feeling homesick, but being around only Church friends, who weren’t really friends, for an entire week seemed like it would be exhausting. It felt like punishment, like community service.

When I got there I was surprised by the number of older boys in attendance. I was barely old enough to be there, so I wasn’t surprised I was younger than everyone, but who were these young adults that stood out like chaperones? Apparently, you could be a Scout when you were eighteen.

“They’re called Rovers,” Brother Kemper told me. “The Church doesn’t have them because we go on missions instead at that age. I bet you’re jealous.”

"Oh totally," I said. Imagine being able to drive and allowed to date, and still choosing to be in Scouts. I pitied them.

I noticed quickly that I was among a very small minority of boys who had hair long enough to be tucked securely behind their ears. Back home, Sam's hair was a quarter of the way down his back. We all knew he'd have to cut it before his mission started in two years, but until then he looked like a rock star. He played the drums in a band and wrote songs for girls on his guitar. When I'd enter his room without invitation—a sacred right and privilege bestowed upon the younger brother—if he wasn't reading his scriptures, then he was fooling around on his guitar. Sam would often offer to teach me how to play, but I never said yes. He had the musical ability. I just read comic books.

Because Sam was nearly six years older than me, when he grew his hair out there was no mistaking his gender, even with the ponytail. On the other hand, I seemed to be getting mistaken for a girl with insulting regularity.

It seemed I was failing at masculinity, and right when it was starting to matter, too, when the opposite sex was becoming much more interesting. I felt sorry for myself whenever I was misgendered, but I felt sorrier for the girl I wasn't. Because, I told myself in the mirror, I was an unfortunate-looking young lady. The people who were mistaking me for a girl just accepted that I was an unattractive one. Bless them for their willful blindness. I was at the point in tweendom when all my adult teeth had come in, but my adult face was still a few years off. Massive chompers and they needed braces. Among them were incisors that had grown in above the rest of my teeth. They looked demonic, which I was a little proud of. My mouthful of teeth, combined with my baby cheeks, made me look chipmunk-esque. I laughed like one, too.

When we arrived at our campsite and pitched our tent, I slipped away from my group to look around. I judged people by how earnest they looked, how happy they seemed to be at the jamboree. If they were wearing their Scouts uniform, they were already lost. Not that I was about to talk to any strangers. This was no place to make friends.

A couple of boys started chanting behind me. Their bodies didn't follow me, but their voices did. I knew they were directing their chant at me, even though there were hundreds of other campers milling around. "BOY OR GIRL!" they chanted. "BOY OR GIRL! BOY OR GIRL!"

Technically, though this was Boy Scouts, it wasn't an unfair question. There were girl Rovers. But these boys were taunting me. They started thumping their fists against their chests to the beat, like they were trying to get the crowd to join them.

I didn't answer them. I tried to give them a dirty look, then kept walking.

"See anything cool?" Brother Connor asked as I got closer to camp. "Were you looking to trade some badges?" Brother Kemper's enthusiasm had gotten to him, it seemed.

"No, I was just looking around," I said. Brother and Sister Conner were the ward's camp specialists. They weren't in our ward, but because neither 4th Ward, where we lived, nor 2nd Ward, where they did, had an overabundance of youth, and because both wards met in the same building, we did a lot of things together. Brother Conner had two sons at the camp with him. Matt was my age, and Josh was the same age as my older sister Mary. We didn't have much in common. Like their parents, they liked outdoorsy activities.

Brother Conner always spoke with his chin and eyebrows slightly raised, as if he were waiting for me to finish his sentences and inevitably get something wrong. "Where is everyone?" I asked.

"I think a few of the guys are tossing a football around back there." He pointed vaguely behind him. "There's a welcome assembly in about an hour, and we'll eat there."

It was the idea of running into the same kind of chants later that made me tell Brother Conner what had happened. I told him what the kids had chanted earlier. It felt like a risky thing to confess.

"Well," he said, "that kind of goes with the territory when you have long hair."

I nodded and went into my tent.

For twelve-year-old boys, life is a cold war in which you are pitted against every other twelve-year-old boy. Every ally is a potential spy, testing vulnerabilities and searching for the biggest, easiest targets while jockeying for power and popularity in any social situation. Puberty looms like a bitter *deus ex machina*; it will save you one day, but not before it first breaks your voice, deforms your face, and brings you shuddering to your knees. It was only by strict adherence to social rules that one had any hope of surviving. This was true in school and, to lesser extent, in church too.

The first organized activity before dinner at the jamboree was an extended object lesson. It involved only our scout troop and was a reminder of who we were as Latter-day Saints. Mormons loved analogies.

Half of us were blindfolded and led away from camp. To get back, we would have to trust one of the non-blindfolded campers from our troop to lead us back safely. But, despite their claims and offers of aid, only one of these would-be guides could be trusted to return us to camp. That person represented Christ. This was meant to teach us about the importance of listening to and obeying the Saviour's voice, despite all the other forces distracting us, pulling us every which way. Some people might seem trustworthy or righteous, but then they lead us astray. With all the temptation in the world, how do we know we're following the right path? What happens when we follow the wrong voice? How can we show that we're listening to Christ's voice?

And so forth.

I was among the blindfolded, carefully led through some woods into what felt like a clearing. Our guides dropped away and we were left alone. After not too long we heard bleating sounds along with snapping twigs and whipping branches. I made out individual names, and I recognized the voices of my fellow campers. Each pubescent squawk called out to a different blind camper. Divide and conquer.

I listened for clues of godliness in the voices.

One of Joseph Smith's favourite hymns was "A Poor Wayfaring Man of Grief." It was one of my favourites, too. The song was about a man who meets his friend in a series of increasingly desperate situations: starving, naked, condemned to die. In each verse, the man attends to his friend's need, including, at the end, by offering up his own life in his friend's stead. It's then that we learn that the condemned, poor, starving, naked inmate had been Jesus all along. "These deeds shall thy memorial be," the Saviour says. "Fear not, thou didst them unto me."

It's a powerful hymn, and not just because Joseph Smith sang it on the night he was martyred while imprisoned in Carthage Jail when a mob stormed the jailhouse and shot him and his brother Hyrum. It is powerful because it tells a story that teaches the basic lesson of the gospel: be kind and good to everyone, especially the poor wayfaring men of grief, because how you treat others is how you treat the Saviour.

With those criteria in mind, I knew exactly whose voice I would follow. In terms of social capital, Steven was the absolute least of us. The Zimmers, the Connor boys, maybe they were cool in their school, maybe they weren't, but I knew they had friends outside of church. Steven had no group. He was unpopular in all settings. He walked like a velociraptor, like his underwear was too tight. When he was picked on, which was often, his best and only defence was to belch as violently as he could in the direction of his tormentors, the way a lion might roar, or a silverback might bang his chest, only he didn't have the physicality to back it up. His belches were impotent. Our leaders made it clear they didn't condone any teasing or bullying, but I could tell that Steven annoyed the heck out of them, too.

The rules of impending teendom had as much sway over Steven as raindrops on a street light. Sometimes that's honourable: rugged individuality, anti-heroes, the road less travelled. But that wasn't Steven (never Steve). He didn't ignore the rules on principle. He wasn't a rebel. Rather, it was like he hadn't been paying attention when the rules were explained. He was curling at centre ice during the Stanley Cup Finals. No one likes that kind of rule-breaker.

He didn't listen to instructions, he spoke out of turn, and he rarely stayed on topic. He was almost a unifying figure: he annoyed everyone. I felt it was important if not to defend Steven, then to at least not add to his torment. But it was hard when he seemed to deserve at least some of it. He was an imperfect victim. But I knew if I didn't try to be nice to him, no one would.

Who in our Scout troop, which was also our Young Men's quorum, better represented the messianic prophecy of Isaiah, that Christ would be "despised and rejected of men, a man of sorrows, and acquainted with grief?"

Confident that I understood the lesson I was supposed to learn, when I heard Steven call to me, I followed him. We didn't move fast. I acted on every direction he gave, through mysteriously tight spaces, over thick grasses, between trees. Every step felt precarious. The other voices faded away. Hopefully this meant we were close to camp.

After a while of this, Brother Connor was also beside us, urging me to follow him, instead. His voice softened like he was a father about to give bad news. But I was more certain with each plea that he was playing a very convincing devil. The more sincere he sounded, the more I knew Steven must be the right choice. Steven didn't sound anything like that. Obviously.

"I can't come and get you, I wish I could," Brother Connor said. "But you have to choose to follow me first." In that moment, he almost convinced me, but I had been too faithful to Steven for too long to throw away that faith now.

Then I heard Brother Connor's voice move closer to Steven's voice. Then aggressive whispering: "Where are you even taking him?"

"Into the lake," replied Steven.

Brother Connor sighed. "Okay, game's over. Take off the

blindfold." With a touch of frustration he explained that he had been the one I was supposed to follow. I was annoyed that this part of the exercise had such an obvious answer. Of course the leader would be the Christ figure.

Inspired by a story Brother Connor had shared about an older group of Young Men he had brought to camp years before, it was decided that the boys would take Steven on a snipe hunt.

Getting Steven on board would not be a challenge.

Had he ever been on a snipe hunt?

He had not.

What were snipes?

Steven was suspicious, a common trait among people who are routinely picked on.

Todd, one of the Zimmer brothers, called to the man tending the campfire.

"Hey, Brother C, what's a snipe?"

"A snipe? It's like a little weasel."

"I thought it was a bird?" Todd said.

"No no, it's like a weasel," Brother Connor said.

"But it has glowing eyes, right?"

"Oh, most definitely. But only at night. That's the only time you can see them at all. Are you going to try to catch one?"

"We were thinking about it," Todd said.

"Are there snipes in the forest around here?" Steven asked.

"There should be," Brother Connor said, then returned to his fire.

Glowing eyes.

Steven was on board.

"We're going tonight?" he asked.

It was decided that, yes, that night was as good as any. The weather was right for snipes. Depending on who you asked, the conditions needed to be either clear and dead quiet or foggy and damp. Steven didn't register the inconsistencies. Small details like size, shape, or species were unimportant in the face of adventure.

The most important job on a snipe hunt was the bagger. That person needed to be extra quiet and still, but also quick and fearless. While everyone else fanned out into the woods, looking for signs of snipes, including and especially their glowing eyes, but also their droppings, which were small and red like berries, the bagger would stay in place, crouched low, holding his stick and, as his title suggests, a sack.

"So, we'll probably all be flushers, and maybe Dawson will be our bagger, since he has lots of experience," Tyson, the older Zimmer brother, suggested. He and Dawson were priests. They were sixteen. They were always tight at church, but they went to different high schools, so I didn't know if they hung out outside of Mormonhood. "Unless you think you'd like to be the bagger?" he asked Steven.

Steven did want to be the bagger, in fact. He would be a very capable bagger. He would likely cry if he didn't get to be the bagger.

"And you won't mind being alone in the dark, in the woods?" Dawson asked.

Piece of cake. Steven was all in. In fact, maybe he would take a walk through the woods that afternoon, to find the perfect snipe-catching stick. "I can get familiar with the area, even though I can actually see very well in the dark. And my hearing is excellent, too."

Steven made hydraulic sounds as he brought a pair of invisible binoculars to his face. He turned his head like an automaton, letting us all get a good look at the spittle pooling on both sides of his mouth. "Heat scan complete!" he said. "Triangulating on target. *Tchuuch tchuuchk.* Just kidding. I am not an android, or a cyborg. Although I wish I was! A cyborg mostly." He made another scan, then finished with a barrage of blaster noises.

"The snipes won't know what hit them," a Zimmer said. Then he laughed more than the situation merited.

I had never heard of snipes either. I was intrigued when the older boys first started talking about hunting them. But the degree to which the boys were trying to include Steven in their fun was suspicious. While Steven and the gang discussed the finer points of snipe disposal and domestication, Josh whispered to his brother and me what was actually happening.

The true purpose of the snipe hunt was to bring an unsuspecting colleague into the woods at night and then leave them there, where it would slowly dawn on them that they'd been duped. As far as pranks went, this one felt both cruel and anticlimactic.

Steven was a test. I was supposed to be kind. We all were. There was really no way around the scriptures. *By this shall all men know that ye are my disciples, if ye have love one to another.* It's just that in none of the scriptures where Jesus talks about caring for others does he mention how frustrating others might be.

I couldn't imagine Sam letting anyone bully his friend Blake the way the boys bullied Steven, and Blake could be a handful, albeit in a different way. It wasn't that I feared the social repercussions of being a killjoy. Popularity only mattered at school—mostly, I only saw church people at church, whereas being a pariah at school would have had daily consequences. No, I didn't always stand up for Steven, because Steven should have known better. Blake had a visible disability, but in my twelve-year-old opinion Steven's behaviour was at least partly a choice, and he could've made a different one.

Steven found his stick and, as the afternoon wore on, his enthusiasm for what were going to be either his new pets or research subjects was exhausting. "I wonder if they can be domesticated. I believe weasels can be trained. We can probably catch more than one. I can come home with a private army of snipes."

My dad was at the jamboree for the night. He arrived after the plans for the snipe hunt had been set. He was allergic to pranks, especially ones aimed at weaker kids.

Walking back from dinner, my dad pulled Steven aside. "They're tricking you, Steven. It's a prank."

"Right," Steven said.

"Look at me for a sec. The snipe hunt isn't a real thing. It's a trick."

"Yeah, I know," he said, like it was obvious.

"They take someone snipe hunting, then they leave them in the forest." My dad said again, "They're tricking you, do you get it?"

Steven assured him one more time that he did. Snipes weren't real. Got it.

We walked on.

"I wonder if you could take out whatever glows in their eyes . . ."

"Steven, they aren't real, remember?" I said. "My dad just said."

"Right. I know. But if they are real, there's likely a substance in their eyes that allows them to glow. It's called bioluminescence. I think it's the same stuff that goes into Timex watches. Or it's a synthetic version in the watches but it's probably based on something in nature. Like snipes."

"Except . . ."

"I know. I meant if they were real. And we'll find out tonight if they are real! Once and for all!" Then he laughed too maniacally for it to be funny.

After word got out that Bishop Hudson had spoiled the secret of the snipe hunt, the enthusiasm to go through with it died out, though not entirely. Steven was still game to wander the woods after dark. The Zimmers obliged him, but without much zeal. It took a group to really leave someone alone.

That summer, along with the long hair, or maybe because of it, I experimented with wearing a bandana. It was white with a pattern of maple leaves on it. I was self-aware enough to understand that it didn't make me look tough or intimidating, even to people my own age. But I liked how bandanas looked on other people. And I had never been mistaken for a girl when I wore it.

After a very long week, the jamboree had ended. We stopped in Canmore on our way back to Edmonton. I didn't want to confuse any of the good citizens of Canmore. I wanted to look like a boy.

Helping in that department, I hoped, was the t-shirt I was wearing. It was navy blue with a Superman symbol on it. Ostensibly there were girls who liked comics, but I hadn't met any. And though Supergirl used the same "S" symbol, for most people it primarily represented Superman. *MAN.* I figured the manly association should be enough for any stranger on the fence about my gender.

Most proudly, I wore my Umbro shorts. All my friends at school wore slightly oversized Umbro shorts. They were like the official clothing of soccer players, and all my friends played soccer. Mine weren't the style of Umbro shorts that were popular at the time, though. They didn't have the alternating shiny/matte square pattern, and they were made of flimsier material, too. They felt like the kind of cheap shorts you might get as a free promotion. But they had the signature double-diamond logo on the knee, and that was all that mattered. They were Umbros and Umbros were cool. Normally, trendy things were out of reach for me, always too expensive for the good they provided, like Starter jackets. These Umbros, which were hand-me-downs from my sister Erin's boyfriend, weren't completely right, but they weren't completely wrong either. And so, I loved them.

Black nylon soccer shorts. Superman t-shirt. Patriotic Canadian bandana. Curly hair that hung down past my chin. Teeth badly in need of braces. The clothes, the face, of a child.

I went with Brother Connor into a small corner store. As he walked the few aisles picking up supplies for the drive home, I moved to the magazine rack to see what, if any, comic books they had on offer. Spinner racks at corner stores were unreliable. The same comics would linger on them for months. But sometimes you got lucky with a store that kept their titles up to date. This store wasn't one of them. I loitered in front of the magazine rack anyway, looking for something interesting.

I still bought *Cracked* every so often. I preferred it to *Mad*, which I decided was the more wicked of the two because it was more popular. I passed similar moral judgements on most consumer goods. Coke and Pepsi were wicked; 7 Up and Sprite were good. This was an easy one since cola had caffeine, which was basically a drug. I knew of no good Mormons who drank the stuff. (Backsliders, known as Jack Mormons, sure.) Beyond the obvious, Nintendo was good, morally speaking, whereas Sega was wicked, proud. The proof was in their hand-held gaming systems. The Sega Game Gear had a colour display, but required six batteries. My humble Nintendo Game Boy had a green-and-greyscale screen, but only took four double-As. Greedy and proud or simple and pure? Energizer batteries were meaner, again more proud, at least compared to the humble, hardworking Duracells. It was harder to pinpoint exactly why I thought Duracells were more inherently *good* than Energizers, but the latter's "z" certainly didn't help them. "Z"s were sharp and cocky.

Basically, if I suspected something was better, or cooler, or more popular, and I didn't already subscribe to it, it was because I believed that I was better for not doing so. Was it a sin to like the Chicago Bulls, or Marvel comics, or to own a Sega Genesis instead of a Super Nintendo? No, of course not, but in a way didn't it show what kind of person you were? It showed what was important to you, whether you stood by your beliefs or followed the crowd.

I scanned the bottom rack, where the kids' magazines normally were, your *OWL*s, *Chickadee*s, and *Tiger Beat*s, then moved my gaze upwards. But the top rack here was different than the one at the convenience store in my neighbourhood. Not only was the adult material—the pornography—not safely behind the counter, but the smut wasn't even confined to the top row. In fact, pornography took up the entire top half of the display. I saw, for the first time, directly at eye level, full covers of *Hustler*, *Cheri*, *Swank*, *Club*, and others.

The first cover I noticed showed a woman partly wearing a wetsuit. I knew from wetsuits; they were neoprene singlets that were worn over a bathing suit. They made the frigid lake slightly less breathtaking. But this woman wasn't wearing hers over anything. She was soaking wet. The top half of her wetsuit was unzipped down to her waist. She was holding her breasts, but her hands were unequal to the task; most of both breasts were visible. It was clear from the woman's facial expression and positioning that she had unzipped her wetsuit intentionally. She was biting her lower lip.

Behind her, on a different cover, was a small inset of a topless woman crawling toward the camera, her nipples covered by little black stars. But for those black stars, she was completely naked. Her gaze was aggressive, like she would taunt me if I looked away.

And so I didn't. I couldn't. While other shoppers bought their treats and supplies, I stood in front of that magazine rack with my legs shaking. It felt like I was backstage at some play, getting more nauseous the closer it got to the curtain rising. Pebbles and glass tumbled together in my stomach. I was short of breath. I felt like I was in trouble, caught red-handed. I hated it.

But also, I loved it.

This was not my first erection. But this one felt different. Could a boner break itself? Was it like making a funny face, where if you weren't careful your grimace became permanent? I worried that looking at the woman in the wetsuit would break mine. Was it going to stay like this: flexed and obstinate? I'd have to go to my parents and tell them what was wrong, even though they'd be able to see it through my flimsy Umbros.

I'd have to tell them how it got that way. That I saw bad pictures and I didn't look away.

My erection didn't go down when I finally turned away from the magazine rack, or when I walked out of the store and back toward Brother Connor's car. My thin nylon shorts were powerless to conceal or contain it. Even if I had known about sweeping one's penis up into one's waistband, my Umbro-lites were too loose to do any good. And they had no pockets, so I couldn't manually keep it down by placing my hands inside them to compensate. The best I could do was sort of lean forward and hope my t-shirt hung over the outcropping.

This was the consequence of sin, wasn't it? Shame. And the loss of the Spirit, too. The Holy Ghost was supposed to warn you of incoming temptation, but it didn't stick around when it was ignored. I had felt that. The warning, and the Spirit leaving. The warning had been that feeling of breathlessness, with nausea around the edges. And I had felt the Spirit leave, hadn't I? That was the stage fright feeling, the nerves. And, to top it off, I probably broke my penis, which I'd have to explain to my parents, which was probably the worst thing I could imagine doing. They would be so disappointed.

I sang all the verses of "I Am a Child of God" in my head until everything calmed down. But something had begun. I was still a child of God, like the song said. But I wasn't innocent anymore.

TRUE TO THE FAITH

(1995–2002)

I BECAME CONSUMED by the hunt. I was like a twelve-year-old gambler, always weighing odds, keeping one eye open for the chance to make a bet and win big.

I was never not hunting. My hunger was constant, insatiable by design. I had my interests—I still read comic books and my scriptures—but the hunt was never far from my mind. It wasn't something I was proud of, or that I could talk about with anyone. It was a battle that raged inside me. No one could know that I was a hunter, not my friends at school and certainly not my family. I didn't want anyone to know that I had become aware that there existed anything *to* hunt. I was equal parts ashamed and committed.

I cared not for bums nor for legs and whatever mystery lay between them. I hunted boobs. I wanted to see breasts, as bare as possible. Cleavage didn't really count. In my limited experience of magazines, posters, and the backs of calendars, I found that pushing boobs together robbed each breast of its shape, creating a far less alluring thing. While hunting, my true hope of hopes was always to see a naked breast. A nipple. One or both, it didn't matter. Muscle mags had some very revealing swimsuit special issues, or maybe someone didn't put a *Penthouse* back on its high shelf.

Of course, I told myself that I'd only look at that which wasn't pornography, namely breasts that had their nipples covered. I knew how I'd feel if I were to look at pornography: like a fugitive, all alone and dirty. I still felt bad looking at scantily clad women, but I knew it wasn't quite as serious. Still, I was like an addict, full of impotent promises to never do it again. But when I was put on the spot, my success rate for keeping my vow was pretty low.

The hunt was stressful. I imagined magazine racks in convenience stores were watched like maximum-security prisoners. I wasn't about to pick up a *Penthouse* or *Hustler* and peruse it in the store. That would be flagrant, illegal, immoral. I'd be caught out for the perverted kid I was but pretended not to be. Besides, more and more of the adult magazines were being packaged in clear polybags, which prevented browsing. This included the ones I most wanted to flip through: the *Playboy Special Editions*—*Playboy College Girls*, *Playboy Lingerie*, *Playboy Wet & Wild*—which were different from regular *Playboy*s. You couldn't say you read them for the articles, as there weren't any. But the women on those covers always seemed the happiest to be there.

In 1995, *Showgirls* came out. The film, about a runaway stripper who claws her way to the top of the glamorous world of topless dancing in Las Vegas, was rated NC-17, which I learned was reserved for movies that were even worse than R-rated. The main character, Nomi, was played by a young woman who had previously starred in a Saturday morning sitcom called *Saved by the Bell*, in which she played feminist overachiever Jessie Spano. The difference between the two characters was so stark that *Showgirls* became an event on entertainment news. *Entertainment Tonight* seemed to have a segment about the movie every night for a month. They showed scenes of Nomi working in a dingy strip club before she gets her big break dancing in a show on the Strip. The clips were always scrupulously censored so as to be appropriate for prime time, but they offered a glimpse into a miraculous world where women danced in the spotlight and aggressively removed their clothes.

I never missed an episode of *Entertainment Tonight*. And while I couldn't always rely on it to cover movies like *Showgirls*—there weren't a lot of movies like *Showgirls*—between stories about Victoria's Secret models, the annual *Sports Illustrated* swimsuit issue, and a new celebrity posing in *Playboy* every month, there was usually at least one segment per episode that would take my breath away.

But the time to go hunting for boobs on TV was Friday and Saturday night. That's when Viewers Choice, the pay-per-view channel that resided in the upper wasteland of our television dial, would start promoting its adult material. Alongside trailers for real movies like *Casino* and *Apollo 13* there were those with parody names like *Babewatch* and *Passenger 69*. On the whole, the porno trailers were less explicit than the *Entertainment Tonight* segments, but the music and carnal sounds from the films quietly underscored the trailers and that was enough.

Around that time, a new comic book company arose to challenge DC and Marvel for the hearts and minds of young men: Image Comics. The company knew what it was doing. It was as though every Image comic book character sprang forth fully formed from the collective horniness and rage of America's pubescent boys. Every character looked so freaking cool and intense. The men carried guns roughly the size of aircraft carriers. Costumes were impossibly detailed, with pouches and superfluous straps crossing this way and that. Faces were pencilled with lines denoting rage or constipation. And the women! The female characters all had proportions that made *Babewatch* seem restrained. Waists were tiny, breasts were planets often barely kept in check by the whisper of a costume. No matter the situation, these women heroes always jumped into action with their butts in the air and their chests out.

The female superheroes—Fairchild, Diva, Witchblade, especially Witchblade—were so hot that Image Comics published swimsuit specials featuring pin-up drawings of their superheroines in bathing suits that somehow provided even less coverage than their usual costumes. These were only a problem/opportunity during my monthly trip to Warp Comics, Edmonton's biggest comic book store, where they were mixed in with the regular new releases. There was no age requirement to look at the special editions. Ipso facto: the pin-up art wasn't pornography. Verdict: looking at them was bad—the nervous feeling in my stomach told me the Spirit was leaving me when I picked one up—but I didn't need to confess to the bishop (my dad). Still, I would try really hard not to look at them, but after some internal struggle, when a new Image Comics swimsuit special came out, I'd pick it up, crouch down, and study it.

Later that same summer, I was in Sicamous, the closest town to our cabin in British Columbia, accompanying my mom as she stocked up on supplies. The grocery store kept its spinner racks pretty up to date, especially compared to what they sold at the Sea Store. They didn't have any new issues of the titles I collected (*Green Lantern*, *Steel*, and, inconsistently, *Batman*) but they had a sourcebook to Image Comics. It was like a guide introducing new readers to the characters and history of the new big comic book company. In the checkout line, when my mom asked me if they had any comics I wanted, I ran and got the sourcebook.

I put it in one of the many grocery bags that weighed down the boat as we went back to the cabin. I waited until we had docked to study my purchase. I stayed in the boat while everyone else went upstairs to put away groceries and start making dinner. I sat down in one of the seats near the engine, flipped open the guide, and began reading up on some of the characters I had never seen before. Each page was a pin-up of a different hero or villain, along with a short bio and backstory. The pin-ups were drawn by different artists, but they all shared a similar aesthetic: exaggerated and slick, detailed renderings of desperate male fantasies. I loved it.

The double-page spread on the WildC.A.T.s, Image's answer to Marvel's X-Men, might have been the coolest two pages of comic book art I had ever seen. Drawn photo-realistically, it looked like a Calvin Klein ad for superheroes. The WildC.A.T.s looked as though they had just finished working out together. They were sweaty and the men were only half dressed. Zealot, a cross between DC's Wonder Woman and Marvel's Psylocke but with stark white hair, was flexing her not-insubstantial bicep near the middle of the frame. She was wearing her costume—sort of a red bikini with red metal shoulder pads and gloves—but her hair was in a messy ponytail. Then there were the men on the team: Spartan, Warblade, and Grifter, who was wearing his trademark trench coat but no shirt. And out front, lying on her stomach, head resting on her hand, fingertip lingering on her teeth, was Voodoo. She was smiling like this whole page was our little secret.

Her purple-and-gold costume was unzipped partway, and two beads of sweat charged bravely into the valley between her breasts. Her bum was raised slightly, as if to make sure it would be in the picture. And here was the illustration's true power, for it was impossible to discern whether her bum was clothed or not. It was a mound of deep amber that didn't quite seem to match the gold on her costume. Instead, her bum seemed to be the same colour as her cleavage and face. It appeared that, improbably, Voodoo wasn't wearing any pants. Now, as I have said, bums held very little interest for me. I could take them or leave them. I knew men were supposed to find them sexy, but I didn't understand why. Nevertheless, I couldn't take my eyes off Voodoo's bum. It was the idea of going bottomless—of being truly half naked, especially during a team workout. And in front of so many people, too.

Then the familiar breathlessness, the pit in my stomach. All the telltale signs that I was looking at something I shouldn't be looking at. Oh, but I couldn't stop. Voodoo wasn't wearing pants! Maybe! Or maybe it was just her costume. I stayed in the back of the boat, alone, trying to figure out what I was staring at for close to an hour. There was no thought to do anything else with the picture, or with my erection. I just looked at the glistening WildC.A.T.s and tried to remember how to breathe.

"I was looking through your comic book," my dad said a few days later. We were all gathered at the kitchen table for lunch. "Some of the women in there sure weren't wearing a lot of clothes."

"Yeah," I said, trying to convey disappointment, as though the sexy drawings had surprised me, too, which wasn't entirely untrue.

"Do you think it's good to look at pictures like that?" he asked. My dad was rarely the one to do the hands-on parenting and he seemed uncomfortable. I assumed it was because my comic book was so wicked. "Is that how we should think about women?"

"It's not a real comic book," I said. "It's like a catalogue, kind of, for other comics."

"Uh huh," my dad said, trying to follow along.

"I don't usually read those actual comics."

"You're saying your usual comics aren't like that?"

"Yeah," I said.

"Well, that's good," he said, though he didn't seem convinced. But he didn't seem to know where to take this parenting moment. He wasn't about to tell me to throw the book away, though I assumed that's what he wanted me to do.

Everyone had found their seat around the table. Dad asked Mary to give a blessing on the food.

Had any child been more fully and relentlessly rebuked than I?

Sometimes there were miracles on my walk home from school. Once, I found a page from a magazine lying on the ground in the middle of the path through the woods behind our house. It wasn't torn. It had been cut out with scissors. On one side, a naked woman rested on a snowmobile, winter weather be damned. And on the other side, a woman was wearing suspenders, but no shirt.

I picked the page up. Studied it. These pictures were much worse than a sexy drawing. This was actual pornography. From a magazine and everything. The less time I spent looking at it, the better.

The war within me raged. If I dropped the picture, I would defeat temptation and be blessed. If I brought it home with me to study later, I would be committing myself to sin, admitting that I was powerless in the face of temptation, weak.

I split the difference. I knew the truth: I would regret either decision. If I didn't look at it, I might never get the opportunity to see naked boobs ever again. So I placed the page at the side of the path, so that it wouldn't tempt or be trampled by anyone else who might pass by. I piled some leaves over top of it for added protection. I wouldn't look at it then. But I anticipated being less strong some other time.

What angel or devil had cut it out of a magazine and left it in the middle of my path, directly in front of me? Bless whoever did.

Has there ever been a boy more obsessed with breasts? What other twelve-year-old searched so hard for even a fleeting glimpse? I was certain that I was alone among my friends in having these perverted urges. They never talked about breasts.

And even if they did, I wouldn't have listened. I was Mormon. I didn't go in for that kind of talk.

And yet here I was, without a doubt the only Mormon boy who thought constantly about seeing naked breasts.

It was lonely, living two lives, serving two masters.

It was easy to get onto the roof of our bungalow. First, you used our fence to climb onto the aluminum shed beside the house, which smelled like old dirt and gasoline and was filled with wasps and disorder. I hated going inside it, but it made the roof accessible. The roof did not offer much more than an elevated view of the street in front of our house. But it still felt special. From the roof, our family home seemed small. It was miraculous that all of us could live under this one L-shape. So much happened underneath my feet.

I could be alone up there.

I wanted to be alone. I deserved to be alone. Earlier that day I had distinguished myself among my siblings by getting suspended from school. It was for a stupid reason, the consequence of some mild thirteen-year-old-boy rebellion that seemed especially stupid when I imagined telling my family about it. My friend had brought a rubber mallet to gym class. While we were changing, he swung it at a column, cracking the plaster. Then he took a few swings at a crumpled pipe that ran along the wall. I borrowed the mallet to do some swinging, too. Apart from cracking some paint, I didn't cause any damage to the pipe. But it had been fun.

That apparently didn't matter to the vice-principal. Vandalism was vandalism. And the punishment for vandalism was a three-day suspension. Rules were rules. The vice-principal, who was not without sympathy, called my mom to pick me up while I sobbed. On the drive home, my mother was quiet. I knew from the silence that she was disappointed in me. What was worse, she said, was that I had embarrassed her.

That evening, it felt right to be on the roof. Batman was always on roofs. It seemed like a place for introspection. A place to find meaning. I didn't know exactly how to think deep thoughts, or what a deep thought would be in this situation, but if I were to think some, the roof would be the ideal spot. Moody music should have been playing, but all I heard were the sounds of a sleeping neighbourhood.

I said a prayer. I asked for forgiveness, not so much for the vandalism, but for disappointing my parents and not living up to my potential. I closed in the name of Jesus Christ, amen.

In the centre of our roof there was a skylight. I got up and walked toward it. It seemed to emanate warmth and cast a small square of amber light in all directions that got eaten up quickly by the dark.

I looked down.

On a table by the closet I could see a framed picture of my parents from a time when my dad wore a beard and my mom was experimenting with a perm. It was posed but they looked genuinely happy. The TV was on and no one walked underneath the skylight. But family life was happening. And I was outside. I was in the dark, in the night. The light could touch me, but I couldn't feel any warmth.

My mom wasn't going to dish out further punishment for what I did with the mallet. She knew that disappointing and embarrassing her had taught me my lesson. No need to make me feel worse, as if that were possible. But she would facilitate my repentance. To that end, I was told to read a sermon that my mother printed off the Church's website. "Making the Right Choices" had been given by Richard G. Scott, one of the Twelve Apostles of the Church.* The title was so on the nose for my current situation that I suspected it was all she had read before hitting print.

Richard G. Scott was a basset hound. The folds on his face were deep, creating heavy jowls that pulled his already grave expression downward so that he appeared perpetually heartbroken and forlorn. He always looked like he had grave news to deliver. "Making the Right Choices," like nearly every other talk directed at young men that I would read, listen to, and study in the years to come, warned about the danger of premarital sex and other sex-adjacent things.

The talk didn't say much else about standing up to peer pressure, which would have been sort of relevant. Instead, Elder Scott turned his attention to a different kind of peer pressure: sexual purity. The apostle wasn't shy. He was direct, but avoided specificity. He didn't name body parts or the particular acts that were verboten. But it was kind of like when a catalogue doesn't list the price of a Patek Philippe. If you have to ask . . .

Scott decried looking at immodest pictures of women, and watching pornographic movies and video cassettes. Then, he emphasized that any sexual activity before marriage was dangerous and forbidden. Experiencing anything sexual before being married would cause spiritual harm, even it we didn't realize it at the time.

---

* The Church is led by the prophet/president and his two counselors. These three comprise the First Presidency. Right under them in the Church hierarchy are the Twelve Apostles.

Even at thirteen, I knew what intimate acts were. It wasn't just sex before marriage. It was anything sexual before marriage. So, if someone experienced intimate acts by themself, for instance . . .

The memory of *Mission: Impossible* suddenly came to my mind.

I thought back to the previous year. Like every other time the memory bubbled up, it stretched to its full, monstrous height and whomped me in the gut with guilt. I hadn't repented yet. Not fully or officially. Not at all.

When I was a kid, baths were still my main source of full body hygiene—though forever up for debate is the degree to which one actually gets clean during a bath—and I was still just barely small enough to lie extended in the tub without much bending. I would lie on my stomach and see how long I could hold my breath underwater. And in that position I could almost pretend to swim. With my legs I'd push off from one end like a swimmer and slide along the bottom, then push myself back with my arms.

Swimming this way felt very good.

So, I did the swimming thing. I slid back and forth in the tub until, breathing heavily, I felt something new and strange, like I maybe had to pee. I got out of the tub as nimbly as I could, worried I was about to piss accidentally, but whatever was about to happen couldn't be stopped.

A small, tender pearl dribbled out, followed by one or two more. My testicles seemed to tighten, as though they had been wrung out and this was all they could muster. The amount didn't matter. To me, or to Heavenly Father. Because that was the C-word. A three-letter word that was too dirty to even say in my head. And I made it happen.

When experienced any other way, they are against His will. I broke the law of chastity.

That night, my sister Mary and I went to see *Mission: Impossible*, starring Tom Cruise. I couldn't enjoy the thrill ride. Every ten minutes, I'd remember what I had done in the bathtub and feel nauseated and doomed. Like I was about to take a test I was entirely unprepared for. The need to repent for what I had done felt urgent; any delay would just soil me more. I spent half the movie praying silently, begging Heavenly Father to forgive me.

But all that praying wouldn't bring me absolution. I was dealing with the law of chastity here. And sins against the law of chastity couldn't be taken care of with prayer alone. I'd have to talk to my bishop.

My dad.

A year after the incident, I still hadn't done that. I couldn't imagine a world in which that conversation would happen. He had been offended by my comic book. And yet I was supposed to tell him, oh, not only do I still look at inappropriate images, I broke the law of chastity with myself, too.

The memory would still take cheap shots at me every now and then, but by that point the constant thrum of guilt had mostly been buried under everyday life.

Mom liked to have important talks while we were driving. It was the rare place where she and I could talk one on one.

A few days after my suspension, we were driving home from church. It had been another Wednesday night playing floor hockey in the church's gym because our Young Men's leaders hadn't planned another activity. I didn't like floor hockey. I wasn't good at it, but I don't think anyone in the group was. Still, everyone else seemed to enjoy playing. Going to Young Men's was not contingent on what was planned. I would always go. But on floor hockey nights, I wasn't thrilled about it. Neither was my mom.

When my mom wanted to speak casually her voice took on a bit of Southern Alberta twang. She sounded more like her rancher father. It was a stark contrast to the smoky enunciation she used professionally. Ironically, when she was angry, the rancher voice crept out, too. Consonants softened and words bumped into each other more.

She asked me how my days at home had been during my suspension from school. I told her that I had finished a whole book in one sitting.

"And what didja think about?"

"It was okay. A little sad," I said, then gave her a rundown of *Of Mice and Men.*

"I wasn't actually asking about the book you read—though I'm proud of you for reading a whole book," she said. Pride was better than embarrassment. "I meant, what did you think about getting suspended. Why did you do it, what are you going to do about it now?"

My mom asked open-ended questions. It was basically what she did as a consultant. She taught courses to engineers about dealing with difficult co-workers and critical thinking. She was always trying to get buttoned-up math types to talk about non-engineering things, like their feelings. I never knew how to answer those kinds of questions. They were meant to be agnostic and non-judgemental. But there was always a right answer.

"Did you read the talk I printed out for you and write in your journal?"

"Yes."

"Well, what did you write about?"

"I don't know, I wrote about the talk." I was always feeling a lot of feelings, but that didn't mean I had words to talk about them. And I knew that I would only have to give three to five shoulder-shruggy "I don't know"s before she'd start offering suggestions of what I was thinking. She was usually pretty accurate in her summaries. Close enough that I didn't have to correct her.

"Why'd you think you did it?"

"I don't know," I said.

"Because you and I both know you're not a bad kid," she began. "You're the exact opposite of a bad kid. You're sensitive and kind. You worry about people's feelings. You take care of people. And you're funny and charming and smart and handsome . . ."

This listing of my qualities was usually how talks ended. It made me feel a little pathetic, being buttered up by my mom, but it never failed to make me cry. "It's okay, Mom."

She stopped.

"When she was suspending me, Mrs. Marshall said sometimes thirteen-year-old boys have their brains just fall out," I offered.

"Maybe. But I think you're too smart for that. Because you've always known right from wrong. And you don't like it when people do things that are wrong. Not even in movies, isn't that right?"

"I don't know. I guess so."

"Why do you think you did what you did?"

I suspected she wanted me to say that it was my friends' fault and renounce the lot of them. The truth was, I would've liked to do that. I didn't like feeling anxious all the time, or dumb. My friends and I were mean to each other in the way thirteen-year-old boys are mean to their friends. We joked together, but usually at one another's expense. I had looked around, though, and there didn't seem to be anyone else to be friends with. The other boys at school were lame. My friends were cool. That probably wasn't a great excuse. Jesus had preached plucking out your eyes and cutting off your hands if they troubled you, since it was better to lose a few body parts than to lose your whole soul. It was better to be friendless than to have bad friends.

That was the right answer. It's what I would say if this were Sunday School. But in practice, it wasn't so easy.

Mom didn't know how much my friends bullied me or how much we bullied each other, and it was important that it stayed that way. I was embarrassed and ashamed that I was the target of so much teasing. My friends teased me about eating sloppy; they teased me about my body. They would pounce on anything someone said, hoping to use it against them somehow. I didn't want my mom to know this, especially when she clearly thought so highly of me.

"I don't know. Peer pressure, I guess," I said. It was half true. They were definitely my peers.

"I think you don't know who you are," my mom said.

Then Mom was off. I knew I wouldn't have to say anything for the rest of the ride home. "The thing that's always been most important to me is that you kids have confidence, self-esteem. A big reason some teenagers get into trouble is because they don't have any self-esteem whatsoever. And it's impossible to have good self-esteem if you don't know who your self is. That wasn't very good grammar, but you understand.

"You might have noticed your dad and I aren't great with rules," she went on. "We don't believe in curfews, or in grounding or punishment. We trust that you'll make good decisions. Joseph Smith was once asked how he kept his growing flock in line. He said, 'I teach them correct principles, and let them govern themselves.' That's why I wanted you to read that talk, because it was about making right choices. But with you, I think it goes a bit deeper than that. You've always struggled with self-esteem, and you worry. Maybe you don't know who you are yet."

My mom probably had a point.

That summer, the summer before grade eight, I had quit comic books cold turkey. Comics were essentially action figures in print. And only children played with action figures. I could justify reading comics when I was a child, but once I turned thirteen I was officially a teenager. I didn't want to be the kind of teenager that read comics. I didn't want to end up like the sad, swollen men at the comic book store. I told myself that comics were no big loss.

However, they had been my only hobby. Growing up, my life had always been defined by my few obsessions: cowboys; G.I. Joes, Ninja Turtles and Dick Tracy; basketball; then comic books. For the first time, I didn't have something to focus on. What could possibly replace comics in my world?

I knew that life would get easier once I finally turned sixteen. That was when the Church said it was okay to date. All these problems with bad friends and no hobbies would melt away with the arrival of a girlfriend.

The Sunday School answer to the question of my identity was that I was a child of God. I had no problem with that, but so was literally every other person in the world. "I talked with Dad, and we think it might be time for you to get your patriarchal blessing," my mom said. Then she waited for a response.

"Aren't I too young?" I asked. "Don't you get that when you're, like, sixteen?" Life started at sixteen.

"That's when a lot of people get them, but there's no rule. The only thing that matters is whether you think you're ready." Then, after I hadn't said anything, "What do you think?"

"I don't know," I said.

"I think you're ready. And your dad does too," she said.

"I'll ace the bishop's interview then. Do you have to have a bishop's interview to get one?"

"Yes, it's basically like a temple recommend interview," she said. "You don't have to decide now. I want you to pray about it. But I think it will really help you to know yourself, and help you know that Heavenly Father loves you. Which will give you confidence to make good choices, no matter what your friends do or say."

Then we were home. Every window in the house was wide awake.

My mom could have just asked my dad to give me a special father's blessing, like he did with all of us at the beginning of each school year. But she pulled out the big guns. A patriarchal blessing differs from a father's blessing in the same way that talking to a friend who's gone to therapy is different from talking to an actual therapist. The trained professional can go deeper and see more, and their diagnoses carry authority. The actual process of getting a patriarchal blessing was the same as getting a regular blessing. The person being blessed sits in front of the person giving the blessing, who puts his hands on the soon-to-be-blessed's head, and then says a kind of prayer. All priesthood blessings are supposed to be messages from God, but patriarchal blessings are more important. They only happen once, whereas I could have gotten my dad to give me a blessing every week.

Patriarchs were usually older men in the Church. By virtue of their calling, they had the power of more specific revelation. People mostly got patriarchal blessings in their later teens because that's when people start looking ahead, toward their future. Patriarchal blessings are a searchlight illuminating the unknown. They contain promises and rewards from Heavenly Father that are conditional on one's righteousness. They are meant to give guidance, to give you a glimpse of your spiritual potential and how to achieve it. But salvation doesn't require receiving a patriarchal blessing.

Still, getting my patriarchal blessing so young hinted at a special sacred calling. Didn't it foreshadow the possibility of being *chosen*? Like a young Dalai Lama. Or like Jesus in the temple, answering questions like a trained rabbi when he was twelve, or David smiting Goliath, or Nephi leading his brothers to get the brass plates despite being the youngest. Joseph Smith was around my age—maybe a little older—when he first saw Heavenly Father and Jesus. Sometimes Heavenly Father anoints his chosen when they are yet unformed. Wasn't getting my patriarchal blessing at such a young age akin to that?

I tried to put that out of my mind. A sure way not to be one of God's chosen is to pine for it. I felt simultaneously special and like a sinner.

On the Sunday of my patriarchal blessing, I fasted for the whole day. It was my first time intentionally missing meals, and the first time I combined fasting with prayer. I was proud of myself for being so adult. It fit with the new spiritual maturity I hoped to cultivate. I wanted my blessing to be a defining spiritual experience.

I had seen small miracles in my life, mostly of the lost and found variety. Special, but pretty common. A few Church videos about families had made me cry, which was often how the Spirit made himself known, but I also cried at the end of every Disney animated feature from *The Little Mermaid* onwards. For me, crying was part of feeling the Spirit, but I suspected it wasn't the entire thing. There was something I was still missing.

In the scriptures, feeling the Spirit was alternately described as a burning in your bosom or a still small voice. Neither description was all that helpful. I knew my chest wouldn't glow like E.T.'s. I wouldn't hear an outside voice like Obi-Wan Kenobi's, but I didn't know where my internal voice was supposed to end and where the Spirit's would begin. And it was too easy to convince myself I felt a slight warmth in my chest. I couldn't fake tears. What I was really missing, though, was certainty. Certainty that Heavenly Father lived, and loved me, and that the Church was true: the kind of truth that didn't require explanation or justification. The *feeling* of certainty that comes fully formed and feels inevitable.

I wanted that. It's not that I had doubts about my testimony, but I understood that my faith was still childlike, dependent. I wanted the power that comes from a direct message from God. I was ready to grow up spiritually.

The patriarch's home was a lot like ours. Family photos hung along the hallway, and paintings of the Saviour hung in the living room. Sister Vilsken welcomed my parents at the door with the Molly Mormon grace that my mother defined herself against.* She led us to a room off the main hall that was dedicated to giving blessings. The room was bare but for a few chairs.

After the patriarch gave a brief refresher about what was about to happen, I sat in a chair in front of him. I saw that around his neck was a small tape recorder. I'd get a transcribed copy of my blessing a few weeks later. My own personal prophecy and scripture, a revelation from Heavenly Father that was uniquely mine. My past, present, and future.

I wanted to remember as much about my blessing as I could, remember the feeling when the patriarch put his hands on my head. The blessing would include promises, gifts I could expect if I were true and faithful; I wanted to remember them as they were spoken. What impressive details of my life might it foretell? Surely, it would give some hint of where I would eventually serve my mission in a few years. Would it sketch the outline of my future wife? Would it tell me who I was?

---

* A mild epithet or backhanded compliment for someone who is a goody-goody. The male equivalent is Peter Priesthood. A Jack Mormon is the opposite.

Patriarch Vilsken had me say my full name. He repeated all four parts of it back to me. Then he placed his hands gently on the crown of my head.

"Gregory William Reed Hudson, as an ordained patriarch I lay my hands upon your head to give you a patriarchal blessing. I pray our Heavenly Father will inspire this blessing that you might realize His great love, that you might realize the important mission that was given to you before you left the preexistence."

My chest shuddered and tumbled. The hull breached open and warmth flowed through. *His great love.* Through my sobs, I listened to all the things my Father in Heaven wanted me to know.

In the years to come, I would study my patriarchal blessing with Talmudic intensity. I would one day read it to girlfriends, and this would be a sign of great intimacy because it wasn't meant to be shared, except with family and future spouses. In future times, I would read my patriarchal blessing after looking at naked breasts, when I felt worthless and wicked, and the blessing would be an astringent: a reminder of my noble potential, and how far from it I was.

But that night, hours after I had received it, all I could do was recall as much as I could of what the patriarch had said while his hands were on my head. A few things had stood out. I wondered if that was the Spirit, helping me remember important bits.

Bits like how I had thought about Becky, although I wasn't a hundred percent positive that she didn't go by Becca. We weren't that close. She lived in a relatively faraway part of the stake. I met her at youth conference; she was a year older than me, and I thought she was the most beautiful girl to have ever laughed at a joke. That is to say, the most beautiful girl ever. She had long, curly hair, which I thought of as the most beautiful of hair types for women. When she laughed at something I said, she'd look at me with sparkling eyes opened wide, as if she couldn't believe I had said what I had just said. Every joke was an audacious little miracle.

The second time we met was at a stake conference.* She came up to me before the meeting started and hit me playfully on the shoulder. We talked about nothing in particular, and then, as the meeting started, instead of finding her family, she sat next to me. For the entire two-hour meeting. If it weren't for the fact that we were at church and that it was nothing like a date, one could almost have called it a date. At home afterward, my mom teased me about the girl at church who was so obviously in love with me. My mom swooned and batted her eyelashes like a mime to show just how smitten Becky had been. As much as I wished, silently, that my mom was right, I was quite certain my mom just didn't know how young people related to each other. It only looked like she like-liked me because that's how all girls were.

I thought of Becky because when the patriarch promised me I would one day be married in the temple to my wife, my mind had gone immediately to her. The patriarch said, *One day you will have the opportunity to go to the temple with your companion*, and it was like a spell had conjured Becky in my mind. I chased

---

* While there was always a devotional component to a youth conference—they were called firesides—mostly they were big activity days with sports, games, and flirting. A stake conference, however, was just a big church meeting for the entire stake that happened twice a year.

her out of my brain as quickly as I could so that I could focus on my blessing. But even as it happened, I wondered if it was a revelation.

There was more important stuff in my blessing.

My patriarchal blessing didn't say I would be a prophet, or give much of a hint of where I'd eventually go on my mission—though I was pretty sure it mentioned something about sharing the gospel with the nations of the world—but I remembered there was still stuff to feel special about. It said that I had been held back in the spirit world, saved for the last days, and that I participated in all the activities leading up to the plan of salvation in the preexistence. I imagined I was a general in Heavenly Father's army in the War in Heaven. Then the blessing said something about how, in this day and age, I would participate in many of the great events that were still to be accomplished in the world. It felt like a confirmation of what I had suspected.

I was important. I would be important. That's what my patriarchal blessing conveyed to me. I didn't know in what capacity I'd participate in these great world events—though I imagined it would be as a diplomat or prime minister—but whatever my role would be, it would pay well. The blessing didn't outright say I would be rich, but it said that in times of famine and desolation I'd be able to provide the essentials for my family.

Did the blessing tell me who I was? It felt like it did. The words were powerful, and I was excited to get my transcription in the mail so that I could review it more carefully. But the question of who I was, especially in relation to who I was at school, had been answered the moment the patriarch put his hands on my head. In that moment, I felt certainty. I was a child of God. He knew and loved me. I was, at that moment at least, worthy.

I went to parties in high school. I partied. Depending on your definition of "party," I totally partied.

And normal parties, too. With booze, and presumably drugs as well. I liked that I went to drinking parties. The parties themselves were fine—shockingly, I soon discovered that being around drunken teenagers could quickly get tiresome—but I liked that I went to them anyway. Some Mormon families didn't allow their adolescent kids to attend anything more risqué than a pop and chip party, where parents were liable to join in on the fun because of course they were home while the party was taking place in the basement. But I trusted myself and my faith. I knew I wouldn't drink or try drugs. I also wouldn't have premarital sex, which, according to several decades' worth of teen comedies, happened all the time at high school parties. Attending non-Mormon parties showed I could hold myself to a higher standard without judging those who didn't. I could be friends with anyone.

You know who else was friends with everyone? The Saviour.

I'd like to bear my testimony that Jesus taught us that we could be *at* the party, but we must never be *of* the party. In the name of Jesus Christ, amen.

This particular party was just outside the city, at the house of a girl in our group at school with whom I wasn't especially close. The house was off a forest road that turned into a driveway made from gravel and small rocks. It seemed to be more like a cottage than a house, though it wasn't quite a cabin. It was out of the way, but it wasn't rustic.

Some church members believed that if an LDS teenager joined a celebration of underage drinking and poor decisions, they would be leaving the Holy Ghost behind. But I didn't believe the Spirit was so powerless in the face of sin. After I was baptized, I was confirmed and given the gift of the Holy Ghost. As part of that confirmation I was promised that so long as I kept Heavenly Father's commandments, I'd always have the Spirit with me. For guidance, for protection. Why then would the Holy Ghost leave you when you needed guidance and protection the most?

It might have been a stretch, but I felt like I brought the Spirit with me to these places. Not that I was perfect.

The day before this particular party, my friends and I were hanging out at Muriel's house. She was an only child, and her single mother often wasn't home in the hours after school. Muriel's place was in a part of Edmonton where the houses were stately and old. They seemed bigger, too, but I often confused height with size. When you lived in a bungalow, any house with a second floor seemed like a mansion.

Someone had brought a hand-held video camera to the gathering and I decided I would take care of it for the afternoon. I soon realized that no one could tell exactly what I was looking at through the lens. No one could tell if I was zooming in on a pimple on someone's face or taking in the entire room. They just saw the red light and knew the camera was rolling.

Young women made up most of our group. This wasn't odd; the ratio of girls to boys at our arts-focused high school was said to be five to one. I began interviewing the girls, asking journalistic questions about their classes, their friends, what it was like to be them. Making jokes.

But I was distracted. From behind the camera, I could see down their shirts. If I was standing, and they were sitting, I could zoom in without their knowing and see a sliver of pale skin and lace. Fortunately for the welfare of my soul, Muriel and her friends all wore sensible bras. If in my peeping zooms I had caught a glimpse of nipple I would have turned to Jell-O, and been damned. But I didn't, so I wasn't.

Drunk on the cleavage of my peers, I forgot that the camera wasn't mine. And that its rightful owner would want to watch all the footage that it captured that afternoon. What had I done? Blinded by bras, I forgot that actions have consequences.

The next day at the party, I entered the cottage house and walked into the kitchen. Muriel was closing the freezer, where she was storing her vodka for the night. Muriel had shortish hair that was frequently held in place by barrettes. She and I shared a similar obsession with musicians. The flavour of our particular obsessions was different, but the intensity was the same. She had covered her bedroom walls with pictures of Sarah McLachlan that she cut out from magazines, I was a fan of British pop star Robbie Williams. Although Muriel was undeniably attractive, until my activities of the previous day I hadn't spent much time considering her breasts. From behind the camera, I realized they weren't insubstantial. She turned and noticed me. She was carrying a red cup.

"Hey, Mr. Camera Man," Muriel said. She was smiling in

the practised way of objectified women everywhere, like she was suddenly training a puppy.

"You watched the tape." I asked the question like a burglar just learning of the existence of fingerprints.

"Well, not the whole thing. It got repetitive after a while. I see my boobs every day," Muriel said. She wasn't mad, she said. She thought it was funny. All the girls in our group did.

"Do you think I could have that tape?" I asked, trying not to sound desperate.

"You didn't get to look at them enough?"

"It's not that. I'm sorry. I want the tape so I can throw it away or destroy it," I said.

"It's not my tape. You'll have to ask Lucy. Her camera, her tape." Lucy was a sweet girl, but she was a gossip. I had definitely looked down her shirt, too. It wouldn't be long before everyone in the universe knew about my cinematography.

I felt guilty for zooming in on my friends' bras, and stupid that I had done it so blatantly. But it was the fact that I had proven myself to be a hypocrite that really sickened me. I had held myself above the grubby deeds of boys my age, both because I was Mormon and because I had been taught better by my older sisters. Let regular boys look down unsuspecting women's shirts or talk dirty when girls were out of earshot. I was a different kind of young man.

That I was Mormon was usually the first thing people found out about me. I imagined everyone I met who knew my faith and was familiar with its strictures was waiting for me to break them. On the surface, I seemed pure, set apart. But it was relatively easy to act that way when everyone was watching. What was the true story? Did I actually practise what my church preached?

Apparently I was as prone to shameful behaviour as any other boy.

I was regular, normal. Natural. And according to a scripture in the Book of Mormon, "The natural man is an enemy to God" (Mosiah 3:19).

I had to get that tape back, not just for me, but for the reputation of the Church. Everywhere I went, I was its ambassador. I was a missionary. I was the product of the true church, which ought to have meant something. We took our rules seriously. It was our lifestyle. Except I had just proven the Church's ineffectiveness. Apparently, it was just like every other church that had rules no one followed.

"Can you talk to her?" I asked.

"Why do you want the tape back so bad?"

"Because that wasn't me."

"No? It sure sounded like you in the background." She was enjoying this. And deservedly so. I had dated Muriel for a couple of weeks in the fall. I was sixteen, and she had been on my list of potential girlfriends for a while. But after making out with her a few times, I decided to break up with her because she wasn't Mormon. It was out of an abundance of caution for my sexual purity. Knowing that I was doing what was right, but scared of breaking her heart, I took her to a café and wrote my feelings on a napkin. I wrote that I liked her a lot, but that I didn't want to get too close to someone who didn't share my values. Then I took her home and had her read it. The napkin was just to get the talk started. Get the wrecking ball swinging. We talked after she read it. I stayed for the tears and such, but I had handled her heart with all the delicacy of a toddler at a wedding.

"No, I know, but it's not who I really am. Please?" The earnestness of the "please" surprised me, and bothered Muriel.

"I'll talk to her. But I make no promises," she said. "But you have to ask her, too. I'm not doing everything for you."

I had a mission: talk Lucy into giving me the tape. After all, I was repenting of the sin, or at least feeling guilty about it, which felt like the same thing. If true repentance meant that once you were forgiven it was as though the sin never happened, shouldn't part of that process be getting rid of the lingering evidence?

Lucy found me first. "I heard you want this?" She was holding the unmarked VHS tape.

"Yes, please," I said. I explained what I had explained to Muriel—that I didn't want there to be evidence of my worst behaviour when I mostly tried to be good.

"It's not even that bad, though," she said with the same condescension as Muriel had.

"It's not good, though. I feel really bad," I responded.

She opened the cassette's flap and pulled at the tape inside, tearing it, then breaking the flap thing off completely. "Happy now?" she asked.

I thanked her profusely. I could breathe again. I could stop shaking.

After succeeding at my mission, I ran into Amanda on the stairs. At school, Amanda lingered at the periphery of our hallway clumps, usually draped across her boyfriend, Jason, barely paying attention to anyone else. She rarely went out if Jason—a year older and perpetually dumbstruck by his luck in scoring Amanda—didn't come with her. They had a healthy little codependency going. A simulacrum of marital bliss.

Jason was at home, she told me, recovering from getting his wisdom teeth removed.

"Did he get any fun painkillers?" I asked.

"Just Tylenol 3s," she said with exaggerated disappointment.

"Did they put him under?"

"Of course. So I guess he got a little bit of fun drugs, if you count that."

"Our dentist doesn't knock people out. My brother Sam said that our dentist had to put, like, his knee up on Sam's chest so he could get enough leverage to pull out his wisdom teeth. And my brother was awake the whole time."

"That's fucked up," she said, then remembered herself. "I mean, that's messed up. Please excuse my language."

I tried to make a benevolent face while swatting her apology away. Like, *Your money is no good here.* But she interpreted it more as, *Why would I care what a drunkard like you thinks?*

"I'm not drunk, you know," she said.

"Cool. Me neither!" I said cheerfully. She thought I was making fun of her.

"No, like you think I'm drunk, and you're judging me because you think I'm drunk, but I'm totally not."

"I'm not judging you," I said.

"Yes, you are, and it's fucked up."

"I promise, I'm not."

At that moment, Rebecca peered over the banister and called my name. She hadn't been at Muriel's house while I was making my film, but I had to assume she had heard about it. "You're here! Great. You can look after Brian. He's outside. He's going a bit cuckoo for Cocoa Puffs."

"Oh boy. Okay. What happened?" I asked as I climbed the stairs.

"I don't know. Seth just came in and said he couldn't get Brian to come back inside," Rebecca said.

"Seth, eh? I keep hearing about this Seth," I said.

"He's nice."

As I put my shoes on, the one they called Seth was standing in the kitchen by the fridge, surrounded by a lot of the girls who had lockers near mine. I didn't know where Seth's locker was. I just knew that it wasn't near ours. I didn't know much more about him than his name, and that he seemed to be friends with very smart seniors, despite being in grade eleven, like me. His name had started popping up in friends' anecdotes about activities I hadn't participated in.

Seth raised his hand at me in an uncertain wave, like I was a detective asking who first called this one in. I was jealous of his hands. Even from far away I could tell they were man-sized. But his body wasn't, quite. He was becoming a man zone by zone. His face, head, hands, and feet were nearly complete. Then, presumably, the rest of him would follow.

It was spring, a risky time to be outside in Alberta. But except for the sharp outcrops of ice in the backyard, standing low and firm in places that didn't get much sun, the snow was gone. The ground was damp. Brian was sitting on the gravel driveway, safely behind his Plymouth Reliant. His ride was a family hand-me-down, like mine. That was the norm at our school, and certainly in our group. Brian was picking up rocks and tossing them into the forest. He had started drinking too early in the evening and with too much zeal. Now he was a mess.

Puberty was being kind to Brian. When we met and befriended each other on the first day of seventh grade, he was chubby in a way I assumed was permanent. But he started slimming down as he grew taller. And now that his braces were off, he smiled with confidence and—was that charm? He had become handsome.

I sat down next to him. He had been crying.

"You don't have to come talk to me," he said.

"What's happening, man?" I asked, keeping things light, testing the bounds of his sobriety—not that I had any frame of reference from which to understand degrees of drunkenness. To me, there were two kinds of drunk: the tipsiness that got people talking loudly, and the horny, sobbing, puking variety. I had no clue how much alcohol got you to one level or the other.

Clearly Brian needed to talk to someone, or wanted to, but I didn't know how valuable a conversation would be. The real, and only, solution to how Brian was feeling—or how I assumed he was feeling—was the gospel. Because with the gospel came an eternal perspective.

I couldn't honestly say that the gift of the Holy Ghost had ever actually provided me with comfort. Nor could I testify with surety that the Book of Mormon would change someone's life. I was reading it. I knew it was true. It was pretty dry. But having an eternal perspective? That did bring comfort. To know that every hardship, every trial and tribulation, is no more than a tiny blip in our eternal existence. Adolescent heartbreak didn't carry much weight when compared with eternity. For a teenager, heartbreak felt like the only thing in the world, but it was actually no more consequential than a toddler crying at bedtime. If Brian understood how little anything we experienced mattered, he wouldn't be outside in the dark, throwing pebbles. "What's up?" I asked him.

"Nothing is up with me. Nothing is ever up for me. I'm awesome. I'm indestructible." Brian picked up another pebble, threw it at his head. He made the laser-like pétanque sounds of bullets bouncing off him. "I'm a survivor, ain't gonna give up. Ain't gonna give in, just working hardeerrrrr."

"Oh my goodness, are you . . . are you in Destiny's Child?"

"Fucking right I am. Destiny was my mother's maiden name." He tossed a few more rocks at his head.

"Hey, hey. What are you doing?"

"It doesn't matter. I'm nothing. *Piu-piu.* Like, what should I do? What do I need to do. It's not like girls are lining up. I'm invisible."

"Are they lining up for me? I don't have a girlfriend."

"But you could. You're sixteen now. You're not invisible. You're untouchable. There's a difference. Perfect Greg Hudson."

"I'm definitely not perfect," I said.

"It's like there's a rotation," he continued, "except I'm not in it. I get fucking skipped every time. Now, it's like it's Seth's turn. Or maybe it's his friends. He's friends with a lot of grade twelve kids, hey? But like who's next, not Brian! Fuck you, Brian."

"Do you even want to date our friends?" I asked.

"I don't know. I want it to be a possibility," Brian said.

"How do you know it isn't?"

"Michelle barely looks at me. I think I'm going to tell her about the *You've Got Mail* thing. It's not working." Brian had recently set up an email address and invented an online identity to go along with it. Over email, he was going to woo the girl he liked by being her perfect match. Once she was safely infatuated with the email personality, he'd reveal that the boy she liked over the internet was him all along. She'd be so flattered by the effort that she would forgive him for lying to her.

"Has McStiffy720 told her how he feels?" I asked.

"I was biding my time, waiting for the ideal moment. But I like her though. I like her a lot. I like that she's a cheerleader, but doesn't act like the other ones. Maybe I should be Mormon, too. Maybe that's why you're untouchable. I'm like anti-touchable."

I thought through what I should say. My first instinct was to take issue with his characterization of me. Like life was so easy for me? But that would be patronizing, and mostly untrue. I was self-consciously enjoying my adolescence. It wasn't without the typical stresses and disappointments: essays still had to be written, I didn't get the lead role in the school play that year. But, during what is often a very challenging time, I had it pretty good.

I probably needed to steer the conversation toward the gospel. Not that it would take much effort. Brian already brought it up. And one had to admit that the contrast between my Mormon life and his non-member existence was, at that moment, very stark. But that seemed opportunistic. *You know why I seem so happy? Let me tell you about another person who had some big doubts and tough questions. His name was Joseph Smith . . .*

I just sat next to Brian. I picked up a few pebbles and tossed them into the dark woods.

"You wanna come to a Mormon dance with me next weekend?" I asked. Every second weekend, the Church held dances for youth in the city. They were normal dances; the only atypical thing was that boys had to wear shirts and ties, and girls had to wear skirts that went below the knee. And they happened in a church gym. "There are lots of girls there. Mormon girls, but still."

"I don't know how to tie a tie," Brian said.

"No one has to know I tied it for you."

He was spent. I helped him up and we walked back into the house together.

The long-suffering party welcomed him back into the fold. Brian joined the cluster of friends in the kitchen. Someone offered him a Mike's Hard Lemonade, which he waved off.

I decided I'd make one more tour of the party before slipping out early.

"Someone got this for you." Seth handed me a can of Barq's Root Beer before I could leave. "It's a trap though."

"I'm allowed to drink root beer. Thanks."

"Yeah, but this has caffeine."

"Well, Barq's does have bite." I opened the can of root beer and drank. I pushed down a belch. For some unknown reason I felt better about drinking caffeinated beverages if they weren't colas. It made as much sense as the permission my siblings and I gave ourselves to eat Coffee Crisp, a chocolate bar that contained actual coffee, but only on Halloween. "It's the thought that counts. Who got this for me?"

"I don't know. I think Muriel."

"That was nice of her."

"By the way, speaking of traps, that wasn't the real videotape," Seth informed me. "They didn't want anyone to tell you, but they still have the real one." The winded nausea came rushing back, apologizing profusely for leaving so early before. "They were watching on the video camera while you were outside."

"Oh. Why do they even want to keep it?" I asked.

"Because it's a good Mormon boy looking at tits," Seth said. I winced at the word tits. It wasn't a swear, but it was probably the dirtiest word for that particular body part. Boobs seemed preferable, at least in adult conversation.

"Technically, I didn't look at any boobs," I said. Seth nodded and smiled a little.

He seemed to have a smile that was purely defensive. It was protection as obvious as a fencing helmet. I looked Seth over to confirm my suspicion: I could totally take him if I needed to, despite having never been in a fight, nor even knowing how to throw a proper punch. But he had those big hands and feet. I suspected I could beat up a lot of people. All without evidence. I never tested my suspicions. Right then, if I had, I'd have learned that, as it turned out, Seth took boxing.

"Well, if you somehow get your hands on it, feel free to accidentally run it over," I said.

"Why are you so sensitive about it?"

"Because it makes me look like a pervert."

"I don't know. I think it makes you look like a human being. And even if God were real, why the fuck would he care about that? He's too busy watching kids die and people murder in his name," Seth said.

"You're an atheist. Why did someone tell me that?"

"Same reason someone told me you were Mormon. I think people want us to fight each other. Don't worry though, I'm a pacifist. Have you read much Bertrand Russell?"

"I haven't read any Bertrand Russell," I said.

"He was a, well actually he was a mathematician, but he was also a philosopher and pacifist. Mormons are pacifists, aren't they?"

"You're thinking of Jehovah's Witnesses. Mormons love serving in the military. The Book of Mormon, full of wars," I said.

"Russell was an atheist, too. He's like my idol. My Robbie Williams, so to speak," Seth said.

"Ha."

"Is that a Mormon thing?" Seth asked.

"What?"

"The love of Robbie Williams," he said.

"No. Why would that make any sense?" I asked.

"Those were just the first two things I learned about you. You were Mormon and you liked Robbie Williams. They seemed foundational to your identity, so I thought they might be connected."

"No, no. Just a fan," I said. Did he have anything else to say about his idol, something Russell, or did he want to talk about mine? I had the impression he mostly just wanted to talk. I felt studied. But I could chat about music.

"So, what about this: how could a loving God make wars?"

Or we could talk about that.

This was a variation of the "Why do bad things happen to good people?" question. It was one I was familiar with, one I'd answered several times in Sunday School over the years.

"He doesn't. We do. He gave us the freedom to choose, and it's not His fault that we choose to do bad things with it," I said. "And apparently freedom of choice is so important that He won't take it away."

"Okay, but let's not even talk about genocide or crime. No, but wait, let's stipulate something first. Okay?"

I nodded. If I wore a watch I would've glanced at it meaningfully.

"Let's stipulate that no matter the circumstance, innocent people dying is bad. Let's say children dying is bad," Seth said.

"Stipulated!" I replied.

"It's evil. And then, if you could stop something evil from happening, but you don't, isn't the bad thing kind of your fault?"

"With great power comes great responsibility," I said. "Parker."

"Alright, then if we agree on all that, either God's real and He's evil, or He's not real. It makes more sense that He isn't real. Or maybe He is real, but He won't stop cruelty because He can't. It would go against His nature."

"Sure." I was being led somewhere obvious. The sophistry wasn't elegant.

"Okay, but then do you see how that would make Him not omnipotent, and thus not a God?" he said.

"You got right into it, didn't you?" I said.

"I'm just saying, if He is all-powerful, and doesn't stop evil from happening, then He's responsible for that evil. Like I said, He's either real and evil, or He's not real," Seth said. "Or ignore man-made cruelty. What about natural disasters?"

Natural disasters were a problem for Mormons to explain. Certainly not as easy to explain as war or genocide. Yet the underlying reason was the same for both. Bad things happened because without bad stuff, we wouldn't have good stuff. We needed opposition in order to be tested. Life, after all, is just about growing and being tested.

There were few things I liked talking about more than religion. But I felt ill about the videotape and, at that moment, unworthy to defend the Lord. Still, I couldn't let that big juicy one float over the plate without swinging at it.

"Good questions. He totally could stop natural disasters. And so if He doesn't, there's probably a good reason."

"I have a related question," Seth said. "Could God make a stone that was so big even He couldn't lift it?"

"He's omnipotent," I said.

"But see, if He can't make a stone that big, then He isn't

all-powerful, because there's something He can't do. But if He can, then He's still not all-powerful, because He can't lift it."

He looked like he'd just pulled off a terrific stunt.

"That's pretty tricky. You win. I don't believe in anything anymore. Congratulations." I saluted Seth. "I'll have to pray about that and get back to you. See what the Big Guy says about it."

He returned my salute. "I hope you aren't offended. I was just asking."

"And I was just getting ready to leave. Don't worry, it takes a lot more than that to offend me."

Driving home, I thought about how I wasn't often called upon to defend the existence of God. I could offer some limited understanding of why bad things happened and I could explain my religion and what it taught about Heavenly Father. All my knowledge rested on the premise that God existed. I might have been ready to split a few hairs, but Seth wanted to pluck them all out. It seemed somehow unsophisticated to attack something as big as God.

I should have known Seth would come back at me with more questions. My quick exit from the party could have easily been misunderstood as a retreat. Of course he'd come back for another round of Stump the Mormon. He was clearly smart. And he seemed to know it, too. After I left the party, he had Brian quiz him about subjects in the volumes of the *Encyclopedia Britannica* that lined the walls of the den off the living room. Muriel said it was pretty impressive.

I hadn't studied to prepare for his attacks. I went to seminary every morning,* read my scriptures most nights, and went to three hours of church on Sundays. If all that didn't prepare me to answer someone's questions or defend challenges to my faith, then what was it all for?

"Yo, what about the Crusades, yo?" Seth shouted at me from the sea of students filling the hall as they headed to third period. The "yo"s were said ironically. When I turned around to see where they had come from, Seth shot me with an intentionally stilted finger gun. He seemed pleased with himself.

"Yes?" I said. I stepped out of the way so that other students could walk down the middle of the hallway.

"And that's just one example. How can you believe in God when, throughout history, God has been the number one cause of all wars?"

"You sure about that?" I asked. I never liked the war argument. It seemed overly reductive. Historically, hadn't access to resources been a pretty popular reason to go to war? Political ideology? Religion was a means of getting one's side revved up for a fight, but I doubted it was always the actual reason for fighting.

"It's all throughout the Bible, too. If you want references, I have them. God commands the Israelites to wipe out an entire city. Women and children," Seth said.

"That's fair. But that's the Old Testament. It's important, but I'm not going to defend it, because there's a lot of messed-up stuff in there, and it's less relevant to Christianity," I said.

"I'm a Christian," someone said as they approached me from

* A Church educational program for high school kids that took place at the stake centre at 7 a.m., Monday through Friday, before school began.

behind. "What about Christianity?" It was Mac, one of a handful of Christian kids at school who took their religion seriously. He was straight-edge, too: he didn't drink or do drugs.

"Yeah, we know," Seth said. He seemed to have no interest in Mac joining our debate.

"Oh, do you two know each other?" I asked. I knew Mac because he was in my drama class and we auditioned for the same parts in school plays. I was pretty sure he'd had a lesson from some hip youth pastor about how Mormonism was a cult that only pretended to be Christian, mostly because I assumed all mainstream Christians had received that lesson. But at least Mac didn't treat me with suspicion.

Right now he continued: "You know what not believing in God is like? It's like thinking a giant wind could blow through a junkyard and—"

"Just happen to make a Swiss watch. Yeah, I've heard that one," Seth said.

I hadn't. Maybe it would come in handy on my mission.

"I was going to say a fighter jet, but a watch works too, I guess," Mac said.

"It's a good one. But it's entirely teleological. It doesn't hold up," Seth countered.

"What doesn't hold up?" Mac asked.

"The argument for intelligent design," Seth said. "You're saying, 'Look at this watch, it tells the time so well, how could it have come together randomly?' That argument works for a watch because watches are made for a purpose. But your argument rests on the world having a purpose, when what science is saying is if it came together for a reason, it's not clear what that reason is. I don't know if I'm explaining myself properly," Seth said. He looked at me.

"I'm just trying to learn a new word," I said. "Teleolo . . ."

"Teleological. It's when you think that something is made for a specific purpose, and you can tell what that purpose is because the thing is doing it. So the purpose of an acorn is to become a tree. It's ascribing order where there isn't any."

"Whatever," Mac said.

"You still owe me an answer to my stone question," Seth said.

"You asked him the stone question, too?" I exclaimed.

"Yeah, it fucking stumps me every time," Mac said, performing dumb frustration as he walked away.

"Why do I find the Christian kids so insufferable?" Seth said.

"Hey, I'm right here," I said.

"I know. You guys actively try to convert people, so you'd think you'd be more annoying."

"And yet here we are, fast friends," I said. "I thought I was special. But it turns out you're having theological discussions with every Tom, Dick, and Harry."

"Mac? He found out I was an atheist in English class, I think, and so now he likes to come at me whenever he's heard a new argument that he thinks will blow my mind."

I nodded.

"But you were saying the Bible is violent," I prompted Seth. The hallway was beginning to clear. I was going to skip my next class—I generally skipped at least one class per day—so I didn't mind. But I thought Seth might have somewhere he needed to be. "And I'm saying I agree with you and I don't really know why God is such a jerk in the Old Testament. It's kind of moot now, since the Messiah came."

"That's a cop-out, but okay. What about the Crusades?

All the torture and murder the church caused throughout history. How can you square that with a loving God?"

"I can't. But I don't have to. The Catholic Church did some horrible things. But you're confusing the fans of the band for the band itself. I don't take the Catholic Church's atrocities as evidence there's no God. I take them as evidence that the Catholic Church isn't true. It's bad. The Church of Jesus Christ of Latter-day Saints didn't go on the Crusades."

"Alright, but what about bombing abortion clinics or justifying racism . . ."

"Every instance of some religion doing something bad will be the same thing. Mormons aren't connected to any other church. We believe the true church of Jesus Christ was lost in the Dark Ages and didn't come back until Joseph Smith came along in the 1830s. You can't judge one church by the actions of another."

The hall was nearly empty now. The polite pings of the late bell woke Seth up.

"Shit. I gotta get to class," Seth said. "Do you have a spare?"

I shrugged my shoulders. "Today I do."

By the third round of our great debate, which came a few days later, Seth had learned his lesson: Mormons only care about Mormons. Countless people have done horrible things in the name of God, but countless people didn't belong to the Church of Jesus Christ of Latter-day Saints. So Seth read up on Mormonism. By the time of our next encounter, he was ready to get into specifics. I decided to take the special attention as a compliment.

It was at a casual after-school hang at Muriel's house. Being there reminded me of the video cassette that someone still had in their possession. But no one had mentioned it since that party.

Muriel and I were in her basement, sitting at her computer and sharing music files illegally while everyone else was upstairs lying in a clump on Muriel's bed. Seth came down the stairs singing a song I didn't recognize, though I suspected it was Weezer.

"Here you are," Seth said. "The collective wants ice cream and so I was sent to inquire whether you had any, and, if you did, if we could have some?"

"What song was that?" Muriel asked.

"I don't know. What song were you singing, Sethy-boy?" I said.

"'El Scorcho,'" he answered.

"'El Scorcho,'" I said. "Is that Weezer?"

"It's from *Pinkerton*," Seth said.

"Can you make me a CD, Muriel? Our computer doesn't have a CD burner," I said. "And I think I generally respect your taste in music."

"I'm flattered you'd think of me," Muriel said. She tapped a few keys on her computer and a title for a song appeared. She clicked on it, and "You're So Vain" by Carly Simon started playing.

"I'm thinking this for a title track?" she said.

"I don't think she's over the napkin yet, dude," Seth said.

"You told him about the napkin?" I asked Muriel.

"I tell everybody about the napkin. The love of my life broke up with me with a napkin!"

"Smooth," Seth said. "Hey, you know who else is smooth? Christopher Columbus."

"I think Seth wants to say something about Christopher Columbus," I whispered loudly to Muriel.

"Hey, you know who else is smooth? Seth making a segue," Muriel said.

"You know what I've always thought was cool about ol' Chris Columbus? How he brought horses to the Americas. Muriel, did you know that? Before Columbus, there was nary a horse anywhere on this side of the world. Crazy, right?"

"Fascinating," she said.

"Also, I'm hazy on dates, but when did Columbus 'discover' America again?" Seth asked me.

"1492," I said without hesitation. "I remember because there was a movie about it called *1492*."

"Right, right, right. 1492. Huh."

"Why's Seth acting all sassy?" Muriel asked.

"I'm not being sassy." Seth looked genuinely worried. "I'm being wry. But whatever. Hey, Greg, when and where does the Book of Mormon take place?"

I didn't know where he was going with this line of questioning. But from his tone, it apparently should have been obvious to me.

At the bottom of every page in the Book of Mormon was listed the year the events described on that page were meant to have taken place. I knew that the Book of Mormon started around 600 BC.

"Ugh, are you guys going to debate religion again? It's like watching the saddest nature documentary. Two betas getting territorial," Muriel said. She got up from her computer chair. Her shorts were very short, and I noticed her legs were tanned. Then, from upstairs, she yelled, "Just fuck and get it over with."

"Ha," I said.

"I'm not gay," Seth said, more seriously than I thought he needed to. "Anyway, the point I was getting at is do you know about all the pretty blatant anachronisms in the Book of Mormon?"

"Probably. Only I don't know what the word anachronism means," I said. It was hard to play ignorance off as coolness, but I tried. I didn't want to disappoint Seth by making it obvious that I wasn't on his intellectual level.

"In like a movie, it's when a thing is in the wrong time. Like, a movie is set in the 1940s, but one of the characters drives a car that was made in the 1950s," he explained.

"Like a mistake someone should have caught," I offered.

"Yeah . . . so like in the Book of Mormon where you have the Nephites and Lamanites riding horses a thousand years before horses were on the continent. Or using steel. The Book of Mormon talks about swords made out of steel and chariots, and none of those things existed on the North or South American continents until after Columbus."

"First of all, it's pronounced knee-fights and laymen-nights. Second of all, how do they know?" I asked.

"They know because they haven't found one example of steel or chariots or horses. No record of any of them."

"Well, there is one record of them: the Book of Mormon."

"Yeah, right. But that doesn't really count. Like, don't you think it kind of says something about the veracity of the book that no historians or archeologists or anthropologists ever use it, or refer to it, or believe it's real at all?" Seth asked.

"Well, sure. If God made the Book of Mormon provable, it wouldn't require any faith, would it?" I responded.

"So, to test your faith, God included dumb mistakes in His

scripture so that it would look like Joseph Smith wrote the book himself, without any research?" Seth asked.

"Okay, but what are you atheists always saying when someone is like, 'Prove there *isn't* a God.' You say you can't prove a negative, right?" I asked.

"Sure, but—"

"But now you're telling me science has proven a negative," I said. "Like, if you were like, 'Prove that horses existed,' I could say, 'Well, prove that they didn't exist,' and you'd be able to. You'd be able to prove a negative."

I didn't know if that argument would hold. It was a bit of a technicality.

I hadn't known that about the horses.

Science would always lose against religion. The prerequisite for faith is believing that there exists a being that is incomprehensibly powerful. And once you have that faith, it's easy to dismiss any human crowing about some proof or argument that proves there isn't an incomprehensibly powerful being. Because that human always misses the point. God's incomprehensible.

"I'll look into it, but my initial response is I don't know," I said. "Except—the anachronisms don't matter, because I already know the Book of Mormon is true," I said.

"That's convenient," Seth smirked.

"The thing is, the Book of Mormon asks readers to question it. To find out it's true," I said. I was dangerously close to bearing my testimony—what I *knew* to be true, and how I knew it. But that would be too earnest to be convincing. I'd come off as a zealot, which wasn't the image I wanted to cultivate. "And I did. So, I'll look into the anachronisms, but I'm pretty sure I know the answer."

"Oh shit. This is what the site said you'd do, by the way," Seth said.

"What?" I said, getting up. Call this round a draw.

"That when you got stumped, you'd resort to repeating your beliefs. What's it called, bearing your testimony?"

"What site?" I asked.

"Some Christian site. Like, 'How to Talk to Mormon Missionaries,' or something."

"Want me to set you up with some?" I said. "They'd be better at answering questions than I am."

"No, thank you," Seth said.

Then we went upstairs to find out about that ice cream.

In my sixteenth year, around the time I first met Seth, my brother introduced our family to a new friend of his. She came home with him after a church activity at the Institute of Religion, which was the semi-ominous name of the LDS Church building just off the university campus. It wasn't a chapel, exactly, though Sunday services were held there. It was where university-level Church classes were held. Whereas high school students went to seminary in the morning before school, college-aged kids had institute throughout the week.

I understood without Sam saying so that when he said *friend* it wasn't a romantic euphemism. It probably meant that she was someone in need of either a place to stay the night, or a ride, or some free legal advice from my dad. She might also be an acquaintance from school who was interested in the Church. Or maybe all of the above.

I met her in the long front hall of our house, where one wall was devoted to pictures of all of us at different ages. Our entryway was a museum of the Hudson kids, aging in reverse all the way to the living room. I liked to pretend that the last picture of me, from the seventh grade—hair tucked behind my ears, baby cheeks, and monster front teeth—was actually a photo of a sister who tragically was no longer with us.

Dianna heard the news about my lost sister with appropriate sympathy, then considered the photo a moment longer. "You're better-looking anyway. I'm sure it's still a loss, but it can't be that big of one."

"She wasn't a very attractive girl, it's true," I said.

"If only she had been a boy. He'd probably be a lady-killer."

Dianna had a black eye that she was hiding with dark-rimmed glasses and the practised application of stage makeup. She acted like it wasn't there. She was a large woman, and I soon learned she was an opera singer, studying music at the University of Alberta.

My guess was Dianna was interested in the Church because she was interested in Sam, that he brought her home so she wouldn't mistake his desire to share the gospel with desire desire. While the "flirt to convert" method of missionary work had a proud history in the Church—a great many Mormon families had been created by a hapless man falling for a righteous Latter-day Saint woman—it wasn't the way Sam would bring people into the Church.

Sam and Dianna didn't run with the same crowd, but they sang in the same choir at school. Sam didn't really have a crowd. Intentionally or not, he modelled what I considered a healthy skepticism of male friendships. Our father had always done the same. Male friends were like sitcoms or fast food. They served no long-term purpose and they contributed nothing to one's eternal salvation. Sam was focused on other, more important things. Namely finishing his schooling and being righteous. And girls. I couldn't blame him. I liked to think I would be similarly focused when I got back from my mission. Other young men mostly annoyed me.

Despite what Church videos dramatized, people rarely came out and asked you whether Heavenly Father had a plan for their life. But Dianna came to Sam with a question so obvious she basically propositioned him, spiritually speaking. She asked him why bad things happen to good people. One of the most difficult and common questions about the human condition, and a perfect on-ramp to Heavenly Father's plan of salvation. The plan of salvation provided an explanation, a reason for life's struggles. More than that, it put those struggles into an eternal perspective. Nothing we faced here on earth could be all that major in the face of eternity, right? Not adolescent loneliness, and not whatever Dianna was going through.

Dianna was the good people. The bad things that happened to her was her father. It was that wrinkle that brought her to question Sam. As a Jehovah's Witness, a member of a religion that shared the Mormon proclivity for door-knocking and so felt like our rivals, Dianna surely had an answer ready for a question like that. But whatever the Jehovah's Witness answer would be, it didn't account for her father—who was an elder in their church—raping her.

When she first told Sam what had happened to her, she made it sound like there had been only one instance of abuse, but it was actually ongoing. It started when she lived at home, and continued after she moved out. It was repeated with sickening regularity. Dianna's father would beat her, rape her, insult and threaten her. When she got pregnant he wouldn't allow her to get an abortion, as that was against Jehovah's commandments. But Jehovah forgave miscarriages. Dianna's father helped God by pushing his daughter down the stairs.

But because the abuse didn't stop with one pregnancy, Dianna would end up getting an abortion.* Afterward, to punish her for doing so, her father filled her existence with gory, visceral anti-abortion propaganda. It would show up in her email, in her mailbox, under the windshield wiper of her Dodge Neon. She'd unfold a piece of paper in a textbook and see an alien amphibian creature, ostensibly a tiny human, smeared with blood and who knows what else, lying among rags and trash.

Although my parents and Sam encouraged her to speak to the police, Dianna said she was too scared to make such a definitive move against her father. It was therefore decided that she would at least begin keeping a record of the abuse, so that when she did have the resolve to turn against her father, she would have evidence. She would still live alone in her apartment, but she'd spend a lot more time with us, and with other Church members at the university, where she could be safe.

Only she wasn't safe. It didn't seem to matter how much time she spent at our house, her father would find a way to meet her. He would rape her in the afternoon, or late at night. He sent her to the hospital by raping her with a hunting knife. He left disgusting messages for her on her answering machine.

---

* Given her situation, getting an abortion wouldn't be verboten, according to the Church. The Mormon Church maintained that abortions were okay in instances of rape and incest, and to protect the life of the mother.

"Dirty bitch, are you too good for me now? Is that Mormon of yours a good fuck?" one message said. "You are my whore. I won't keep waiting for you. Come back now or it will be worse than you remember."

Witnessing Dianna's abuse was like watching someone struggle with an addiction. Every step toward recovery was precarious and fearful, a battle of attrition. Our family didn't see the invisible thread tying Dianna to her father, and couldn't understand how it could be so strong. It wasn't that I doubted Dianna's desire to be free from abuse, but it seemed impossible that anyone could have the kind of control Dianna's father had over her.

She'd leave our house for the night, intending to go straight home and get some sleep, only to come back the next day with new shades of purple and green around her eyes. Her father had a preternatural ability to be where Dianna was and we weren't.

"What was Satan's plan from the beginning?" Brother Woodrow asked my priesthood class one Sunday.

Brother Woodrow wore his hair in straight bangs in the front, then long enough in the back to just brush his collar. It was neither a bowl cut nor a mullet exactly, but an unholy hybrid of the two that looked medieval.

"He wanted to force us to live righteously. We wouldn't have to choose, not one would he have lost, but we would've had to give all the glory to him," I answered.

"Right," he said. Then, reflexively, "And what is God's glory?"

"This is my work and my glory—to bring about the immortality and eternal life of man," I recited.*

"So what Satan was really saying was that he wanted Heavenly Father's job," he said, getting back on track. "Satan has always wanted to take away our free agency. How does he do that?"

"Sin," someone suggested.

"Addiction," said someone else.

"Yeah. Sin—addiction comes from sin, so it's kind of the same thing. So sin and fear. I like to think of Adam and Eve," said Brother Woodrow. "After he tempted them to sin, what did Satan do? He pointed out that they were naked, and that Eve should hide from the Lord. Instead of encouraging them to turn to their Father, Satan made them scared of Heavenly Father. Satan's great power is fear."

"I thought it was pride?" I said.

"That's his great sin, but he uses fear to control us," Brother Woodrow said.

"And fear and pride aren't that far apart," Brother Lowry said. He was there to help Brother Woodrow. He didn't have much to do while Brother Woodrow taught the lesson, so Brother Lowry broke in when he could. Like a lot of people called to interact with youth, Brother Lowry was in his twenties with a couple of young kids. He seemed to be settling nicely into his softer, wider body. "Pride is basically fear that you won't get what you think you deserve."

"So, if Satan controls people through fear, how does the Lord get us to follow Him?" asked Brother Woodrow.

---

* Moses 1:39. The book of Moses is a retelling of Genesis that was revealed to Joseph Smith. It is in the Pearl of Great Price, the fourth, least studied book in Mormon scriptures.

"A different kind of fear?" I offered, only half joking. "'Work out your salvation with fear and trembling.'"*

"Where's that from?" Brother Lowry asked. It was a friendly challenge.

"Somewhere in there, probably near the back," I said, holding up my scriptures. "I don't know where it says that, but I know it says that." Brother Lowry rolled his eyes. He mouthed the word "Philippians," but it was impossible to make out.

"Okay, sure, but actually doesn't God just *ask* us to follow Him? We want to obey because He loves us. And love is always a more powerful motivator than fear," Brother Woodrow said.

"Always?" I said. "I don't know if that's right."

"Why not?" Brother Lowry asked.

"I'm just thinking fear is a pretty powerful motivator. I don't think, like, the Nazis were inspired by love."

"And they didn't win, did they?" Brother Woodrow said.

"Sure, but that's not why," I said.

"I promise you, love is a stronger motivator than fear. Every time," Brother Woodrow repeated.

"Then why don't dictators use love to inspire their people? Hitler seemed pretty powerful, was it just because of love? Were the Gestapo really secret love police?" I asked, sounding more annoyed than I had meant to. My voice had that whining certainty of an arrogant teenager. "It seems like fear is more powerful, at least in the real world." I didn't often disagree with my teachers; there was never any reason to. But this lesson on love seemed dangerously naive.

"Fear is powerful, I'm not denying that. But fear can only

* Philippians 2:12.

take you so far. The control that fear brings, it's temporary. It always fails in the end," Brother Woodrow said.

"Like think of Darth Vader," said Brother Lowry. He understood the convincing power of a pop culture analogy. Plus, the fictional space fascism of *Star Wars* was more pleasant to talk about than the real-world genocidal fascism of the Nazis. "The Dark Side was all about fear—that's how Vader and the emperor ruled. But in the end, that wasn't enough. It was love that brought balance to the Force, wasn't it?" Then he put on his best Yoda voice and quoted *The Phantom Menace*: "Fear leads to anger, anger leads to hate, hate leads to suffering."

"I guess," I said.

"You don't sound convinced," Brother Woodrow said.

"I'm sure you're right."

"Well, why do you keep the commandments? Is it because you're scared of what would happen to you if you didn't?"

"Kind of," I replied, which was more honest than I meant to be. I rephrased: "It's because I know the Church is true. And I don't want to disappoint anyone."

"And how do you know it's true?" Brother Woodrow asked.

He was building to something, so I gave him the answers he was expecting. "The Spirit," I said.

"And how do you know when you feel the Spirit?" he asked.

"A burning in my bosom, obviously," I said.

"I know that's what the scripture says, but I don't really know how a burning in your bosom is supposed to feel." He paused. "This was the scripture we used on my mission: turn to Galatians 5:22–23. It lists the fruits of the Spirit. Would you read that?" Brother Woodrow asked.

I got to the passage quickly. Seminary really was helping me master my scriptures. "But the fruit of the Spirit is love, joy, peace, longsuffering, gentleness, goodness, faith, meekness, temperance; against such there is no law."

Brother Woodrow spoke again. "I can't speak for anyone else, but that's how I know the Church is true, because I've felt my Saviour's love testifying that it's true. And because I received that witness, I'd do anything for Jesus Christ. Or I'd like to think I would anyway."

Having borne his testimony, Brother Woodrow was satisfied he'd convinced me of my error and probably saved my soul. I was still skeptical of the fear/love conundrum, but I nodded my head. I could accept that love had a slight power advantage over fear and hate, but I knew the contest was a lot closer than Brother Woodrow made it sound.

Dianna didn't want to go to the police. She didn't want the humiliation of explaining her situation to suspicious police officers, and she didn't want to drag her mother through a criminal trial. If it would even go that far. Despite all the injuries she'd sustained, she didn't have any incontrovertible proof that they were caused by her father. But something had to change.

The plan was for Dianna to go to Montreal in the fall of 2000 to finish her schooling at McGill, the Harvard of Canada. Her apartment wasn't safe, so she started living with us until she left for school in the east. She was not the first troubled young woman to take up residence at the Hudson house. It seemed my mom would bring one in every year or so. Dianna fit in better than most. She was a performer. She didn't get swallowed up by the goofy sibling energy that turned so many other guests into spectators. She was funny and confident.

By this point, Dianna's relationship with my brother had become complicated. He got frustrated that she still spoke to her father and that she'd still meet with him when he asked her to. Then she'd come back from the meeting with another black eye. And Sam knew the black eyes were probably the least of it. He had spent hours on the phone with Dianna on nights when she had threatened to end her life. He took her to the hospital when her father took a knife to her privates, and he stayed the entire night with her. The threatening calls that Dianna had been receiving were coming to the downstairs phone line, which was a separate line for us kids to use. The alarming messages were filling up Sam's answering machine daily.

Sam reasoned that the voice leaving the threats didn't sound old enough to be Dianna's father. It was probably some friends of his, or other members at his church calling for him. That way there could be deniability if Dianna ever tried to use the messages against him in a court case.

"There's actually a pretty good doctrinal analogy in them, as twisted as it is," Sam said. Mormons love analogies. I had interrupted him studying. Dianna was singing in the chorus of an Edmonton opera company, so she wasn't home. I hadn't heard the messages and I didn't want to. But Sam was giving me an update. "Whoever they are, they are acting in the name of Dianna's father. They are probably saying what he wants them to say, and they say it in his name. Get it?"

"Like with Jesus, I get it," I said.

"Yeah. We act in Christ's name, and say things He would say."

"That's clever," I said.

"Obviously, it wouldn't work for a lesson. The calls are really gross."

He wouldn't admit it to Dianna, but Sam was losing his patience. With the messages, the black eyes, the general hopelessness. He was exhausted. He had been Dianna's main support system for nearly a year.

When my brother would get impatient with her, Dianna would turn to me. She knocked on my door in the middle of the night, all the theatrical bigness and sass emptied out of her. She stood in my doorway, wounded and mousy. She cried about disappointing my brother, but didn't know what else to do, because her father was still her father. And she was the only thing preventing him from hurting her mother and/or her sister.

And thus it came to pass that even though Sam had first brought her to the Church, and he did attend each missionary lesson with her, when she was getting ready to be baptized into the Church of Jesus Christ of Latter-day Saints, she asked me if I would do it. I don't know if Sam had told her he wouldn't feel comfortable baptizing her, or if she had picked up on that feeling herself. She saw me as a little brother, and being baptized by her brother felt special.

I could baptize. There was nothing that said I couldn't. It didn't happen often, but sixteen-year-old boys with the priesthood could perform baptisms. Mostly baptisms were performed by dads, if the family were already church members, or by missionaries, if the baptizees were converts.

I told Dianna that I'd be honoured to baptize her.

I was still looking for my own powerful conversion story. One that would be genuine and convincing to use when I became a missionary in a few years. Deep in my bones, I knew the Church was true because that's all I ever knew. And I knew I'd felt the Spirit before. I thought of my patriarchal blessing. The Spirit was undeniable. But I didn't think the story made for good missionary material. To tell it, I'd have to first explain what a patriarchal blessing was, and it just wouldn't work. But if I could feel something at Dianna's baptism, that would make for a perfect story.

Obviously, Dianna's baptism wasn't about me and my spiritual journey. But in my sixteen-year-old mind, it kind of was. Since my desire was for increased faith, I didn't think Heavenly Father would mind that I was thinking of myself.

Nothing that was happening to Dianna was her fault. Whatever horrible things her father accused her of, she hadn't sinned. And yet it was still special to think of baptism washing her entirely clean. Like maybe all the pain that came with her father's cruelties could be washed away, too.

But even more selfishly, I was looking forward to having *my* sins forgiven. There was ample scriptural evidence that when one brings someone to Christ, two people are saved. It's the Lord's incentive program—your bonus for the referral is that your sins are forgiven.

It wasn't a guaranteed trip to the celestial kingdom, the way dying for someone was. I still had to endure to the end after getting the clean slate. I liked the idea of starting at square one. Because the truth was I still hadn't confessed and forsaken my first great sin.

Masturbation, I now understood, wasn't the chastity breach I had worried it was when I was twelve. It wasn't as serious as actually having sex. The problem was I still didn't really know how serious it was. The Book of Mormon is very clear about fornication. According to a scripture, sex outside of marriage was "most abominable above all sins save it be the shedding of innocent blood" (Alma 39:5). But masturbation wasn't sex. Could I get excommunicated for what I'd done to myself? I didn't think so. But would it endanger my ability to go on a mission? I was pretty sure it would.

Because it's not like I had been perfect since my *Mission: Impossible* moment. I had sinned in the same way three more times since then. It was like an annual tradition. Sin, then feel worthless for an entire year, until I did it again. Of course, when I say I sinned in the same way, I mean I committed the same sin, but not in the same manner. Let's be perfectly clear, I only made love to the bathtub that one time.

I didn't think much about the meaning of Dianna's predicament. I never once stopped to consider why Heavenly Father saw fit to put her through such an ordeal. Maybe it was because Dianna never seemed to wonder about it either. She seemed able to differentiate between the things God allowed to happen and things He caused to happen. Her issue wasn't with God for sending her to be her father's daughter. It was that her father was wicked.

And maybe I recognized that she had some agency, even in her situation. Why did she keep meeting him? Why did she seem to make choices that weren't in her best interest?

The severity and constancy of the abuse Dianna was experiencing was unique, but the general plot wasn't. Dianna was a familiar character in a story I understood. The damsel in distress, the lost soul, the seed planted on good earth but surrounded by weeds and thorns. She confirmed what I already thought I knew: Mormons were the only ones who had all the truth, and so we were the only ones equipped to rescue her. Of course Dianna's dad was a monster. He wasn't Mormon. He didn't have the priesthood. He was an elder in a false church.

She made me feel like a protector and follower of Christ. Her hopelessness, her plight: they gave us the opportunity to serve God. "Inasmuch as ye have done it unto one of the least of these my brethren, ye have done it unto me."

At night I said my prayers. In the privacy of my room, I was better at speaking freely—almost conversationally—when I prayed. I prayed for Dianna, for her safety and strength. That she'd be okay. And I prayed for forgiveness for whatever sinful desire I had had during the day—usually involving staring at a magazine cover for too long, wishing I could just flip through its polybagged pages for a moment—and asked for strength to keep my thoughts pure. Like when I was a child, I didn't always know what to say to my Father in Heaven, so out of habit and an abundance of caution I still asked that my city be spared from any tornado that should come in the night, and that my slumber be unmolested by bad dreams. I had been asking for the same favours since I was five.

What if those requests weren't granted? What if a tornado touched down on my street minutes after I closed my prayer in the name of Jesus Christ, amen? Would I stop believing in Heavenly Father, or begin doubting His ability to hear and answer prayers?

I didn't think so.

Heavenly Father didn't send tornadoes any more than he sent Dianna's dad over to her place. Granted, there was a difference between a natural disaster and an abusive parent. Tornadoes weren't sentient. The devastation they wrought was indiscriminate.

I was in Sam's room, listening to him play a nonsense song on the guitar. From the basement we heard Dianna open and close the front door. We heard her steps as she walked underneath the skylight, toward the stairs. Then she was a blazing brown blur of hair and gown moving past Sam's door. She didn't quite slam her door behind her. She came out again a second later and stood in Sam's doorway. The gown, which was her costume for the opera in which she had been performing, was silk and shiny and displayed ample cleavage. It was meant for a red carpet, not a basement rug.

She had been crying, and she was crying still.

"What's wrong?" I asked.

"I can't go to Montreal," she said. I didn't think she had heard my question. We both knew that she had more to say, so we didn't ask her a follow-up. "I know how much everyone wants me gone. To go. I know I've basically taken over your life, and I realize that. I do. And I see the damage my life causes to other people. That's why I don't ever want to be taken care of. It's too hard for people to deal with. It's too much."

She looked up from the ground. She smiled a little through her tears, like she wasn't expecting to see us there. "And of course the Hudsons have been different, but I know even the Hudsons have a breaking point. And that was probably several points ago. But I just really think I shouldn't go to Montreal."

I wanted to see what Sam would say. He couldn't admit that, yes, she had taken over his life and, yes, he would like a bit of a rest. He wanted some time to just be a university student, not a full-time counselor. If he tried to convince her it was okay if she stayed his heart wouldn't have been in it. He ran the risk of looking like a liar, but only because he would be lying.

"I know it's been hard, don't you think it's been hard for me, too?" Dianna said. "It's my life. I'm the one actually living it. The insults and abuse." For a bit, her voice became her "woman" voice. It was deeper. It had body. It was the voice she used with people from the theatre, or with me when we bantered. I always thought that if she were ever a guest on a talk show, she'd use her woman voice. But then she slipped back into the girlish voice she used when she was sad and scared and hurt. "I don't want you to think that I'm not grateful for all you've done for me. That would be the worst possible thing."

"What if we leave the Hudsons out of it," Sam said. Dianna looked chastened. Not, it seemed, by what he said, but by his speaking at all. She nodded. "Let's not worry about what's best for the Hudsons. We're on your side. We're a given. So, the Hudsons don't matter, stay, go, we're here for you, right?

"So," he said, shifting positions in his chair, as if to restart the scene. "What's this I hear about you not wanting to go to Montreal?"

"It's not that I don't want to go. It's not what I want. Of course I want to go. But it's like everyone keeps forgetting! What about my mom! And what about my sister! What about my family? Everyone thinks it should be so easy to leave my family because of my father, but what have they done? They'll just be hurt."

"Okay," Sam said. "But aren't they not supposed to talk to you anyway? They can do that just as easily if you're in Montreal."

"That's true," Dianna said.

"Which incidentally is another point for Mormonism, not that anyone's keeping score," I said. "But, yay for no shunning."

"But at least I know that if my father's doing it to me, he's not doing it to them," Dianna said.

"How do you know that though?" Sam asked.

"Because I know."

"Right, but how?" he repeated.

"Because he doesn't need to," she said.

"Is it because that's what he told you?" Sam asked.

Dianna steeled herself for the admission, then nodded solemnly.

"And your dad, he's a pretty trustworthy guy?" I asked.

"No. Obviously not."

"I just thought of a scripture. Would it be lame if I broke out my scriptures for a sec?" Sam asked, already opening his copy of the Doctrine and Covenants.

Sam adopted the overly earnest cadence of a missionary, since he was acting like one. It was exaggerated, though, to show that he was in on the joke. "Brother Hudson, will you read verses 22 and 23?" Sam asked. Missionaries always began their requests with a "will you."

"Of course, Elder Hudson. I'd be happy to," I said, matching his over-the-top earnestness. We were putting on a little show. He handed me his scriptures. "Verses 22 and 23, you say?"

"If you could."

"Of course," I said. "*Verily, verily, I say unto you, if you desire a further witness, cast your mind upon the night that you cried unto me in your heart, that you might know concerning the truth of these things. Did I not speak peace to your mind concerning the matter? What greater witness can you have than from God?*"

"Brother Hudson," he said, pausing the way missionaries did when they wanted to say something with the Spirit. "What does that scripture mean to you?"

"Well, Elder, I don't know much about these things," I said, putting on a bit of a Southern accent because it seemed fitting. "But it sounds to me like Joseph Smith was asking Heavenly Father for some, I guess, reassurance. Maybe wondering if all the persecution he was going through was really worth it. And Heavenly Father answered in a pretty cool way. He was like, 'Remember that other time you asked about this, and remember how you felt?' And He was like, 'What more do you want from me?'"

"And what about you, Sister . . ."

"Fellows. Sister Fellows," Dianna said, joining the scene.

"Right, right. Sister Fellows, what does that scripture mean to you?" Missionary Sam asked.

"I get it," Dianna said. "That's not a bad scripture, Elder Hudson."

"That Joseph Smith, not a bad guy," I said.

During the first week of classes at McGill in September, 2000, Dianna met Reuben. He was a non-member, obviously. But he was kind and funny and seemed supportive of her new religion. At least he was at first. It was like he had been waiting for her. Like a predator, he knew what he was doing, must have known the secret signs of victimhood, and he saw them all, flashing in neon, in Dianna. Within a month, Reuben proved to be just as vicious as her father had been.

And the cycle of abuse started up again.

Sam started fielding Dianna's suicidal phone calls again. And we felt despair. We couldn't protect her while she lived with us, and now we had encouraged her to trade one abuser for another. And we couldn't do anything from across the country. All Sam could do was make sure he was always ready to answer her call. She'd be coming home for Christmas in a few months. Dianna was no longer a Jehovah's Witness. She was a member of the Church of Jesus Christ of Latter-day Saints, now. And Mormons celebrate the hell out of the Saviour's birthday.

Dianna's conversion to the Church was sticking, despite being so far from the ward she knew. Despite Reuben, too.

When Dianna got home from Montreal, she immediately volunteered to drive down to Utah to pick up my sister Mary from school at Brigham Young University and bring her home. They had never met, and Dianna wanted to make up for lost time during the eighteen-hour drive. With the high number of Canadians (mostly Albertans) at BYU, there was a culture of getting rides from strangers to and from school. So, for Mary at least, it wasn't that strange to drive home with a person she had never met.

Dianna called once on the way down. She had hit some bad weather in Idaho and she'd spun her Neon off the road. She wasn't hurt, she said, but she didn't know how she was going to get going again.

"Of course she went off the road," I muttered under my breath when I heard the news.

"That's sort of what I thought, too," my mom said, as if she was confessing something embarrassing. I hadn't expected her to agree with me.

"If a bad thing is going to happen to someone, it'll happen to Dianna," I said. I was being insensitive. But it felt morbidly predictable.

That incident, small as it was, felt like it was too much. Spinning off the road strained credulity. No one could have worse luck than Dianna. It was like every time Dianna tasted freedom, she was punished. How much humbler did she need to be? What lesson was she still meant to learn? She was being tested to the same degree as Joseph Smith or Job.

Or was something else going on? We didn't dare give voice to what that something else could be: that Dianna was lying.

Even contemplating that possibility felt gross. My parents weren't naturally suspicious, and they passed their general faith in humanity—some might call it naïveté—down to us. It felt like our faith was being tested.

But why would Dianna lie? Why would anyone lie about the things Dianna experienced?

What else could she be lying about, other than spinning off the highway?

Maybe Reuben didn't exist. That would have been a little strange, even worrisome. Had she felt she needed to make up an abusive boyfriend to keep our interest? But even if Reuben were fiction, we knew her father wasn't. She wasn't lying about that. We had all seen the evidence of their encounters too many times.

With Mary in the passenger seat, Dianna and my sister were able to drive home without further incident. Everyone came home that year. My sister Erin and her husband, Ryan, with their new baby, came all the way from Singapore, where they lived as expats, and it was our family's turn to host Gill and her husband, Andrew, too.

To create some distance between her and Reuben, Dianna was going to stay in Edmonton with us instead of returning to McGill after the holidays. While she had been away, she had left her car behind in Edmonton for Sam to use. To thank her, Sam gave the Dodge Neon a good cleaning. He lugged our vacuum out to the driveway, along with several rags and garbage bags. He would get rid of all the evidence that he had been driving it. Dianna didn't expect him to do it, but he thought it would be a nice gesture.

Sam was vacuuming, shifting the front seats back and forth in order to get all the detritus. Underneath the driver's seat there was a CD. He read the label on the case. It came from a recording studio in town. The CD had the words "Mean Guy Phoning You" written on it.

Curious, my brother slid the CD into the car's stereo. Suddenly, he heard the same messages he had been getting on his answering machine, only now they were coming out of Dianna's car speakers. Track after track of awful words we had heard on our phone, including the hit: "You can't protect her, the bitch is mine." He ejected the CD from the car stereo and brought it into the house to play it in his room.

These were the messages from Dianna's father, or allegedly from her father. They were from a CD made by a local recording studio.

Sam tracked down the studio. He asked the people there if they knew anything about the CD.

The man from the studio took a look at the label and smiled. He told Sam that it was just a project they were hired to do for Dianna, whom they knew.

My brother asked the studio guy if he knew what the CD was for.

He said that he didn't ask people a lot of questions when he was doing his job. But he had assumed it was for a drama class.

As Sam left the studio, the man encouraged him to say hello to Dianna for him. My brother said that he definitely would.

There was no satisfying explanation for the CD's existence. It seemed impossible to imagine a world where the abuse Dianna experienced was real, while the phone messages that threatened it weren't. The most charitable interpretation was that she had the CD made so that we wouldn't finally turn her away. Maybe she really was being abused, or had been abused in the past, and this CD, written and directed by Dianna Fellows, was a backwards way of ensuring we stayed on her side by keeping the threat ever-present and palpable. If the danger wasn't imminent, we might lose interest. And then where would she be?

But even if that were true, did her unfounded fear that we'd suddenly reject her justify deception?

The CD hadn't been made on a whim. Dianna would have had to rent the studio, write the script, and get the producers to perform according to it. Then she'd have to have paid for the finished product. And every day or two, she would have had to pick from a track list of threats and go to a secluded place where she could play the CD into a phone receiver, so as to leave a message on Sam's answering machine. There were so many points at which she could have stopped and reconsidered what she was doing. But she didn't.

I wasn't there when Sam and my mom confronted Dianna about the CD. About all of it. I didn't want to be there. I wanted to be anywhere else. So I stayed in my room. I heard the muffled arguing coming from the basement, then frantic wailing, sobbing.

Dianna first tried to feign innocence. She didn't know anything about that CD. It was probably made by her father. Then she confessed her fabrications in reverse order. First, Reuben didn't exist. She had never had any abortions. She had never been pregnant. Her father hadn't penetrated her with a knife. It turns out she had done that to herself and she had given herself all the black eyes.

After my mom threatened to call the police, Dianna finally gave her her mother's number. My mom called her mom to come and pick Dianna up, like the playdate was over. When Dianna's mother came around, she was smaller than Dianna, with short, curled hair and granny glasses. My mom apologized to her. After all, we had all believed some pretty horrible things about her. Her mother waved the apologies away. This wasn't the first time Dianna had gotten carried away. She used socks full of pennies to hit herself and blacken her eyes, her mother said. But she offered no clear explanation for the behaviour.

When her mother arrived to pick her up, Dianna changed entirely. She wasn't the brassy dame, or the mousy victim. She was rage. She refused to leave with her mother. She wouldn't leave the house. Dianna gnashed her teeth as my mom wrestled her out the door. Dianna bit her arm hard.

The fight left her when she saw her mother in our driveway. She shut down and let her mother lead her to her car as my mom apologized some more. Later that day, Dianna's father stopped by to pick up her things. He had been this nightmare figure, this calculating, heartless monster. Now he was just someone's dad. Her parents seemed older than my parents. He didn't talk much while he was packing her things into black garbage bags. We never got to ask him any questions. We never got any satisfying answers.

The closest thing we got to the truth was something Dianna said after confessing to all of it. "If I told you the truth," she said, "you wouldn't think what happened to me was all that bad. But it was to me."

Dianna leaving was a little like getting off a crowded bus. Her turmoil took up a lot of space. The constant tragedy and danger had been stifling. But we only really noticed how uncomfortable it had been once we were off the bus. After all, what was a little discomfort compared to the hell Dianna was living through. After she was gone, we could stand up straight and breathe.

Dianna also left us with a lot of questions. We decided that the only explanation of her behaviour was some vague mental illness, which is to say: she was crazy. She had to be, didn't she? It couldn't have just been a desire for attention, or some backwards attempt at marrying my brother. It had to have been something pathological.

It wasn't a perfect explanation, but it was enough. Actually, the questions we were left with couldn't be answered by Dianna at all. They were questions for Heavenly Father: what did it all mean?

Wasn't the Spirit supposed to help discern truth from fiction? With all his scripture-studying and efforts to live righteously, shouldn't Sam have been warned that something was amiss?

To the contrary, Sam said he often felt the Spirit inspiring him when he tended to Dianna. It was the same with her bishop, her institute instructor, and my parents. They all had felt that they were guided by the Spirit in their words of comfort and counsel. And while it hadn't been as epic as I had hoped, I had felt the Spirit at Dianna's baptism. But was her desire to be baptized even genuine? Surely the Spirit knew that Dianna had been lying. Shouldn't He have let her bishop know? Meanwhile, as youth we were told never to lie to a bishop, a) because it was tantamount to lying to the Lord, and b) because it would be a fool's errand. Thanks to their special calling as bishops, they'd know if someone was trying to hide something from them.

I didn't have an answer. The meaning I took from the Dianna drama was that people will lie with or without motivation or explanation. About anything.

I HOPE THEY CALL ME ON A MISSION

(May–September 2002)

I LOOKED AT the papers Bishop Flowers gave me. These were my papers. My whole life I had heard talk of young soon-to-be missionaries "sending in their papers," and here were mine. I filled out a reasonable number of forms asking about my education, work experiences, extracurricular activities, and proficiency in languages. Hint hint. I got letters of recommendation from my family ward bishop. I got shots for tuberculosis and as many hepatitises as I could. I had blood drawn. I got my picture taken both for my passport, which I was getting for the first time, and to accompany my papers. I was going to need all of this to embark on my mission.

I was told it worked as follows: the prophet, the leader of the entire Church, who at that time was Gordon B. Hinckley—or one of the Twelve Apostles, if the prophet was busy—would sit in a room either in the Salt Lake Temple or across the street in the Church's office building. That part was unclear. But the process was always described in the same way. The prophet would study the picture of the potential missionary as it was projected on a wall in front of him. He would read their papers, look into their eyes, and take in the entire potential missionary. Then the prophet would be told by the inner still small voice of the Spirit where I needed to serve. It was important for me to convey as much as possible with my photo: faithfulness, eagerness to work, willingness to serve in foreign lands, humility, and the joy the gospel brought me. I needed to look like I had a burning testimony that I was eager to share with the world. It was a lot to ask of a photo.

I would answer every question asked of me and send my papers off to Salt Lake with my stake president's blessing. Three weeks to a month later I'd get a small package in the mail: my mission call.

Timing was important. I timed things so that I would send my papers in while I was still eighteen. Then I'd get my call and leave on my mission as close to my nineteenth birthday as possible. That showed eagerness and obedience. Young men went on missions when they were nineteen. That was the instruction. People who seemed cavalier about sending in their papers—waiting until after their nineteenth birthday to fill them out and send them in, for example—made me wonder. What were they waiting for? Every day that I was nineteen and not on my mission would be time wasted.

There were a lot of Mormon hymns and Primary songs about missions and missionary work. "I Hope They Call Me on a Mission" was a popular one in Primary. It had a "Home on the Range" vibe, and little kids looked especially cute when they sang it. Of course, I preferred "We'll Bring the World His Truth

(Army of Helaman)." It had a dramatic hook and it compared missions to military service, which I always appreciated.

Helaman (*Heal-a-min)* was a Book of Mormon prophet and military leader. The combination wasn't unique—most political and military leaders in the Book of Mormon were also spiritual leaders. Although he was a Nephite, Helaman led an army of young Lamanite men—stripling warriors, they were called*—into one of the many battles in the middle of the book. But weren't the Lamanites wicked, you ask? Most were. Lehi's family had separated into two camps when they first got to the promised land. The Nephites were righteous, while the Lamanites were cursed because they were wicked. But these Lamanite soldiers were a minority. Although they were very young, they fought in battle because, years prior, their fathers, a group of righteous, pacifist Lamanites, had been murdered by wicked Lamanites for their refusal to fight. As a result, the stripling warriors had been raised in the faith by their mothers. And because of their faith, not a single stripling warrior was killed in the battle. It was a good story. Like all the best stories in the scriptures, it depicted faith as a kind of superpower. But this one was especially cool because the protagonists were teens themselves. A popular t-shirt among Mormon youth depicted the stripling warriors with comic book bodies. Underneath the muscled-up teens were the words "Momma's Boys."**

I still thought of faith as a superpower sometimes. Or, more accurately, I imagined faith as the means through which extraordinary powers were bestowed on a person. It was the magic in Magic Stick's magic stick.

---

* Alma 53:20–22.

** Alma 56:47–48.

Two final steps in the process of completing my papers scared me. I'd always known they would come and I'd been dreading both since elementary school.

Before I could receive my mission call, I had to 1) get a full physical and 2) have a final interview with my stake president for the metaphysical equivalent: a full spiritual. If there was lingering sin I hadn't dealt with properly, anything I had neglected to tell Bishop Flowers in one of the many other interviews I'd had with him, this would be the time to unburden myself. And I knew, with shame and fear, that I had one major sin still weighing on my chest that threatened to keep me from my mission.

Yet I was probably more worried about the physical exam. It would be the first time I'd be naked in front of another person, outside of a locker room—and even in that situation I was very adept at maintaining modesty through expert towel manoeuvres. This would be the first time another person would take a good hard look at my late-adolescent penis. If I were examined by a male doctor, fine. It would be awkward, but I imagined it would feel clinical. But what if the doctor were a woman? And what if that female doctor were pretty and relatively young? Or buxom? How would I not get an erection when a woman was looking at my member? And once I inevitably got an erection, what was the protocol then? What was expected of me? Was I to apologize profusely? Laugh it off—*what, this old thing? Ha ha.* And just as importantly, what would the doctor do? Would they laugh? Would they scold me? Would that scar me? My sister Erin said that when one of her male friends stiffened during his physical, the doctor just grabbed the dick as if it were a microphone and bopped it on its head to settle it down instantly.

I didn't know if that story was true or not. But it meant that there was the possibility that this would be the first person not only to see my penis, but to touch it as well. Mostly, I didn't want to catch the doctor stifling a laugh.

Whether intentionally or not, the first thought anyone had upon seeing my stubby fingers and Muppet feet—the smallness of both accentuated by the fact that I was over six feet tall, with shoulders that were starting to broaden—was that I must be packing a distressingly small dick inside my cargo pants. And for all I knew, I was. How would I know any different?

I had concerns not just about my penis size, but about its look, too. From television I learned that the uncircumcised penis was a wretched, unwanted thing. Elaine and Jerry basically said so in a very hurtful episode of *Seinfeld*. As with questions of size, I didn't know exactly how much of a freak my dick was for sporting his turtleneck.

Now, obviously I was grateful for all the Lord's commandments. They were how the Lord showed He cared. But I was especially grateful for the law of chastity because of all my anxieties around my penis. It wouldn't matter how small or uncircumcised my penis was, it would be the first and only one my eventual wife would know. She would fall in love with me without seeing my penis, so chances are she would continue to love me afterward. I imagined my future wife would feel about my penis the same way she would about opening up something practical on her birthday, like a toothbrush or a gift certificate for an oil change. Thoughtful, and not unwanted, but by no means dazzling.

Between the ages of eight and eleven, I exclusively called my penis "my nevermind." As in "Ouch! I just got kicked in the nevermind." I did this not because anyone told me I should, and not because I'd heard anyone else call it that or because I was explicitly taught penises were shameful. I did this because I felt yucky using the accurate term. It sounded weaselly and wet and rotten.

By the time I was nearly nineteen, I'd gotten better at calling a penis a penis, but I still wasn't confident enough to put mine on display. Even if, according to Sam, all I'd have to do was allow the doctor to cup my testicles while I turned my head and coughed, the whole thing seemed too intimate and embarrassing to handle.

But such were the sacrifices a faithful young man had to make in order to serve the Lord.

When I was eighteen, I started going to a young single adult ward. My excitement at being surrounded by so many new people was tempered by the fact that I would be leaving on my mission soon. But on the plus side, Bishop Flowers wasn't my old basketball coach or next-door neighbour, or my father, who had stopped being my bishop when I was about fifteen. That meant I no longer had a reason to be shy about talking to my bishop and clearing up my major sins.

Mormons never talked about dry humping. It was inappropriate to talk about your transgressions with anyone other than your Church leaders, so it's not like it would be brought up in Sunday School. But even in the *For the Strength of Youth* pamphlet, which laid out the Church's standards for young people, dry humping was absent. Instead, *For the Strength of Youth* cautioned young people against necking and petting, both heavy and light. These were words teenagers last used when Eisenhower was president.

It's not that I thought I had been the first to discover dry sex, but I assumed I had stumbled on an act few other Mormons were desperate enough to commit. In my mind, it was an act so shameful the Church wouldn't mention it lest it give young people ideas.

I only dated Lainey for a couple of months, at the end of twelfth grade, but in that time we fell into a routine where our dates would end on her couch. The dry humping happened naturally. Once we did it so furiously I made my dick—my nevermind—bleed. It seemed like just punishment.

Bishop Flowers really liked my brother Sam. I didn't look forward to offering up so clear a contrast, but what else are younger brothers for? I still had time to be as good as Sam was. My impending mission would help. And so would talking to the bishop.

And it did. I was worried I'd have to explain what I meant by dry humping, but to my surprise Bishop Flowers was familiar with the practice. There was no immediate absolution, no "say ten Hail Marys and you're forgiven," since that's not how Heavenly Father actually works. That might be how the Catholic Church worked on TV—something of which I was deeply jealous—but in reality, Heavenly Father expected us to work a little bit for forgiveness, by forsaking the sin and living righteously after copping to it. I was taught that forgiveness, when it came, would come privately: sometimes when you were praying or reading the scripture, the still small voice would silently let you know that you had been forgiven. The repentance process for serious transgressions like breaches of the law of chastity required priesthood mediation, but forgiveness was entirely personal. After confessing my stupid sordid sins I felt less alone. It wasn't that Bishop Flowers said anything special, rather it was his lack of reaction that made me feel better. I wasn't abnormal. I wasn't the only young man who succumbed to temptation. I felt like I was fully back on the path.

It was a straight shot to my mission. I would be one of the Lord's missionaries, working to bring the world His truth.

Only, maybe not. There were some sins that were so serious they disqualified you for missionary service. I was unclear exactly what those sins were, but I knew they were related to the law of chastity.

The final stake president interview to come still scared me. There was something I still hadn't dealt with, that I hadn't confessed to anyone. Something so shameful and serious I had withheld it from my talks with Bishop Flowers. Even after telling him about the pantomimed sex.

I touched a breast.

Technically, I had actually touched a bra. A purple bra with floral swirls of lace that I would remember for the rest of my life. But that bra had boobs in it. They were Lainey's. After we broke up during the summer I turned eighteen, I promised myself that she'd be the last non-member girl I'd ever date. The law of chastity was too easy to bend and break without both parties diligently defending each other's virtue. It was a glass table that needed all four hands to carry safely.

Could such a transgression keep me from my destiny? Deep

inside, I felt like it could, or maybe should. It seemed to me that the seriousness of a sin grew in proportion to the pleasure it offered. In which case I could hardly imagine a more serious infraction.

At the beginning of the summer, my brother and I moved to Calgary to live with our parents, who had moved there in the winter for my dad's work. It was a cruel and horny irony that one of the best spots to park and make out in Calgary—an activity with a long and glorious tradition even, and maybe especially, among Mormons—was across the street from the Crescent Road Chapel of the Church of Jesus Christ of Latter-day Saints. There were six parking spots there that looked out over Calgary's skyline.

To get to the spot, first you drove along a winding road lined with expensive-looking houses. Then the houses stopped on one side and there was a precipitous drop. Down below, the Bow River wound through Prince's Island Park on the northern edge of downtown. Roads and bridges rose and turned toward the city centre like tentacles. The skyline was crowded and peppered with cranes, and the lights on the skyscrapers looked like Christmas, even in June. Off to the side, ostracized, was the Calgary Tower, a free-standing structure built in the style of Seattle's Space Needle or Toronto's CN Tower, but noticeably shorter. Lamer. It looked like it was meant to loom large among the other buildings, to be the city's steeple. But taller buildings sprang up around it.

I didn't have anyone to make out with. But I wanted to take in the view. The best place to do that was the roof of the church.

I very much liked being on roofs. They offered a clearer perspective. Getting onto the roof of the church was as easy as getting onto my roof back home in Edmonton. It involved roughly the same process, too. First I clambered onto the roof of a shed that was practically attached to the church, and from there I could easily pull myself up onto the peaked roof.

Up there, the street disappeared along with the makeout spots. I sat on the tallest peak, near the front of the building. Underneath me was the chapel. I looked out at the proud, half-blinking concrete buildings.

This was a spot made for reflection and profound thinking. I still didn't know what that was supposed to feel like, or what exactly would constitute a deep thought, but from my understanding, it was mostly about finding analogies in, and for, everything.

There were so many lights below me. All the skyscrapers were advent calendars whose surprise gift, every day, was office furniture. I could see neighbourhoods practically aglow with street lights, headlights, kitchen and living room windows, and buzzing neon signs from strip malls.

Let your light so shine before men, that they may see your good works, and glorify your Father which is in heaven (Matthew 5:16).

All those lights represented a child of God, I thought.

And from where I was sitting, if one of those lights went out it wouldn't make a single bit of difference. I wouldn't notice. Not from the roof of the church. The city would be just as bright. From a distance, every individual light was unimportant and unremarkable.

My life was as insignificant as a street light. If I didn't go on a mission, if I somehow disappeared entirely, it wouldn't make a difference to the city below me.

This wasn't an uplifting analogy. From this vantage point each individual light *seemed* like nothing, I said to myself, but the closer you got to each light, the more you'd notice if it went out. And the more the light mattered to you, the greater the shock would be if it went dark.

Sure, on a grand scale, my light didn't matter. But the people around me, my family mainly, would notice if my light went out. Right?

That was almost hopeful. Though I still felt my insignificance. Of course, the miracle of Heavenly Father's love was that He could see the lights of the entire planet—every one of his billions of children—and He didn't think any light was unremarkable. He noticed every time one of His kids flickered.

That was a pretty thought.

I probably needed to temper my expectations about how epic my mission would be, and about how powerful I'd be on it. My patriarchal blessing promised me leadership positions and that I would "serve in foreign lands, bringing the gospel to those who have yet to receive the blessings of eternal life."

Complicating where I would be sent on my mission was the fact that I had been diagnosed with diabetes the year before. I seemed to be tired—what seventeen-year-old doesn't like to take frequent naps?—but since diabetes ran in my family, especially on my dad's side, my mom bought a test to check for sugar in my urine, which is a telltale sign of diabetes. And that was that. In a day or two, the doctor confirmed the diagnosis and suddenly I was a diabetic. I didn't think I was a very serious case. It wasn't as though I was a type 1 diabetic. I was diagnosed as type 2. My body still produced insulin, it was just resistant to it. It preferred my insulin with a side car of the genetically synthesized stuff. I had the diabetes of an out-of-shape middle-aged man, only I got mine as a young person, and not as a result of excess weight or a sedentary lifestyle. Yes, I had type 2 diabetes, but it was type 2 with an asterisk.*

Because it was such a light form of the condition, I didn't think it would affect where I would be called for my mission. I held out hope I'd get a foreign call. Lots of countries had insulin.

Most people in the ward who knew I was diabetic clucked their tongues when I talked to them about my impending mission. "So you're going somewhere in Canada," they'd say. "Where do you think you'll go?"

I refused to play along, not wanting to let myself believe that my mission call would be anything but pure revelation from God, signed by the prophet. Because if diabetes was going to keep me close to home, why did the Lord give me diabetes? I had the same type of diabetes that my father had. He almost surely had diabetes when he served his mission in the late 1960s, but wasn't diagnosed until he was in his thirties and married with children. That meant he was able to serve his mission in France. I'd had a 50/50 shot of inheriting my condition from my dad. It was a genetic crapshoot and I lost. And yet the Lord saw fit to expose my condition to my doctor when I was seventeen. Why?

I couldn't rule out sin. Gillian, who went to Russia on her mission, was also diagnosed with diabetes after coming home. She was definitely more righteous than I was. If I had lived a life more like Gill's I would definitely be going abroad.

---

* I have what's called MODY, maturity-onset diabetes of the young. It's a result of a genetic mutation that is unavoidable. Some doctors refer to MODY as type 3 diabetes, because it's pretty different from types 1 and 2. There are different types of MODY, too. I have MODY 3. Interesting trivia: apparently the gene that makes me a MODY 3 also ensures that I have small hands and feet. I never stood a chance.

That mission calls were a reflection of one's righteousness went unspoken, but was undeniably true. Having an incurable chronic condition might provide plausible cover, but I knew that I wasn't an exception to the rule. In terms of mission calls, I firmly believed that the more difficult the local language, the more drastic the cultural differences, the fewer local Mormons, the more righteous the missionary. Obviously there was room for miracles on the margins—the slacker who gets serious about the gospel while in Japan, say—but mostly mission calls were a spiritual meritocracy. And that made sense. Why would Heavenly Father send unprepared shepherds to tend His most precarious flocks? Gill went to Russia: difficult language, different culture, fledgling Church. She was clearly righteous. Sam went to France, where everyone seemed to dislike any organized religion, especially one from America.

Latin American countries offered an interesting exception. There was the foreign language aspect, sure, but that was softened by how easy the missionary work apparently was down there. According to reports from returning missionaries, people lined up to get baptized in Mexico.

Up on the church roof, I sat silhouetted by the city. I had no say in the matter, but of course I thought about where I wanted to go, along with where I didn't. I was intimidated by Asian languages, so I didn't want to go there. Because the Church was already so well established in states like California, Nevada, Idaho, and, of course, Utah, missions in the United States were on easy mode. Show me a kid called to one of those missions, and I'll show you someone who didn't take their faith seriously as an adolescent, who probably hadn't even read the Book of Mormon all the way through, who had probably started dating before they were sixteen.

My dream was a place like Haiti or South Africa, where I would be a distinct minority. I wanted culture shock. I wanted to be called to a place that would confirm my suspicions that, aside from some mistakes, I was mostly righteous. I took the gospel seriously.

When I talked to my stake president, I rehashed the sins I had covered with Bishop Flowers: the dry sex with my ex-girlfriend and my infrequent but troubling viewing of inappropriate material. I couldn't bring myself to also mention the breast-cupping. It was altogether too risky. I told myself that if I was really unworthy, he'd feel it. The Spirit would let him know. And since he felt good about me going on a mission, I decided that I was probably okay.

But I still had to get my physical.

The day arrived. The male doctor (phew!) had me lie down. He asked me to pull up my shirt and undo my pants but not pull them down. He tapped on my tummy a few times, listening. Then he told me I was good to do my pants back up. "That was it?" I asked.

"Yep," he said and handed me back the forms he had filled out.

"I thought there was going to be like a turn and cough thing." I had been worried about this appointment for years. The anticlimax was staggering.

"Oh, no," he said, "that might scar you. Good luck on your mission trip."

I immediately assumed I hadn't been clear about what I needed when making the appointment. Had he given me a partial physical instead of a full one? He had signed all the forms, so he must have read them. I left the doctor's office without a single person looking at my penis.

You can open a mission call letter publicly or privately. The public option is slightly more iconic, but it requires planning, patience, and proximity to friends and family.

In this scenario, Mother brings in the mail (because she is probably a stay-at-home mom) and finds an envelope addressed to her son from the Church of Jesus Christ of Latter-day Saints. Knowing that it is her boy's mission call, she sets to work calling Grandma and Grandpa, Uncle Roy and Aunt June, the Cards and the Bennetts and of course the bishop, too. While she waits for her son to come home from his part-time job—some kind of honest manual labour—she opens a couple bags of potato chips, then checks her ice cream supply and finds it sufficient.

If the boy gets home before his father or any of the guests arrive, he'll stare at the envelope, wishing for the eight millionth time in his young life that he had X-ray vision.

Once everyone has arrived at the house, they'll gather around the young man. The men will peer over his shoulder from behind the couch, while the kids, the nephews and nieces, will push in tightly on either side. With shaking hands, he'll tear the envelope open, careful not to accidentally rip any of the materials inside. Someone will make a joke that this envelope looks smaller than the one they got. "Maybe it's a rejection letter," Uncle Roy will say to guffaws. Then the soon-to-be missionary will clear his throat and read in a shaky voice:

"Elder BLANKETY BLANK, you are hereby called to serve in the [country, city] Mission. It is anticipated that you will serve for a period of 24 months . . ." And the letter continues, but everyone has started cheering and joking, repeating the mission name over and over so that it becomes familiar. There is hugging and crying and, in the days before smartphones, calls to dig out the globe or atlas so everyone can take a look at pictures of the country and city where the boy will serve.

The second way of receiving a mission call pays more attention to the spiritual aspect. In this scenario, the soon-to-be missionary finds the envelope in the mail but doesn't tell anyone about it yet. He takes his call to his room, or some special spiritual spot, such as the parking lot of a temple if there is one nearby. He says a prayer, then tears the envelope open. And in that moment, he feels as though the Saviour himself has sent him this letter, and he knows beyond the shadow of a doubt that the [country, city] Mission is exactly where he needs to be. The celebrating will come when he gets home, but in that moment, he is a humble servant receiving orders from the King.

Of the two options, I preferred the latter. It felt altogether more serious. But more than that, opening a mission call was like opening a Christmas present. No matter what, it wasn't okay to show disappointment in where you had been called. Opening it alone took away the pressure to perform.

When I received my mission call, I only wanted to feel humble and grateful.

In June, Sam and I got jobs at an upscale casual dining restaurant called Earls. I had always imagined doing some kind of manual labour to pay for my mission, but no lucrative construction jobs fell into my lap. Still, Earls often gave me two shifts a day, so I made overtime, plus a whole day's worth of tips. Some days I'd serve tables for fourteen hours straight. By the end of those nights, out of exhaustion I approached diners as if I were an eccentric party host and they my doomed guests. I spoke louder than I needed to and used dramatic hand movements, acting as if their experience with me was just as important as getting their food.

But all that talking to strangers was good training for the mission.

Normally, I had a couple of hours between the lunch crowd petering out and the start of the dinner rush. I had enough time to go home, make and drink a smoothie, starch and re-iron my white shirt, and maybe rest for a few minutes before heading back to the restaurant, smelling as though I had never left.

The day I got my call was no different.

One afternoon in July, an envelope was sticking out of our mailbox when I came home between shifts. I had been serving quesadillas and chicken clubs to unimaginative lunchers while a few kilometres away a simple mail carrier delivered a message from God. It was addressed to me and it was from the Church of Jesus Christ of Latter-day Saints in Salt Lake City.

I didn't have the patience to craft the ideal scenario for opening the letter, let alone wait for any member of my family to come home. I had to be back at the restaurant in an hour. But I could at least take the time to pray. If my mission call was from Heavenly Father—and I knew it was—then the Spirit would confirm that just as powerfully whether I was kneeling in my parents' living room or on the roof of the church. The important thing was faith.

The prophet had already signed the mission call that was

hiding in that envelope. No prayer would change what the letter said. It was the same as facing a storm or incurable sickness. Heavenly Father's will was being done; the only thing left to pray for was understanding, comfort, a sense that things would feel okay even when they weren't.

"Dear Heavenly Father.
Thankful for my many blessings. Thankful for this day.
Heavenly Father, I'm so grateful that I get to go on a mission.
Please bless that as I read my mission call, I'll know that it is from Thee.
And that I won't be disappointed.
In the name of Jesus Christ, amen."

Inside the envelope were a booklet and a letter. I knew from Sam's call that the booklet was like an orientation package that included instructions on appropriate haircuts and wardrobe. In big type at the top of the letter was the name of the Church. Then, just under that, in a smaller-sized sans serif:

FROM THE OFFICE OF THE FIRST PRESIDENCY

DEAR ELDER HUDSON,

You are hereby called to serve as a missionary of the Church of Jesus Christ of Latter-day Saints. You are assigned to labor in the Canada Toronto West Mission. It is anticipated that you will serve for a period of 24 months.

You should report to the Missionary Training Center in Provo, Utah, on Wednesday, 18 September 2002. You will prepare to teach the gospel in the English language.

You have been recommended as one worthy to represent the Lord as a minister of the restored gospel. You will be an official representative of the Church. As such, you will be expected to maintain the highest standards of conduct and appearance by keeping the commandments, living mission rules, and following the counsel of your mission president.

You will also be expected to devote all your time and attention to serving the Lord, leaving behind all other personal affairs. As you do these things the Lord will bless you and you will become an effective advocate and messenger of the truth. We place in you our confidence and pray that the Lord will help you meet your responsibilities in fulfilling this sacred assignment.

The Lord will reward you for the goodness of your life. Greater blessings and more happiness than you have yet to experience await you as you humbly and prayerfully serve the Lord in this labor of love among His children.

Sincerely,
Gordon B. Hinkley

The Canada Toronto West Mission. The Church's administrative practice of listing the country first felt a little like a punch to the gut. Like the Lord wanted me to know right away that I wasn't going anywhere fancy.

Toronto.

I had never been to Toronto. It was the home of MuchMusic, CBC, and CTV. Toronto was where, according to the address on the boxes, cereals were made. The biggest city in the country.

You will prepare to teach the gospel in the English language.

Still on my knees, I waited to see how I felt. Did I feel

disappointment or maybe rejection about the assignment, like a foreign-speaking mission was a school I didn't have the grades for? Did I feel a wave of warmth and calm, a feeling that I was known and loved? Did I know as instantly as love at first sight that this mission was the only place I needed to be? Did I feel the Lord whisper to me a little apology as I tore open the letter?

I felt okay, that I was going to be okay. A thought came to me: Heavenly Father didn't see some of His children as more or less exotic or, for that matter, more or less in need of the gospel. He knew the people in Ontario just as well as He knew the people of France, Russia, or South Africa, and knew what—and who—they needed. I would be okay.

I said another quick prayer of thanks before getting up. I would have no excuses, I thought. When foreign-speaking missionaries get to the field, it's understood that they'll be next to useless for at least the first three to six months. They get to be good missionaries when they can properly communicate. That was one of the reasons coming home had been so hard for Gill. Sister missionaries only serve for eighteen months, and she didn't feel like she could speak Russian fluently until she had been there for a year. She only had six months of effectiveness.

I wouldn't have that kind of slack. My goal for the next three months was to prepare like a chess student—know the scriptures, the doctrine, the language of missionary work, the arguments and counter-arguments—so as to be a great missionary on my first day, in my first area.

After letting the news sink in, I got ready to go back to the restaurant for a closing shift that loomed long into the night.

The benefit of a closing shift in addition to a day shift, of course, was the money. You got there first and you left last. Not only did you have the most tables, but you also had the best tables: the coveted booths along the front windows. The best shift was to close the patio. It was the same deal—first on, last off—but even in the summer it was rare for people to want to sit outside much past 11 p.m. It was roughly the same amount of money, same coveted tables, but I got to leave earlier and be outside. People on the patio were happier, too.

There was a substantial number of Mormons in Calgary. Most of the servers had at least one LDS friend or acquaintance that had already left for their mission. They knew the drill, roughly.

"Why Toronto?" Cassie was waiting for a table from lunch to leave. She was eating noodles in the break area near the kitchen, in an old corner booth that was always covered in newspapers and people's belongings.

"They don't get a choice," Struggles answered. I had worked there for too long to ask what his name actually was. "Right?"

I adjusted my shirt, then my apron. "Yeah, I filled out like an application and sent it to Salt Lake. They decide where I go."

"Who's they?" Cassie asked.

"Church leaders," I said.

"You believe the prophet decides, don't you?" Struggles said, looking proud he knew the inside lingo.

"Yup," I said, hoping that we could avoid discussing living prophets at work. Best to keep it vague. "Yes, the leader of our Church does it."

"And they said Toronto. Why Toronto?" Cassie repeated.

"Why anywhere? There are people who need to be Mormon in Toronto, too," I said.

"Huh, I guess so."

"Also, I'm diabetic, and they like to keep people with medical conditions close to home."

"Oh, yeah, totally. That makes sense." Appeased, Cassie

returned her focus to her noodles. "You want to check if my table has put down anything when you go out there?"

I headed outside to start my shift. One of the Sarahs was rolling cutlery into napkins. It was her last side duty to complete before leaving and handing the patio over to my care. "I heard you found out where you're going on your mission."

"Yeah, Toronto," I said.

"I dated a Mormon guy in high school," she told me. "He ended up going to the Philippines on his mission."

"That's cool."

"He came back a little weird though," she said. "He reached out after he got home. I hadn't seen him since high school."

"Did he want to marry you?"

"I think so. He told me he wanted to see me when he got home because he had a dream about me on his last night on his mission. He thought that was a sign," she said.

"Was it?"

"Not a good one. I never saw him after that," Sarah said.

"He married already?"

"I think so, actually." She picked up a stack of trays to bring them back inside. "When do you leave?"

"I'm still here for another couple of months. I leave in September."

"Well, congratulations."

I had one mission before my mission: prepare to be a good missionary.

That meant being prepared for any concern or pointed question. I would be knocking on a lot of doors. Some of them wouldn't be friendly. And some might even be waiting to pounce on a Mormon missionary. I wanted to learn the best defences against any doctrinal attack. But I couldn't study possible attacks on our doctrine without running into books or sites that were anti-Mormon, or had what we called anti-Mormon literature. Most often, it was simply called Anti. I would never actually look up Anti on the internet in the name of research. That would be like having a person with Ebola lick my eyeballs to fight off infection. Someone once said that anti-Mormon literature was worse for one's soul than pornography. And considering how often I was taught about the evils of pornography, that meant reading Anti was one of the most awful, destructive things I could do. I wasn't about to risk that kind of damage before my mission. I knew I'd get Anti-ed on my mission (Anti was both a verb and a noun). No doubt some evangelical would tell me lies about Joseph Smith dabbling in the occult or boasting about being better than Jesus. Nonsense about us not believing in the real Jesus. But by then I'd have an indestructible testimony and it wouldn't matter. Still, I didn't want to be surprised by anything.

To that end, until I left for the Missionary Training Center in Provo, Utah, in September, 2002, my daily schedule was pretty much set. I woke up late—a habit that would be easy to break once I stopped working the night shift at the restaurant—worked a lunch shift, then came home to read my scriptures and study until I had to go back to the restaurant.

Along with the scriptures, there were only four books that missionaries were allowed to read while in the field: *A Marvelous Work and a Wonder* by LeGrand Richards; *Our Search for Happiness* by M. Russell Ballard; and *Articles of Faith* and *Jesus the Christ*, both by James E. Talmage. Together they made up the Missionary Reference Library. All the authors either were, had been, or would become one of the Twelve Apostles of the Church. Talmage had the reputation of being the brainiest Church leader. *Articles of Faith* was a book of essays that explained gospel principles. I didn't read it. *Jesus the Christ* was a deep dive on the life of the Saviour from an LDS perspective. I planned on reading that someday, but it seemed too advanced—and too long—for me to complete in the two months I had left before leaving for my mission. *Our Search for Happiness* was the most basic of the four, outlining the history of the Church while also explaining doctrines. I finished that one quickly. The one I really studied was *A Marvelous Work and a Wonder.* It wasn't apologetics, per se, but it did explain LDS doctrine in the context of the Great Apostasy—when God's true church was taken from the earth after Peter, James and John, and all the rest of them were martyred. It was about how and why we were right and the rest of the world was wrong.

I studied with purpose. I wanted to be able to show evidence of every Mormon doctrine, from the basic to the advanced, in the Bible. I knew the Bible wasn't perfect—we Mormons believed that a lot of sacred truths had been lost from it over the centuries due to poor translations—and I was under no delusion that this would convince a non-believer. But it needed to be possible and I needed to be able to do it. It was the closest to testing Heavenly Father I could muster. If we really were the true church—a reboot of the one Jesus Christ founded when He was on the earth—then there ought to be traces of it in the Bible.

Meanwhile, the temple loomed.

The Cardston temple had no spires, which meant no golden angel Moroni blowing his trumpet atop it. Other temples looked like castles or bright white Kryptonian cathedrals, but the one in Cardston—which was the first temple built outside of the United States—looked like a superhero's secret headquarters. It was a stone fortress, rolling out of a small hill. A gleaming cement fist.

For me growing up, the temple was a mystery and a goal.* People spoke of how beautiful and meaningful going to the temple was, but they weren't allowed to describe what happened inside. As such, temples were concrete symbols of the expression "You'll understand when you're older."

Improbably, the Church had managed to keep the secret of what exactly happened inside the temple for my whole life. Only, of course, it wasn't a secret. It was kept hush-hush because it was *sacred.* So sacred that to talk about the specifics of what happened inside it—anywhere other than inside it—was verboten, and asking about it was taboo. It would be dragging the sacred and pure into the dirty everyday: tossing pearls before swine.

I did all I could to keep the wool over my eyes in place. Because I wasn't supposed to know what happened in the temple, I didn't do any digging. I was careful not to ask questions that couldn't be answered. The temple was a Christmas gift under the tree that I didn't want to shake or handle lest I prematurely find out what was inside and ruin Christmas. Of course I was

* The word "temple" is always preceded by an article, unless it is followed by the word "work." It's "going to *the* temple," never "going to temple." But one would say "I have devoted my life to temple work," not "I have devoted my life to the temple work."

curious. I strained to imagine the secrets of eternity that would be revealed inside the building. How the world was created. How God came to be, and how we mortals could do the same. I imagined I'd learn more about the premortal life, who I had been—a general in God's army, naturally, but what kind?

In terms of my eternal salvation, going to the temple was more important than going on a mission. It was a commandment for young men to serve a mission, but if I didn't fulfill that commandment for whatever reason, I could still make it to the celestial kingdom. The same wasn't true for the temple. Going to the temple was a requirement for exaltation.* Still, as mysterious and essential as it was, going to the temple felt like one more thing I needed to cross off my mission preparation checklist.

People went to the temple to get their endowment, which is what the temple ceremony, for lack of a better term, was called. In our last meeting, the full spiritual I had been nervous about, President Percy, who ultimately decided if I was ready to go to the temple or not, shared with me this quotation by Brigham Young, second prophet of the Church of Jesus Christ of Latter-day Saints:

> *Your endowment is, to receive all those ordinances in the house of the Lord, which are necessary for you, after you have departed this life, to enable you to walk back to the presence of the Father, passing the angels who stand as sentinels, being enabled to give them the key words, the signs and tokens, pertaining to the holy priesthood, and gain your eternal exaltation in spite of earth and hell.*

---

* This is slightly different from salvation. Everyone will be saved to a certain extent. But exaltation is like salvation plus. It's living with God in the highest level of the celestial kingdom.

There were parts of that quote that I didn't understand—I had never heard people in the Church talk about signs and tokens, for example—but the gist of the quote was obvious: whatever I was going to do at the temple, whatever I was going to learn, would stay with me for the rest of my life on earth, and into the next.

Luckily, going to the temple and going on a mission required the same preparation: reading scriptures, reading talks,* books, all the same stuff.

What I knew: the temple was a place where you made sacred covenants with God (as if there were any other type). A covenant, as I was reminded often, was a two-way agreement between a person and Heavenly Father. We promise to do something, and God promises a reward in return. But what with all the secrecy and head-tilted seriousness, I understood that the covenants I'd be making in the temple were more potent than the covenant I made when I was baptized. I didn't know if that meant they would be more specific, or if they just came with greater consequences. For instance, breaking the law of chastity was always bad, but, as far as I understood, if you did it after having been to the temple, there was a good chance you'd be excommunicated from the Church.

As a symbol of the seriousness of those covenants, people wore garments (short for garment of the holy priesthood) after going through the temple. The special Mormon underwear, which look like an extra-long pair of boxer briefs and a t-shirt, are white. Men's and women's were often made from different materials—my dad's were just plain cotton, but my mom's were satiny—and the women's shirt had more of a cap sleeve, but

* Another word for sermons.

apart from that men's and women's garments were the same. I knew all about garments because I had parents who wore them to bed. And our parents would often stumble out of their bedroom late at night wearing only their garments, looking like rumpled swimmers from the 1920s, to tell us kids to keep it down.

Temples were like heaven's embassies on earth. As such, they were where you could feel the presence of God most keenly. But from an administrative perspective, temples were also where you conducted the essential business of eternity.

Whatever nerves I had about going through the temple for the first time didn't change how I felt about temples generally. They were monuments to God's mercy.

The endowment ceremony took place over several different rooms of the temple, meant to mirror stages in the plan of salvation.* First, I was ushered into the creation room. On the walls were paintings depicting the Creation—animals, nature scenes. The room had cinema-style seating and a plain altar at the front that looked like an especially tall ottoman. I had seen pictures of what the rooms in the temple looked like in pamphlets and church magazines, so at that point, nothing was too strange. Like every other man at the temple that day, I was wearing white pants, a white shirt, and a white tie. I had been given a cloth packet; inside were my temple clothes. I had heard that there was more to temple clothes than just the white base layer

* You'll recall the plan of salvation is God's plan for our eternal existence. It begins in the premortal life and continues through life on earth, life after death, and the assignment to one of three kingdoms: the celestial, terrestrial, or telestial, with the first being the goal.

I was wearing. But other than knowing the term temple clothes, I did not know what they were. Naturally, I initially pictured flowing wizard robes.

Men and women sat on opposite sides of the room. The lights dimmed and the film portion of the service began. Using professionally sourced B-roll, a video took us through the creation of the world right up to the Garden of Eden. In voice-over, we heard the pleasant American voice of Elohim, our Heavenly Father, speaking with Jehovah, who would become Jesus when He was born, narrating the Creation. When it came time for Adam to show up, the video ended and we all got up and migrated to an adjoining room, which had the same private-screening-room seating, but no paintings on the walls. This room was mostly beige, with ornate curtains that opened to reveal another movie screen at the front of the room. This room had a velvet altar as well.

The lights dimmed for the next video presentation. While I hadn't been surprised by the first video, I wasn't prepared for the production values or the quality of the acting in the second. Church movies could go either way. The ones the Mormon Church made for missionary purposes were often as well done as any TV movie, but this one felt like it had been shot on an old *Star Trek* set, like the film crew knew a guy who let them use the studio after hours. It looked cheap, flimsy.

The actors in the video went through the motions of the Fall: a scene-chewing Satan beguiled Eve; Eve lazily convinced Adam to join her; they were both kicked out of Eden and sent off to explore the New World. I was then encouraged to open up the cloth packet I'd been given and pulled out a small green apron. The apron was knee-length. The voice narrating the endowment explained that the apron represented how Adam and Eve, once they had eaten the fruit in Eden and realized they were naked, made simple coverings out of leaves. Helpfully, there was a leaf pattern sewn on each apron.

Up to that point, the film hewed pretty close to the scriptural account in Genesis and the Pearl of Great Price.* But then, without warning, the plot turned allegorical. At least I hoped it was an allegory, because it wasn't scripturally accurate at all. We watched as God and Jesus, in a room meant to represent heaven, wearing identical high school play–quality wigs and beards, called for the apostles Peter, James, and John.

Jehovah sent Peter, James, and John on a mission. They were to go down to earth to test Adam and Eve, give them further instructions, and then return and report how it had all gone. Never mind that the apostles wouldn't be born for more than a thousand years or so. This bothered me. In my personal studies, I had been trying to align, or at least find, Mormon doctrine within the Bible. These time-travelling apostles flew in the face of all that.

I told myself that it must be allegory. It had to be.

When the apostles met up with Adam and Eve in the harsh New World, they all stood together, talking to Satan.

The apostles ask Adam and Eve, but mostly Adam, if he has any signs or tokens. Before answering, Satan interrupts and, speaking for Adam, offers to sell them to the apostles for money.

---

* The Pearl of Great Price is a small book of scripture that contains additional revelations from Moses and Abraham. Joseph Smith translated it from some Egyptian papyrus that came into his custody. Unfortunately, the papyrus, which the Church still has, has since been translated by Egyptian scholars, and it's not at all what Smith said it was. Nevertheless, the Church still consider it scripture.

But Adam faithfully rejects Satan's offer and tells the apostles that, while he does have some signs and tokens, he would never sell them for money because they are sacred.

See? There was never a scene like that in any scripture. I decided Adam and Eve represented us, God's children generally, and members of the Church specifically. The apostles must have represented priesthood? The prophet and apostles of the Church? It was a little hazy. But it was clearly allegory. Right?

And yet what if Mormons believed that encounter actually happened? After all, we did believe the Bible had been corrupted over the centuries. The fact that I couldn't be sure if the film was an allegory or what Mormons literally believed happened at the beginning of the world meant something. It was as if I didn't trust the Church not to secretly have some deeply silly, far-fetched, even stupid beliefs. And if it did, I knew it would be on me to accept them. That just seemed demeaning.

The participation portion of the ceremony, which I had been vaguely warned about, was maybe more distressing than the revisionist take on Adam and Eve. I'd had a Sunday School teacher who had been a convert to the Church. When he taught us about the temple, he said that he hadn't been confused by it at all. He was raised Catholic, he said, he was used to religious ritual. As a result of this tidbit, I had expected what would be asked of me to feel like a Catholic mass—or what I imagined a Catholic mass to be: kneeling, standing up, some call and response, maybe a Mormon equivalent to crossing oneself. That was not what it was.

In each room, at different moments the video would stop and we would learn a different handshake grip. These were the tokens alluded to in the film. Each one had a name: the first token of the Aaronic Priesthood, for instance. At other times we were instructed to put on a new article of clothing from the white satchel. Soon, over my white pants, shirt, and tie I wore a toga-like robe that hung off one shoulder like a curtain, over which I reattached my green apron, and on my head something that looked like a cross between a baker's hat and a graduation cap. I saw that the women, who stayed on their side of the room, wore the same outfit except for the hat. They wore a face covering instead.

The end of the endowment symbolized our final judgement. We approached the veil at the front of the room, which was a white curtain with holes at various points for a temple worker's hand to reach through. With that hand, which represented God, you ran through the different grips you learned earlier, and followed a very specific script.

The voice on the other side of the curtain would ask for a grip, then ask its name once I performed it. An old temple worker—they are all old—stood beside me to help with the answers.

After I had run through all the hand positions and names, the signs and tokens, and thus proven my faithfulness, I was pulled through an opening in the veil and welcomed into the celestial room. It didn't feel like an ancient religious ceremony. There was no Latin, no burning incense, just secret handshakes and rote recitations. It felt new, and, frankly, dumb to think that, in the end, getting into the celestial kingdom would come down to knowing some different ways to grip another man's hand.

In most temples, the celestial room is a study in white and crystal. It is, after all, meant to symbolize the celestial kingdom. But the Cardston Alberta Temple is a bit different. It's hardly white at all. Instead, it's covered from floor to cathedral ceiling in rich mahogany. The only white to be found is a few couches in the centre of the room. It's as though heaven were an old-fashioned steakhouse. I took a seat on one of the couches and looked over at my mom, who had been part of the ceremony, dressed like a frumpy bride, like all the other women. During the endowment, there had been a part where the women had to cover their faces. I didn't like seeing my mother appear subservient. That wasn't who my mom was; she didn't veil her face. That was when the thought first came to my mind, as clearly as a revelation.

I looked over at Sam and my dad, their hats flopping to one side like deflated crowns, which is what they were meant to suggest, just not the deflated part. Everywhere I looked there was someone praying, or whispering, or shuffling around like a ghost in a green apron. All acting like they didn't look supremely goofy.

Then I had the thought:

Why didn't anyone tell me we were in a cult?

If I saw another religion dress like this, that's what I would call it—a cult—without doubt or remorse. There were lots of religions that incorporated special clothing into their worship, obviously. But those clothes were part of ancient traditions. The clothes we were wearing looked like cheap knock-off versions of them. You could only buy temple clothes from the Church, so all the robes and crowns and face coverings seemed mass-produced and chintzy.

"You okay?" Sam asked.

"Yeah," I said.

"It's a lot to take in, isn't it?" he said. I nodded my head. "It usually takes a couple of times."

"That's not how it really happened, is it?" I asked.

"No no, it's a metaphor," Sam said. And I felt a little better.

"For what?" I asked. "What're they metaphors for?"

"What do you think?"

"Seeing as how I've seen it exactly one time, I'm going to guess probably priesthood authority or something."

Sam nodded his head, but didn't say yes or no.

After sitting in the celestial room a little longer we changed out of our temple clothes and had lunch in the temple cafeteria.

Afterward, on the drive back to Calgary, I decided that the temple was like kissing. One could reasonably assume that if you had never seen kissing before, and were then suddenly made to kiss someone—even someone you had fond feelings toward—it would feel strange and unnatural, this meeting of feeding holes and spit. The tongue suddenly acting in ways entirely unrelated to speech or food. And in that world, if I stopped kissing after the first strange encounter, I'd never learn how great kissing could be.

I doubted the temple would ever be as fun as kissing, but the metaphor was apt. It was okay that I hadn't liked my first temple experience. Sometimes it takes a few times. The important thing was to go back.

On one of my last Sundays at home, my dad sat at the kitchen table and flipped through my orientation package. On its cover was a Caucasian missionary, dressed all in white, naturally, standing in water getting ready to baptize a Latino man, also dressed in white. The missionary's right arm was lifted and bent at a ninety-degree angle, as if he were about to swear on the Bible in open court. This was the position one's arm had to be in when performing a baptism. My dad was turning the pages casually, sometimes stopping to read, but rarely for a whole page. He came to the page that outlined the borders of the Canada Toronto West Mission. He took a closer look at the map.

There was Ontario, like a hermit crab facing east. And there was the border of my mission, travelling down from James Bay through the area of Ontario where there lived only trees and rocks and lakes, past North Bay and Sudbury, both definitely in my mission, until it got to the province's dangling bit, where Toronto and all its populous bedroom communities reside.

"And see how the line just skirts Toronto. It looks like the closest your mission gets to Toronto is Markham."

"Huh, you're right." It turned out I had been lying to people about going to Toronto. "Weird that they call it the Canada Toronto West Mission then."

"It really should be called the *West of* Toronto Mission," Dad said. "But Brampton is where the temple is, even though we call it the Toronto temple. And . . . Brampton is in your mission."

"That's cool," I said. I tried not to be upset. After all, it was better that I find out now, rather than stepping off the plane ready to hit the mean streets of Canada's largest city only to be brought low on my first day.

I wasn't going to do any teaching on a subway, or make friends with a street gang, or fight off massive cockroaches for the last scrap of cheese in my fridge. I wouldn't come home with crazy stories from a big multicultural city that had a neighbourhood devoted to every ethnicity I could think of. That wasn't the mission Heavenly Father wanted me to go on.

Instead, I was going to be humbled.

I always knew that, of course. You couldn't be a good

missionary without being humble. Humble enough to follow all the mission rules, humble enough to live peacefully with a companion not of your choosing twenty-four hours a day. Humble enough to be worthy of the Spirit's constant guidance, since He was the one doing the actual converting.

But what I didn't anticipate was how specific my humbling would be. Or that it would begin before I left home. Because if I were honest, if I heard that someone I barely knew had been called to the Canada Toronto West Mission, I would have made some assumptions about that person: that he was only barely worthy to go on a mission, or that he wasn't fundamentally serious about the gospel.

This all reminded me of something a high school friend had asked me once.

We were waiting in the wings for our cue to go onstage so that we could pretend to be Russian Jews in a production of *Fiddler on the Roof*, singing about tradition in front of a theatre full of parents and siblings.

"Would you die for someone you loved?" my friend asked me.

"Of course," I said. Secretly, I longed for just that opportunity. Not because I wanted to die, per se, but because I believed that dying for someone else guaranteed entry into heaven. That kind of altruism was an all-expense-paid trip to the celestial kingdom. I daydreamed about pushing strangers out of the way of speeding automobiles or shielding members of my family from a mysterious hail of bullets, accepting a tragic fate so another would live.

My friend had anticipated that I'd say that. "But," he said, "what if they didn't know you were dying for them? In fact, what if everyone hated you for doing it? And they never find out the truth. They always hate you."

It was an interesting proposition. How much of my altruism was ultimately self-serving? Did I actually care about the person for whom I was hypothetically dying, or was I more interested in being legendary?

In that same spirit, would I go on a mission even when no one looking on from the outside would be impressed? Did I care about being a good missionary because I knew the Church was true, and wanted others to be part of it, or was I training to be a good missionary so that other missionaries would see how smart and powerful I was? That's how I would be humbled.

My mission would be simple, ordinary.

In the Book of Mormon, Lehi, the patriarch of the eventual Nephites and Lamanites, has a vision. In it, he stands at the foot of a tree "whose fruit was desirable to make one happy."[*] After tasting the gleaming white fruit, he wants to share it with his family. He calls to them from the other side of a great chasm. Then he notices a path leading from where they were to the tree, and along that path is a "rod of iron." No description is given of the iron rod, but it's understood to be a kind of railing. Lehi sees that his family has held on to the rod while they walked the path and made it safely to the glowing tree, whereas those who didn't wandered into dark mists and were lost. It's not a complex analogy, which is why it's effective. The tree represents eternal life, and the rod of iron is the gospel, the commandments that keep you on the straight and narrow. The name of this vision is called the tree of life.

* 1 Nephi 10.

Because I was going to an English-speaking mission, I would only be at the Missionary Training Center for three weeks. Still, it would be an intensive study period, filled mostly with classes and devotionals and almost no free time. At the MTC in Provo, the showers were also called the tree of life. Each locker room had two showers, and each shower had eight heads. The Hydra-inspired design and the fact that all the missionaries at the MTC were on the same schedule meant that it was nearly impossible not to shower uncomfortably close to the other missionaries sharing your floor. There was always a long line snaking around the wall of the bathroom and out the door and down the hall. As you showered, you were surrounded by other elders. Folks reacted to this in different ways. Those who had been athletes in their civilian lives were practised at being naked among other men. I envied their easy nudity.

I felt about the tree of life the way I felt about the MTC in general. It was necessary and maybe even cleansing—a kind of detox from the world that I definitely needed after spending all summer at Earls selling people alcohol of various hues—but, at the same time, there were frankly more men here than I felt comfortable with. The campus itself was bland and friendly—like an inexpensive convention centre and hotel decorated with pictures of Jesus Christ and Joseph Smith. Walking around, I saw a sea of vanilla ice cream men with the same haircut, each wearing his own tie and carrying his own set of scriptures. They were copies of each other. I wasn't any different. When we left the MTC campus to walk across the street to attend the Provo temple, we gave off the vibe of an impossibly young-looking Secret Service detail without anyone to protect.

Mostly, we only spent time with our district, the group that we would be travelling to our mission with. The twelve of us who were Toronto-bound ate, attended class, exercised, and slept together, six bunk beds to a room. We prayed and sang and attended giant MTC-wide devotionals together. At the end of three weeks, we boarded the plane together, and flew to Toronto.

On an early morning in October, 2002, the assistants picked us up at Pearson airport in Toronto, as I knew they would. Because of Sam, I felt like I had private knowledge of how missions worked and who these missionaries were. I didn't know these particular assistants, obviously, but I knew that they were likely the most righteous missionaries in the mission. They were special assistants to the mission president, just as Sam had been on his mission.

There was a type of returned missionary—usually men in their thirties and forties—who talked about assistants the way detectives on cop shows talk about Internal Affairs. They always sounded jealous. Bitter that they weren't chosen to be assistants themselves. And thus, to them, assistants were narcs. I saw the assistants differently: they were stand-ins for my brother. It was unrighteous to think it, but I secretly wanted to be one. It went beyond want: I expected to be an assistant to the president by the end of my mission. Of course, I'd never admit to something so crass and vain. But I believed that Heavenly Father knew the desires of my heart. Thankfully, He was pretty discreet.

The group of us stood outside the airport like a huddled mass of freshly birthed businessmen, still blinking from all the lights. We were a dozen strong. Mostly from Utah, but we also had a Brit, and two Canadians. An assistant with curly hair, Elder Wiley, grinned at us as we piled into a van, while the other assistant, Elder Boyd, whom I instantly and mysteriously liked less, packed our luggage into a matching van.

I sat in one of the back seats, by the window, quietly dignified. Behind the wheel, Elder Wiley chatted with Elder Wexley, from the UK, and Elder Branton and Elder Whitmore, both from Utah. I looked around the van. This was my MTC group. We'd be connected throughout our mission as though we had all enlisted in boot camp together, which is essentially what the Missionary Training Center had been.

Now we were driving to the mission home together. Our mission home. It was where the mission president and his wife and family lived while they were in Canada. It was kind of the heart of the mission. There was a mission office, too, which was the administrative centre of the mission, but the mission home was special. There, we'd each be assigned our trainers, and then be sent to our first areas. Some of us might end up serving with one another again but mostly we were seeds about to be scattered across Southwestern Ontario.

We escaped the maze of airport roads and headed west on the highway toward Brampton. Our mission president and his wife would be our surrogate parents, ecclesiastical leaders, and general bosses for the next two years. All I really knew about Paul and Lynn Sybrowsky was that they were from Utah. Mission presidents served for three years, and like us were expected to leave their work and their regular lives behind for that time.

Then I saw it.

Standing watch over the traffic, waving majestically in the fall wind, was a Canadian flag. A large retaining wall along the side of the highway made it impossible to see who was flying the flag, whether it was a car dealership, strip mall, or government building. I just saw the flag furl and flap, True North, strong and free.

I admired the elegant simplicity of my country's flag. After being surrounded by Americans in America during my time at the MTC, I felt like the flag was reassuring me that I was safe now. And through the flag, I felt the Spirit, in its wordless way, tell me that I was where I needed to be. That whatever got me here was irrelevant. This polite little country was exactly where the Lord wanted me.

I cried one or two tears, but I didn't let anyone in the van see.

HE THAT THRUSTETH IN HIS SICKLE WITH ALL HIS MIGHT

(October 2002–September 2004)

THE MISSION HOME was a sprawling mid-century ranch-style bungalow. It was decorated with the generic timelessness of a church building. It was functional and clean, with a plush white carpet that seemed to have never met anything as heavy as a shoe. There were ample prints of the Saviour on the walls, along with family photos. The Sybrowskys had many children, it seemed. Many appeared to be married, with families of their own. At least one was presently on a mission somewhere. President and Sister Sybrowsky, along with two of their younger children, had been in Ontario for a year by the time we got there. They had two more ahead of them.

The assistants escorted us down to the basement. It looked like a campaign office. There was a table set out for us near a large map of Ontario that hung on the wall. It was big enough to clearly show the borders of both the Canada Toronto West Mission and the Canada Toronto East Mission.

"See, our mission doesn't actually cover Toronto," I said to Elder Simonson. I had told my fellow missionaries this a few days ago at the MTC, but I hadn't had visuals then. With the map up on the wall, it was very clear that we were a mission of small towns. The CTWM border looked like it was afraid of Toronto, favouring the safety of more manageable cities like Waterloo, London, Sudbury, Barrie, and Niagara Falls.

"Dang it, Elder, are you saying we don't get Etobicoke either?" Elder Jake said. He pronounced it with a hard *coke*.

"I think it's pronounced Etobi-KO," I said. "And I'm sorry. I know how much you dreamed of serving in Etobicoke."

"I think we all did, Elder. I think we all did," he said. Elder Jake was from a small town in Arizona.

"It was prophesied that I'd serve here," Elder Cameron said.

"Oh, yeah?" Elder Simonson said. "Where?"

"Here," Elder Cameron said.

"No, I mean where was it prophesied." Like me, Elder Simonson assumed this was a setup to a rambling shaggy-dog story or a real groaner of a joke. That was Elder Cameron's style. On preparation day at the MTC, the one day we saw each other in street clothes, Elder Cameron wore overalls and a newsboy cap, like he had been working on the railroad, all the livelong day.

"Well, my dad, see, after I put in my papers, my dad said he knew where I was going to go. And so he wrote it down, sealed it in an envelope, and put the envelope in our safe . . ."

"Your dad's quite the showman," Elder Jake said.

"But anyway, once I got my call I read it out and my dad starts tearing up a bit. And he says, well he calls me by my name, but for now I'll say he says, 'Elder Cameron, go on and get that envelope out of the safe. And wouldn't you know it, I opened the envelope and on a piece of paper was my dad's handwriting: Canada."

"He didn't give a city?" I asked.

"No, he just said Canada. But still."

"That's powerful, Elder," Elder Simonson said. "My patriarchal blessing says I'll serve in a foreign land. I figure Toronto counts. I mean Ontario."

"Mine says the same thing. And yet," I said.

"Don't get me started on patriarchal blessings," Elder Jake said quietly.

"No, let's!" I said.

"Let's just say I don't as of yet have perfect faith in all things." I liked Elder Jake's cynical streak. He was more serious than a lot of elders in our district, but he was sarcastic and seemed to have as much patience for unserious missionaries as I did.

We were fed taco soup with thick sour cream for dinner at a group of tables set up for us. Then we were brought up to the living room on the main floor. We each took a seat, some on couches, but most on folding chairs. In the dining area that was directly across from us, but raised slightly, sat the experienced elders who would go down in our personal histories as our first real missionary companions. We had had companions at the MTC, but that was mainly for practice. For the next two years we would never be without a companion. We would never be alone.

Standing betwixt the two gangs of elders was President Sybrowsky. We'd met him before dinner, but he was more official now. Imposing, though not at all physically. His voice was pitched slightly high, and he spoke with a distinctive cadence; throughout my mission, when elders would inevitably break out their impression of him, they almost uniformly sounded like they were doing a bad impression of President George H.W. Bush.

President Sybrowsky spoke on predictable subjects—faith, obedience, baptisms, following the Spirit—then he slowed down.

"Elders, let me tell you a story," he said. "As some of you know, I was in the Army. I was enlisted, but we still had to do training camp. I know some of you have military experience. Where's Elder Majors? Well, of course you have military experience. You look like a recruiting poster. *Semper fi*, Elder.

"Everyone in my platoon got along perfectly. Like brothers. Except for one young man. He was smaller than the rest of us, and I don't think it's too uncharitable to say that he didn't have the best hygiene. But other than that, I don't really know why we didn't like him. I guess in every group there's someone on the bottom. He just rubbed us the wrong way.

"After not too long, we were told that we were going to receive an inspection from a high-ranking commander. We set about cleaning our bunk so that it was immaculate. We made sure our beds were perfectly crisp and tight. And then we put on our dress uniforms, making sure that every detail was perfectly in order. Shoes gleaming. We even got fresh haircuts. When inspection time came, we stood proudly next to our bunk. We were ready and we knew it.

"The commander walked through slowly, stopping in front of each of us. Noting the knots in our ties and the shine of our boots until he came to that one young man that every platoon has. He looked the boy over from head to toe. Finally, he looked him in the eye and said, 'Private, you don't have a friend in the world, do you?'

"'No, sir,' the soldier replied.

"Then he reached out and wiped a bit of fluff from the young man's uniform. It was a glaring aberration, one that any one of us could have helped him with if we had but cared to look. 'You must not have a friend in the world.'

"Elders, we were chastened that day. Judged as a unit, we failed because we failed him. We turned our back on a brother. *You don't have a friend in the world*. Oh, how those words cut me.

"Elders, be good to each other. Be friends with each other. A companionship is a blessing, even when it doesn't feel like it. Elders, you're good. Go, and be good." He closed with his testimony and had us do the same.

When it was my turn, I opened my scriptures to 2 Nephi. I was conscious of how pristine the pages still were. I had marked them up while I studied, but I knew they'd look a lot more worn in a couple of years.

"There are obviously a lot of traits I love about the Saviour. But one trait I depend on, or that I'm sure I'll depend on throughout my mission, is His enduring belief in me. It's an image that comes up a few times in the scriptures, but I like how Nephi says it, I guess quoting Isaiah. He says, 'I will be merciful unto them, saith the Lord God, if they will repent and come unto me; for mine arm is lengthened out all the day long, saith the Lord God of Hosts.'

"He's waiting, arms out, always there, waiting for us to reach for Him," I said. I bore my testimony: that I hoped I would remember that He is waiting, always, with His arms outstretched. And finally, that I knew that this was the essence of the gospel. That we do all we can, and the Lord meets us where we are and helps us finish.

Then, as he did with every new missionary who had gone before me, President Sybrowsky asked me what I hoped my trainer would teach me.

"Humility," I said.

"Elder McDaniels," President Sybrowsky called, and one of the missionaries in the front row across from us stood up. He wore glasses so he looked smart.

"Will you help Elder Hudson learn humility?"

"It's done, President," Elder McDaniels said, just like every other trainer who had gone before him. That was how we were to respond to President Sybrowsky's commandment; as if we were so obedient time was irrelevant. I was informed I'd be beginning my mission in Sarnia, a town that sounded like the land of Christlike lions and interdimensional wardrobes.

I knew how I wanted to learn humility.

I would be paired with someone who made all my pre-mission studies seem quaint and remedial. This companion would pair encyclopedic gospel knowledge with a quiet dignity and compassion that would make my waiterly charm ring hollow. He would be like a Mormon monk who used the priesthood the way a Jedi used the Force. He would have answers to every question that I or anybody else had. And he would be indefatigable and prepared for any eventuality. No mission rule would go unfollowed. And not just to the letter of the law: he would embody the spirit of the law, too. He would always know what to do. He would lead and I would follow in awe.

Elder McDaniels wasn't that missionary. He wasn't a bad missionary. He didn't willfully break mission rules. He strove to be obedient, diligent. He wanted to work hard. He knew his scriptures, and communicated clearly when he taught. But he sometimes spoke with his eyes closed, mostly when answering questions. It was probably meant to convey wisdom and sincerity, but I thought it made him look like a know-it-all. Though his worst habit was that he sometimes lost track of time when families from the ward had us over for dinner. We were supposed to spend no more than an hour at members' houses, but sometimes that stretched to two. It was more out of politeness than laziness, but I counted it as a moral failing. Plus, in the six months he had been on his mission, he hadn't had a single baptism.

All this was enough to make me feel hard done by. I had had a feeling before leaving for the MTC that, since I tried to be nice to everyone, I would be entrusted/saddled with difficult companions on my mission: the lazy, the disobedient, the arrogant and loud. That I had Elder McDaniels right off the bat was a compliment, in a way. By giving me such a challenging first companion, the Lord was essentially saying that I didn't need to be trained.

I was not learning humility.

My problem, apart from my natural arrogance as a beginner, was that for the first month I was in Sarnia, I was homesick. Suddenly and shockingly homesick. I ached to be with my brother, mostly, and with my mom. The last time I had felt so far away from my family and forgotten had been at the Scouts Canada Alberta Jamboree, when I was twelve. That had been the first time I had been away from home for longer than a sleepover, and by Wednesday of Jamboree week

I wanted to go home. That morning I woke up early, before anyone else in my troop, and I used a pay phone to call my mom. I wasn't going to ask her to pick me up, but I wanted her to remind me that I was loved and missed. I had been a little hurt that, in the background of the call, life sounded like it was continuing on without me there. I didn't want my mom to know how sad I actually was, but I probably wasn't crying that discreetly.

I used to hide in our pantry. I must have been eleven. I could fit comfortably on the bottom shelf, in front of the cans of tomato sauce, beans, and pineapple slices. The goal wasn't to hide, exactly. I wanted to be found, but more than that I wanted to be looked for. I wanted to hear someone ask someone else if they'd seen me. I'd hear confusion start to grow, then concern, as voices moved about in the kitchen and living room, thumping up and down the stairs, calling my name. They'd list out loud all the places where I wasn't and wrestle with where I could be. When I sensed they were actually worried, I'd emerge from my hiding place and be met with joy and gladness.

Of course, no one in my family ever noticed I was gone, let alone worried I was missing. It was a game they didn't know they were playing, and the stakes were surprisingly high. When I would eventually clamber out of the glorified closet, I'd try not to be hurt. After all, it was just a failed prank. It wasn't further evidence that no one cared if I was around.

I felt the same on my mission, only it was more pronounced. I wanted to be missed. I wanted to know that home wasn't the same without me. Only now I couldn't call. We were only allowed to call home on Christmas Day and Mother's Day. I had to rely on receiving reassurance in the mail and, for whatever reason, letters from my parents were slow to reach me in Sarnia. It was proof that I had already been forgotten.

Seeing as how I was unimportant back home, I felt extra pressure to make my time meaningful. I wanted to be important to the work and important to the Lord. Therefore, I needed to work harder than I had been. And it was easy to blame that on Elder McDaniels.

As the only missionaries in Sarnia, we lived in a small one-bedroom mother-in-law apartment that was attached to the home of a family in the Sarnia ward. The rug was brown shag, and the one couch was old and damp.

Our days were structured, but how we filled our time was up to us. To help us keep our attention on the work, we prayed often. Unceasingly. We rolled out of bed. Prayed. Then we blessed our breakfast. Once changed into our missionary attire (white shirt, tie, dress pants, name tag) we prayed before personal study. Then we prayed before companionship study. Then again before we left our apartment for the day. Before every appointment. At the beginning of each appointment. Over lunch. And on and on. Somehow my mind was still able to wander. And when it did, I would inevitably ache to be home.

At those moments I thought of Steven back home, he of snipe-hunting fame. We had gone on our missions at roughly the same time. He went somewhere stateside, in the Northeast. He was so unprepared for adult life, defenceless. It was competitive and unchristlike, but as long as Steven was still on his mission, then I had to stay on mine. I wasn't about to be worse at something than Steven.

But then the work seemed to pick up. That's what helped the most: we found some investigators. We started teaching the Hills, a family of four, though the youngest child, who was maybe three, didn't really count. Mostly we were teaching the family's matriarch, Tricia, who had grown up in an offshoot of the Mormon Church called the Reorganized Church of Jesus Christ of Latter Day Saints, but her husband joined our discussions, too. By the time Tricia and her eight-year-old daughter agreed to be baptized, my homesickness was gone. Learning how long a letter from Calgary took to get to Sarnia also helped ease my angst. And seeing success with Elder McDaniels made me re-evaluate him as a missionary. Admitting I was wrong, even to myself—my family hadn't forgotten about me, and I hadn't been saddled with a Problem Missionary (not yet, anyway)—took some humility. But I didn't think I'd had a change of heart yet.

After two transfers together in Sarnia—totalling about three months, a pretty standard amount of time to be with a companion—Elder McDaniels was transferred to Barrie.

My new companion, Elder Grey, was going to continue my lessons in humility. Technically, he was the senior companion, having been in the field just over a year, but Elder Grey had no desire to lead. It wasn't that he was lazy, exactly, or that he didn't want to be a missionary. He just didn't want to make decisions. Although he was probably half a foot taller than me, Elder Grey was a sidekick. He was game for anything, so long as he didn't have to take charge. It was as though the Lord had heard all my complaints about Elder McDaniels (of course He had) and decided that if I thought I knew so much about being a super-missionary, how about I prove it? Lead the way, Elder Hudson. Be the missionary who runs from door to door, who always has a backup plan. Be the missionary who baptizes a new convert every single month.

The missionary handbook was a little white booklet every missionary kept in his front pocket. We were to read all fifty-six of its pages once per week. We broke it up into daily chunks. On one of its pages it listed, in order of effectiveness, fifteen finding methods a missionary should use. First on the list was "recent converts." You couldn't do that every day, though, and Elder McDaniels and I had asked our recent convert Tricia for referrals; she had given us a phone book from her old RLDS church, but it had yet to prove useful. Tracting—a.k.a. knocking on doors—was number thirteen on the list. Only "street contacting" and "speaking to everyone" were less effective.

It made sense. Cold calling door-to-door was too random to be effective, which admittedly was one of the reasons I liked doing it. It was like channel surfing. Would the person who answered the door be a man or a woman? Would they be in a good mood, or a miserable one?

On one particular morning, none of the effective methods of finding possible investigators seemed doable. But we could always tract. Tracting would be less random if the Lord told us exactly where to go. He knew Sarnia and its citizens better than we did. When it came time to say a prayer before leaving our apartment, I pulled out a map of our area. It covered all of Sarnia and the surrounding towns. It was laminated with clear packing tape. I put the map in between us, and Elder Grey and I knelt down. I asked Elder Grey to say a prayer. He asked the Lord to lead us to someone prepared to hear our message.

After I said "amen" at the end of the prayer, we looked over every street and residential polygon, waiting to feel *something*. Like a shot to the heart, or a wave of serenity and love emanating from a particular cul-de-sac. A neighbourhood that might glow almost imperceptibly.

Although no angel descended and highlighted the right neighbourhood with his flaming sword, we both felt *something* about Camden Street, which wasn't too far from our apartment. That we independently felt good about the same street was clear confirmation that that was where we would find someone Heavenly Father had prepared for this exact situation. The Lord was timing everything just so. Who knew what actions He was inspiring and orchestrating on Camden Street, but He was doing something to ensure that we'd knock on someone's door at exactly the right moment. We drove our mission-supplied Cavalier over to the street, said one more prayer before stepping out of the car, and began knocking.

The first few houses were non-responsive, which was to be expected on a cold winter weekday morning.

We knocked on the storm door of the cream-coloured house that was next in line. David answered with a smile. I was still relatively new to the field, but I already knew to be suspicious of the smiles of strangers. People who were happy that we'd knocked on their door were often as deeply committed to saving our souls as we were theirs. Only they were meaner about it.

David wasn't mean. He had black hair that swept across his forehead and a beard that struggled in places. He was a kindly troll. If he wouldn't talk about the gospel, I was pretty sure, based on his glasses, weight, and subtle devotion to proper enunciation, that I could get him talking about *Star Trek.* He introduced himself and read aloud our name tags while he shook our hands. "Elder Hudson and Elder Grey. That sounds like it could be a law firm. Hudson and Grey, attorneys-at-law.

Listen, you don't need to waste your time. We already agree on almost everything," he said, opening his storm door.

"That doesn't sound like a waste of time," I said. "You gotta know that'll only make us curious: what do we already agree on?" I expected him to say something vaguely ecumenical, that we all prayed to the same God, or something.

"How about that Joseph Smith is a prophet and that the Book of Mormon is true?"

"You're already a member," Elder Grey said.

"Nope."

"But you used to be," I said.

"No. I've never been a member of the Mormon Church. How's that?"

"Would you like to be? It sounds like you might," I said.

David let us in and showed us to two seats in his living room that seemed to be arranged expressly for sales presentations. He explained that he had been a member of the Reorganized Church of Jesus Christ of Latter Day Saints. "It's called the Community of Christ now," he said.

"Yeah, I used to drive past a Community of Christ church back home," I said. "I saw when they changed their name."

"One of the many problems with that denomination," David said. I wasn't all that familiar with the teachings of the Community of Christ. I understood that they were an offshoot of our Church, which split after Joseph Smith died. I knew that, unlike in our Church, in the RLDS Church women could hold the priesthood.

Obviously, David was the person the Lord wanted us to find. My brain was shouting so loudly it was hard to speak, to know what to say. I felt impatient. I knew how this was going to end. It would be like a spiritual romantic comedy. David would resist a bit at first, then he'd acquiesce to another meeting, mostly on a lark. But everything would change after that.

That was how it had gone down with Tricia and her family. She had been raised in the Reorganized Church of Jesus Christ of Latter Day Saints, but had stopped going, too. When Elder McDaniels and I knocked on her door, she let us in out of curiosity and nostalgia. She hadn't expected to convert. But a month later, she had. And a month after that, her husband, Don, who had never been religious, got baptized, too.

Like Tricia, David would notice how different he felt when we talked about the Church, how we made his home feel different when we visited. We'd identify that as the Spirit. He'd come to church. There, he'd meet someone—I wasn't sure who—that would be able to answer his questions about Church history, to show that the Mormon Church (a name none of the offshoots of the Church ever adopted) was Joseph Smith's church, and no reorganization had been necessary. And once the ward realized the depth of David's knowledge about Joseph Smith's early church, they'd welcome him into the fold with open arms. Tricia would befriend him. Maybe they already knew each other.

Maybe my mission would be full of Community of Christ converts. Why didn't we target them specifically? They believed nearly everything we did—all the God-talking-to-a-farm-boy stuff anyway—and if Tricia had been any indication, they were eager to learn all that they had missed growing up in the almost-true Church.

For Elder Grey's benefit, David gave a brief tutorial on the Reorganized Church. How after Joseph Smith was killed by a mob while in jail in 1844, most of his followers threw their lot in with Brigham Young, who was the most senior apostle of the Church at the time. He led them across the country, from

Illinois to the state of Utah, where they famously settled. But a man named Sidney Rigdon, who had been close to Joseph, also claimed to be the true successor to the mantle of prophet.

"But Sidney Rigdon and Joseph Smith's widow, Emma, didn't believe in polygamy, which Joseph had begun instituting, and they hated Brigham Young," David said. I knew that none of this really mattered. The Church had abandoned plural marriage in the 1890s. And any other claim Rigdon had to the leadership of the Mormon movement must not have been that convincing, since the majority of Joseph's flock believed in Young. Really, what mattered was that one Church was true, and the other wasn't. It came down to one thing.

"The only question, though, is who had the priesthood authority," I said. "Who had the permission from God to act in His name. You know our history pretty good," I said.

"That's another part of the problem. I probably know your history better than you do."

"There's no doubt about that," Elder Grey said.

"Then you know how important the Book of Mormon is," I said. "I heard that your Church was distancing itself from the Book of Mormon."

"I never said the RLDS Church was true. It's not. The problem is, neither is yours," David replied.

"But if you believe in Joseph Smith and the Book of Mormon, what do you do? There aren't a lot of choices if you believe the Book of Mormon is scripture. It seems like it's gotta be either us or the Community of Christ. And you don't seem too thrilled with them. Besides, what do you have to lose?" I offered.

"Time, really. And I consider my time precious, I'm afraid," he said. He glanced toward his wrist.

"What's a little time if we're right?" Elder Grey said.

What was supposed to happen wasn't happening. He was being friendly, but he wasn't softening.

"But you aren't. There has been another apostasy," he said. One of the central claims of both churches—basically their raison d'être—was that Christ's church fell into darkness and confusion after the apostles died along with their priesthood authority. This was known as the Great Apostasy. It's why so many Christian denominations sprang up, each holding a piece of truth. It's why God needed Joseph Smith to restore His Church to the earth. "What needs to happen is there needs to be another restoration. Until then, there are no churches on the earth that have all the truth."

I felt like I was watching God's plan unravel in front of me. I was too new a missionary to know what to do in this situation. David had concerns, but I didn't yet know how to resolve them.

"What are we missing?" I asked him.

"The miracles," he said. "Joseph Smith spoke with angels, he prophesied. And it wasn't limited to Joseph. Other people bore witness to angelic visitations in the Kirtland Temple. When was the last time that happened? If the gospel has been restored, why doesn't it still look the same? Why did it stop with Joseph?"

"It didn't," Elder Grey said. "We still have a prophet."

"Sure, but when was the last time he prophesied? He's a prophet, seer, and revelator, right?" David said.

We nodded. That was the title that went with his office.

"What was the last thing he revealed?" David challenged.

"Proclamation on the family?" Elder Grey suggested. I shrugged. It was the standard answer when someone wanted to know what a prophet—a real-life prophet—had done lately. But the proclamation on the family was more of a vision statement than a vision.* It laid out the Church's doctrine on gender (unchangeable) and family matters—including who could and should be married to whom (man + woman only). But while it was a handy document, it didn't reveal anything new. It quoted scripture, but it wasn't scripture. Compared with the entirety of the Doctrine and Covenants, which was section after section of the Lord speaking directly to and through Joseph, the proclamation on the family wasn't very impressive. It felt less like it came from the mouth of God and more like it was birthed by committee.

"Or, better, what was the last thing your prophet *saw* as a seer?" David asked. "Did you know why Joseph was called a seer? It's because he used a seer stone to translate the Book of Mormon."

David didn't know everything about Joseph Smith's history, since I knew that was false. Joseph didn't use a seer stone, whatever that was. He used the Urim and Thummin, a biblical device that had been buried with the gold plates. He sat on one side of a table with the gold plates, wearing the Urim and Thummin, which was described as a kind of breastplate with rudimentary spectacles attached, and read out the translation to whoever was transcribing for him. There was a strain of anti-Mormon literature that claimed Joseph had been immersed in the occult. A seer stone sounded like it was part of that.

Still, the only answer I could think to give was that maybe the big blockbuster miracles like angel visitations and holy fire, like the translation of ancient languages inscribed on metal pages, were never intended to be ongoing; after all, Moses had only

---

* Technically, the document is called "The Family: A Proclamation to the World," but everyone called it the proclamation on the family.

spoken to a burning bush once. There were no free refills when it came to miracles. It was a foolish and wicked generation that sought signs. The big stuff, that was usually a one-time event.

But my explanation didn't persuade David. His mind was made up. "Will you at least pray about it? Ask which Church is true, like Joseph did," I asked.

He got up, letting us know we should, too. "Oh, I never pray," he said.

"Sounds like you don't want to know the answer," I said as he led us back to the door.

"You better believe it." He let out a self-satisfied chuckle as Elder Grey and I departed, then closed the door behind us.

Knocking on doors along the rest of the street seemed anti-climactic. We couldn't pretend to believe that there would be *two* perfectly prepared souls on one street. We were meant to reach David. And we didn't succeed.

Elder Grey was quiet as we walked back to the car. I didn't feel like talking either.

Maybe all we were supposed to do was plant a seed. That was the refuge of the defeated missionary. It gave context, at least. A bit of hope. It might be an unsatisfying answer but maybe it was part of a larger operation and plan. Or maybe this was just a lesson for me to understand the frustrating power of free agency? The Lord can lead you to water, but He can't make you get baptized. There were positive spins I could put on the morning, but I suspected the truth was harsher. Some smarter, better prepared missionary would have been able to break through David's defences. A missionary more in tune with the Spirit would have known the exact right combination of words to unlock his heart. But neither I nor Elder Grey was that missionary.

The term used for people we were teaching, who were interested in the Church, was investigator. Our only investigator at that time, Wendy Gilmore, mostly liked having us around for her sons: Aidan was thirteen and Christopher was fifteen. She was a single mother and I assumed she liked the positive male influence we represented.

Wendy sold cars at the Honda dealership in town. Apparently, Wendy had originally been referred to missionaries by her friend, Randy Bachman, lead guitarist of the Guess Who and Bachman-Turner Overdrive, who was one of the most famous Canadian Mormons I knew of. They knew each other from Wendy's days working at a radio station in Sarnia, I assumed as a host of some classic rock show, though she didn't specify.

But Wendy was hard to pin down for appointments. She was always apologetic about her limited availability, and she knew she owed it to Randy to hear us out, so we kept trying to set up times to meet with her and her sons.

On our weekly day off, called preparation day—which was when we were supposed to write our families, buy groceries for the week, and clean our apartment—Elder Grey and I made dinner for Wendy and took it over to her home. Elder Grey had spent a few transfers in Brampton and had learned how to make authentic curry from some of the Indian members of the Church there. He spent all day cooking, filling our small apartment with the fragrance of rich spices.

The meal worked. After eating it with her and her boys, we got a firm date for our first lesson.

I wanted to teach Wendy something that would be immediately meaningful, that would highlight why Randy Bachman, lead guitarist of the Guess Who and Bachman-Turner Overdrive, had wanted her to check out Mormonism in the first place. Typically, lessons with investigators began with what was called the first discussion, which, building on common Judeo-Christian beliefs, covered the existence of God and the mission of Jesus before telling an abridged version of Joseph Smith's First Vision and the coming forth of the Book of Mormon.* It was all important stuff but it was like teaching music theory instead of how to play an instrument.

Better to start with the plan of salvation. This would typically be the fourth discussion, but it was okay to skip ahead.

And so that's what we did. Most elders had their own visual aids for the fourth discussion, little cards illustrating every step along the path. Mine were drawn in the style of *Calvin and Hobbes*. Elder Grey and I created a kind of map of eternal existence by laying out the cards. I moved a Calvin through the premortal life, then birth into a physical body, followed by life, then death and judgement, until the little Calvin was finally assigned to one of three potential heavens, or degrees of glory: the celestial kingdom (best), terrestrial kingdom (where most people would go), or telestial kingdom (where bad people went).

At the end of our lesson, all our cards were laid out on the coffee table in Wendy's living room. This was the point in the fourth discussion where people usually got excited, seeing the journey and purpose of life all laid out right in front of them. I imagined.

"This makes so much sense," I imagined people would say. "I always suspected God didn't send people to hell."

* The six lessons missionaries taught to people interested in joining the Church were called discussions.

Investigators could get excited about how those who died without hearing the gospel had a chance to hear it, and accept it, in the afterlife. Wendy, I assumed, would wonder at how insignificant life's problems on earth could seem when considered in proper perspective.

Wendy looked at the cards strewn across her coffee table. "No," she said.

"No," I said. "What's no?"

"No. I don't believe that."

"Our message is that if you ask God, you can believe it. You can know it," I said.

"No. That couldn't be right," she said, still looking at the drawings in front of her.

"What part is bothering you?" I asked.

"Besides all of it?" She laughed a bit. It felt like she was being blunter because her kids weren't there. "Why would God send us here? If we lived with Him before in the premortal existence and He knew how bad the world was, why would He send us here? Why would He send us away from Him?"

I pointed to the card that showed earth with the words "Mortal Life" written around it. "Well, we wanted to become more like our Heavenly Father, but we were lacking a couple of things: 1) unlike God, who had an immortal body, we were just spirits. We needed to get a body. And 2) we needed to be tested, to learn and grow. I know that that's why we were sent to this earth."

"No, I remember. I just can't believe that God would do that to us."

"Send us to earth?" Elder Grey asked.

"Send us away at all. But yes, send us to earth."

"Because that was always His plan," he said.

"That's not really an answer," she said. "I read a news story the other day about a girl, she was eight, I think, or maybe younger. And her parents were part of this sex ring where they passed her around, like every weekend she'd be raped by another man in the neighbourhood. The wives were part of it, too. Disgusting."

"That is disgusting," I started.

"So why, if God knew that was going to happen to that little girl, would He still send her to earth?"

"Well," I said. "We believe that our Heavenly Father gave each of us agency—the ability to choose—so that we could choose to follow Him and keep His commandments. That's such an important part of the plan that He would never take it away. Even though people sometimes use their agency to do horrible things, He isn't going to take it away."

"No," Wendy said. "I'm sorry, Elders. I think you're both wonderful boys, but I can't believe in a God that would do that. I just can't."

"Will you at least pray about it? Ask Heavenly Father if what we talked about today is true. I know He can answer your prayers. I know because I've also asked. And I know it's true," I said.

"Fine," she said, getting up. "I'll pray about it."

It wasn't until we were outside of Wendy's home and walking toward our apartment that I realized the problem with her argument. The question I should have asked was: why did she have kids? It's not like she didn't know the world was bad when her two sons were born. Why go through with bringing a kid into this world? Wasn't that basically the same thing she was asking?

"That was a pretty messed-up story, hey?" Elder Grey said as we walked home.

"Yeah. People suck," I said.

"You think it's true?" Elder Grey asked.

"Who knows. Probably. I wouldn't put it past people."

"Yeah, and why would anyone lie about that?" he said.

"Pretty messed-up," I said.

After six weeks in Sarnia with Elder Grey, it was time for transfers. That didn't mean one of us was going to a new area necessarily, but it was a possibility.

Transfer calls started around nine-thirty, right when we were supposed to be coming in from a night of tracting or teaching. Getting home late was a clear transgression of mission rules, but almost as bad was coming in too early. It showed a lack of work ethic and planning. I wanted to come in at exactly nine-thirty every night.

Obedience with exactness was something President Sybrowsky talked about.

If you got a call from one of the assistants, it meant you were making a lateral move, so to speak. You would be leaving your current assignment and moving to some new area but not moving up the leadership chain. If the president called, it meant you were getting a leadership position. You were training others or becoming a district or zone leader. Or an assistant.

President Sybrowsky called a little after ten.

"Elder Hudson," he said in his oft-imitated voice. "How are you doing?"

"I'm good, President."

"That's good. You are good, Elder Hudson. You're going to be a district leader in Barrie. Will you go to Barrie and help your district baptize?"

"It's done, President."

"That's what I thought," he said. "The assistants will call you shortly with more details. We love you, Elder. Tell Elder Grey that we love him, too."

"I will. Thank you, President." I hung up the phone. "The president wanted me to tell you that he and Sister Sybrowsky love you."

"Aw, that's nice. Where are you going?"

I told him that I was going to Barrie. To be a district leader.

"How big is the district?"

"I don't know. He said the assistants would call with the details," I said.

"And they'll tell me who I'm getting," said Elder Grey, wondering who his next companion would be.

"Maybe you'll train someone," I said, though I knew if that were the case, President Sybrowsky would have asked to speak with him.

"Ha" was all he said.

When the assistants called, Elder Knight told me that my companion in Barrie was going to be Elder Fields. "The one I'm related to?" I asked. My first cousin once removed had been sent to the CTWM a year or so before me. He also was diabetic, and a big man.

"Which one are you related to? You're all three from Alberta."

"The big one," I said.

"Ah, no. Your Elder Fields isn't very big. But he's good. I think he came out the transfer after yours. This will be the second area for both of you."

"We're getting double transferred into Barrie?"

"Exciting, right? Elder Hudson, we're so excited for this transfer. It was one that was arranged entirely by the Spirit.

We knew we were going to put Elder Fields there, but we didn't know who the district leader would be. Then we all looked up and saw your picture, and we all just smiled. It was powerful, Elder."

"Thanks," I said, getting a bit tipsy from the compliments.

"This is going to be that point in your mission where you'll look back and think: that was the moment. That was the best area of my mission. I hope you're excited."

"I am."

"Good. It's not everyone who gets called to be a district leader in their second area. You've been out for how long?"

"Like four and a half months."

"Amazing. I mean, don't let it go to your head. But you're going to do great things in Barrie. We're really looking forward to it."

Somewhere along the highway near Owen Sound, Ontario, the birthplace of Canadian World War I flying ace Billy Bishop, there is a pair of giant Muskoka chairs. If you served in or around Owen Sound, it was customary to have your picture taken seated in one of them, looking like a baby missionary balancing precariously atop a grown-up's chair. If you served further south, in St. Thomas, or had occasion to travel there, you had your picture taken in front of the statue commemorating the death of Jumbo the Elephant, P. T. Barnum's star attraction, who was hit by a locomotive there in 1885. The photo backdrop was the giant Canadian nickel if you served around Sudbury. If you were passing through there on your way to Timmins, where country superstar Shania Twain was born, you could take a picture under the street sign bearing her name.

The closest thing to a roadside attraction in Barrie was a large spirit catcher, standing sentry along the western coast of a bay that connected to Lake Simcoe, between the city's quaint and cracking downtown core and the parks and marinas along Lakeshore Drive. The spirit catcher served a purpose similar to that of a dreamcatcher, only, as the name suggests, it filtered out spirits instead of dreams. Judging from the design, it seemed that spirits were dangerous. The spirit catcher stood as an architectural notion of some winged thing made of iron. From its outstretched wings hung blades like kitchen knives that swung and creaked in the wind. Its head was like a crescent moon lying on its back, giving the creature horns. All the better to scare away naughty spirits and protect visiting, non-violent ones.

We would pass the spirit catcher on our way to the south end of the city, where it seemed like most of the members in the ward lived. The walk around the lake took about an hour. When we got to Barrie it was late January, 2003. It was still very much winter, and the path tracing the shoreline was always slippery. I fell often. Every time I went down, it felt like a punishment, only I knew that it wasn't. Heavenly Father might not grant me success in terms of baptisms, but he wouldn't literally knock me on my back. On days when I felt humbled because the spiritual work wasn't progressing as I imagined it would, slipping on ice felt like mockery. But I liked walking by the lake, and by the spirit catcher.

Elder Fields was raised on a farm in Southern Alberta. Mormon country. Back home he drove a truck to earn money for his mission. A real truck, the kind with many wheels and an infinite number of gears, made for carrying big boxes full of corn, or oats, or wheat, or cows to be butchered. He had been very sick before his mission. Now, he wore a bag under his shirt, attached directly to one of his intestines in a way I never saw because of our garments. But as a result of his illness, Elder Fields was twenty-two, a little older than the average missionary in his second area.

Our apartment was in Barrie's downtown, which consisted of about three or four blocks not far from the shore of Lake Simcoe. The downtown felt adolescent, like it was in the middle of a slow, awkward transition. It wasn't quite the quaint old Main Street you saw in smaller towns. But, while it had a surprising number of law offices and was home to City Hall and a few buildings that tickled the sky without scraping it, the downtown wasn't an urban core full of professionals either. Along the principal street there was a movie theatre, a strip club, a handful of restaurants and bars, and independent stores that always looked on the verge of closing for good. Barrie had a couple of malls, but they weren't downtown, and so neither were the chain restaurants or big-name franchises. We lived a few blocks north of Five Points, an intersection with, get this, five streets converging, which was the official centre of the city.

On nights when we were at risk of getting in too early from a dinner appointment or tracting, we walked down to Five Points and then up and down Dunlop Street, bearing our testimonies to everyone we stopped.

We kept track of testimonies. A testimony in the Mormon Church is like court testimony, but for spiritual things. It's what you *know* to be true. Other Christian denominations might use the word witness, another court term. Testimonies were one of our missionary performance indicators. We set goals about how many testimonies we'd share in a week, and report that number to our district leader, who would report it to our zone leader. Then, at the end of the week, we'd report back on whether we hit our goal or not. President Sybrowsky ran the mission like a business, but most missions had some way of tracking how often missionaries spoke to people. Missionaries back home in Alberta called it GQing—golden questioning—as in asking someone if they wanted to know the purpose of life, or learn more about the Church of Jesus Christ of Latter-day Saints. Counting testimonies, or the number of times we shared our faith with people, was one of the ways we held ourselves accountable. Elder Fields carried in his pocket a golf swing counter that made a satisfying clicking sound whenever we shared one. Ideally, for an interaction to count as a testimony, the words "I know" and "true" would be worked in. For example: "I know the message we're sharing today is true." But if all you managed to get in was the latter, that still counted. Ultimately, it was up to the individual missionary to decide whether they had shared a testimony or not. Our goal was twenty-five testimonies a day.

I liked being downtown because people in Barrie always seemed to be outside, even in the winter, even after dark. This was mostly thanks to the bus station at one end of Dunlop Street. It injected a constant stream of troubled men and lost women into the city's streets. There was no shortage of people wandering about who needed the gospel.

"Hi!" I smiled like I was teaching a baby the word happy.

"Hello," the man holding the other man's hand said. He was taller.

"How are you guys doing tonight?" I asked.

"We're fine. Thank you," said the other man.

"Only fine?" I said.

"We're fine, thank you," he said again.

"We're doing great," I said, pointing to Elder Fields. "That's my friend, Elder Fields. I'm Elder Hudson. We're doing great because we're sharing a true message about Jesus Christ."

cliclick!

The two men missed their light to cross the street. They were stuck on our corner for another minute. Defeated, the shorter one turned to face us. "Mormons?"

"That's right! How did you know?" I said.

"I've spoken with elders before. You all just have that glow."

"Virginal glow," the taller man whispered so we could hear. "Why are you both named Elder?"

"It's just our title in the Church. It's what we go by while we're missionaries. Would you like to talk to elders again?" I asked. "Because I could totally make that happen. I know our message brings happiness."

cliclick!

"What makes you think we aren't happy?" the shorter man said.

"That's the wonderful thing. No matter how happy you are now, I know our message can make you even happier."

"I don't think your church really wants us to be happy," the taller man said. He had been holding the other man's hand, but had now casually dropped it.

"No way. Why don't you come to church on Sunday and I'll show you," I said. If I had thought there was even an infinitesimal chance that this couple would take me up on my invitation, I wouldn't have said it. We had been in the city for two weeks. I hardly knew the ward at all.

The light changed. They took each other's hands. "Thanks. We're good."

"You are good! God loves you!" I called to them as they crossed the street. As I turned back to Elder Fields, I nearly hit a man going in the same direction. "I know God loves you, too," I said.

No response.

The thing was, I knew the Church wouldn't really be the best place for that couple. Not as a couple, at least. Individually, maybe. After all, it wasn't a sin to *be* gay, but it was a sin to *do* gay things. Joining the Church would be tantamount to taking a vow of celibacy.

"Oh hi!" I said.

There was a woman walking toward us, smoking. She was in her forties, probably. Possibly she could be a mother. She could also be homeless. It was impossible to guess sometimes. As she got closer, I was pretty certain she wasn't homeless, and she didn't have any visible signs of mental illness.

"I'm Elder Hudson. This is Elder Fields. We're missionaries from the Church of Jesus Christ of Latter-day Saints. We're . . ."

"Fuck off. Not interested."

"Are you sure? Be honest," I said.

"I said fuck off."

"Okay," I said. "We will EFF off, but I want you to know our message is true."

cliclick!

"God loves you!" Elder Fields called.

"I say we count that," I said.

"As a first discussion?"

"Yeah. No, as a testimony."

"I don't know. I didn't technically testify that I knew God loved her."

"Yeah, but you expressed a true principle, and you said it as though you knew it was true. You didn't have to say 'I know.' The fact that you're saying it means that you know it. You know?"

cliclick!

"What's the score? I mean, how many pure and powerful testimonies have each of us borne today?"

"Fifteen to eight," Elder Fields said. "Two more for the day."

"They're all yours," I replied.

A small group approached, two men and a woman. They looked like the kind of people that hung around the bus station. Bus station people were ageless. Their faces were old apple cores. They could be in their thirties or in their sixties. It was tough to tell. The woman's winter coat was open, revealing a t-shirt that was too small for her, and jeans that at one time probably didn't hang so low. One of the men was telling an involved story. I could only make out that the main character seemed to be named Fuck. The men wore flannel shirts of different colours under their denim jackets.

"Hello!" Elder Fields said. I felt a pang of parental pride and worry when Elder Fields showed enthusiasm. It wasn't that it felt forced or fake, just untested. I imagined he'd one day sound the same at his wedding reception. There wasn't a huge difference between bearing your testimony and confessing your love publicly.

"We're missionaries for the Church of Jesus Christ of Latter-day Saints. We're walking around, actually, sharing a true message about God's plan. Do you have a minute or two to hear it?" Elder Fields said.

cliclick!

"Don't need no religion, thank you very much," the man who wasn't telling the story said. "You know what religion is for, don't ya? Religion is for people who are scared of going to hell. Spirituality is for people who have already been there."

"That's what we got," the woman said. "Maybe we should share a message with you?"

"Oh, well, we'd love that. When would be a good time for us to come over and hear it?" Elder Fields said.

The group reminded me of an investigator Elder Fields and I had briefly met, and who we could no longer get hold of. He was a recovering alcoholic, and was a deep believer in AA. He had a lot of neat little maxims like that. *Whenever you point your finger at someone, you are pointing four back at yourself.*

I liked the guy's sentiment about spirituality, but I didn't think that religion and spirituality needed to be mutually exclusive. You might have lived through hell, but that didn't mean you didn't need to be baptized.

"HA. Yeah, right," the woman said. They kept walking and didn't slow down. We watched them turn toward the bus station.

"The question is, did I just bear one testimony or three," Elder Fields said.

"I was taught that that counts as one. But I see your point. It's like man-hours," I said. "Just to be safe, why don't you get one more. We've got ten minutes."

We wandered east to the side of downtown that we went to less often. We didn't avoid it because of the Hooters restaurant, but I did know that it was there. There was plenty to distract us in the west. That was where the strip club, the Silver Star, was. Not to mention all the posters on display in front of the movie theatre, with their mysterious titles and famous actors looking out at us. They might as well have all been foreign films. Over the course of my six months in the field, pop culture had become inconsequential and inscrutable, which seemed miraculous. That was what happened when you couldn't watch or read or listen to anything that wasn't approved by the mission president.

We crossed the street. As we began walking back toward our apartment, Elder Fields stopped a young man wearing a flat-brimmed cap and baggy sweatpants, the backs of which he had tucked into his socks. I had seen other people, mostly young men, wearing this look around town. I first thought it was a utilitarian thing, a way of protecting the hem of your pants when they would otherwise be too long and drag in the snow and salt. But I was beginning to wonder if this wasn't some misguided Barrie fashion trend.

"Where you headed this evening?" Elder Fields asked him, sounding a bit like a dad.

"I'm hitting up the Silver Star actually," he said. His name was Ben. He had just gotten off work. He was a line cook at Hooters.

"Busy night," I said.

"Just got paid," Ben said. He walked a little quicker but Elder Fields kept pace. I walked a few steps behind. I couldn't hear everything that they were saying, but I didn't want Ben to feel crowded, either. Plus, it's not like we were going to get very far with a guy who we met on his way to the strip club. Sad, I thought, because he could probably really use some of the Spirit in his life.

"Alright, we'll give you a call tomorrow and set something up," Elder Fields said, walking back to me. "Oh, and God loves you."

"Hey, nice work," I said. "We have an appointment?"

"Not yet. Just his number. He said his roommate might be interested, too."

"That's awesome. That just goes to show me, *judge not lest ye be judged*," I said. "I wrote him off after he said he was coming from Hooters. Ever eat at Hooters?"

Elder Fields looked as though I had asked him about the frequency of his wet dreams. His face was visibly red, even in the dark. "No. Of course not. What's the Silver Star?" he asked.

"Are you joking?" I said.

"No. He said he was going to the Silver Star. I told him to have fun. He laughed and said he would. I don't know what the Silver Star is, though."

"We walk past it like every day. It's a strip club just down the street."

"It's a strip club? How do you know it's a strip club?" He was looking toward where the Silver Star was.

"I guess I don't know for sure, for sure," I said. "But its sign has that silhouette of a woman wearing a cowboy hat, riding a shooting star. Kind of seems like a strip club."

"I never noticed that. I guess I haven't seen too many strip clubs."

"No? Not a lot of them in Raymond?"

"Surprisingly not," he laughed.

"What about at truck stops?" I asked. The life of a long-haul truck driver was a mystery to me.

"Oh, you get the lot lizards for sure. They'll knock on your door and ask if you wanna party or whatever."

"What are lot lizards?"

"Prostitutes that work truck stops. They'll usually sell you drugs, too. If they aren't looking for drugs themselves. But I've never seen a truck-stop strip club."

We started walking up the hill toward our apartment.

cliclick!

"I forgot to count the last one with Ben," Elder Fields said. "That's twenty-five."

We didn't have a baptism set for the month of April, and the other pair of missionaries in the district didn't either. Elder Fields and I had a few serious investigators, but none were going to be baptized by the end of the month. Sister Lopez and Sister Oakley were in a similar situation. Their most promising investigators were a young, unmarried couple. Since they were living together, they would need to be married before they could be baptized. But their urgent need for nuptials was complicated by the fact that the bride-to-be was only sixteen years old. Her fiancé was a twenty-three-year-old man with a goatee who looked like he owned several novelty samurai swords and was always on the lookout for more. Getting married would require parental permission, which her mother wasn't keen on giving, because of the whole teen bride thing, and because she knew that a baptism would follow shortly after the wedding. Probably the very next day. Her daughter would become a Mormon. She might lose her daughter twice over in a single weekend.

Two weeks prior, to show the Lord that we were serious about the work, and serious about getting His help in it, the elders and the sisters of the district put forward some specific terms for a special deal between Him and us. Sacrificing was a way of supercharging our work, of receiving extra blessings from Heavenly Father. We would make sacrifices like in the Old Testament, only instead of the flesh of livestock, we'd put our thoughts of home and our idle chatter on the metaphorical altar. And if the Lord accepted our sacrifice, we were sure He'd bless us with opportunities to baptize some of His children. We decided our sacrifices would be that we would only open our mail on preparation days, we would cease all talk of home amongst ourselves, and we would wake up an extra half hour early every morning to study the scriptures just a little bit more. With these sacrifices we would demonstrate our humility and desire.

But either we weren't doing something we should have been doing, or we were doing something we shouldn't have been, because there had been no change in the work since our sacrifice. No great influx of investigators. No baptism-ready old investigators calling out of the blue, wanting to become a member of Christ's true church. Nothing.

Sister Lopez was reporting all this nothing at our weekly district meeting, which we held at the church every Tuesday. It was called District Development Council, or DDC. Sister Lopez was blonde and from California and I was a little in love with her. She was updating the district both on her companionship's numbers—investigators added, discussions taught, testimonies shared—and how she and her companion, Sister Oakley, were doing with regard to our district's special sacrifice.

Sister Oakley was brand new to her mission and was having a hard time not talking about home, which for her was back in Utah. Waking up early was also a new challenge for her. But both sisters were trying their absolute best. After Sister Lopez wrote her numbers on the chalkboard, I could tell she was upset.

"Is everything okay?" I asked.

"It's fine," she said, but she didn't take her seat. She started to cry. "It's just . . . Where is the grace? When does that part come in?"

"The grace?"

"We memorized Ether 12:27 this week. To keep us focused and not talking about home. 'And if men come unto me I will show unto them their weakness. I give unto men weakness that they may be humble; and my grace is sufficient for all men and women that humble themselves before me; for if they humble themselves before me, and have faith in me, then will I make weak things become strong unto them.'"

"Elder Hudson, I memorized it, too," Sister Oakley said.

"I feel like He's shown us our weakness. I feel like I've been humbled. When does the 'my grace is sufficient' part start? We aren't perfect, but we're trying really hard, and still nothing?" Sister Lopez said.

I didn't know what to say. I had an uneasy relationship with heavenly grace. I think we all did. To openly rely on grace seemed like trying to put one over on God. As if missionary work were a group project and we were leaving all the work to Him. That way, you could blame Him if no one was baptized. I knew that the scriptures were true, and so I knew that grace saved us *after all we can do.** I believed it was important to never be satisfied that I had fulfilled my end. At best that led to complacency, and at worst to pride.

But grace was easier for me to understand when it was directed at others. No one deserved grace—that's what made it grace—but Sister Lopez's heart was broken and her spirit

---

* 2 Nephi 25:23.

was contrite.[*] Certainly, she was trying her best. I didn't know why Heavenly Father seemed so exacting. I didn't have an answer. So I did what we taught others to do when they didn't know something.

If any of you lack wisdom, let him ask of God, that giveth to all men liberally, and upbraideth not; and it shall be given him.[**]

I invited all four of us to kneel together. Kneeling, especially when it wasn't convenient, pushed prayer into a different category of seriousness. Technically, Heavenly Father heard all the prayers of His children, regardless of volume or position. He answered according to need, and His own perfect plan. But kneeling was humbling. We each took a turn saying a prayer. They were all some version of the same plea for grace, for help in moving the work forward. We prayed for understanding and peace, that we'd know how we could help our investigators feel the Spirit and want to be baptized.

We prayed for each of them by name.

We prayed for Maged. He was homeless, but always kept himself presentable and clean. Our zone leader had approached him in front of the library about a month prior. Elder Garmin, who had since gone home, had taught Maged a first discussion. Then Elder Garmin had passed him to us, since the library was in our area. Maged was from Egypt and was a Coptic Catholic, which meant very little to me. He listened to the discussions as if we were feeding him ice cubes in the desert. Every word out of our mouths was beautiful and precious. Sometimes he would close his eyes to savour what we were saying. He was converted fully to everything we shared and accepted every new principle

---

* 2 Nephi 2:7.

** James 1:5–6.

instantly. I worried we weren't understanding each other fully. His English was good, but it wasn't his native tongue. Maybe the language barrier was larger than I understood. I also thought our message was beautiful. And I obviously knew it was true, too, but I was wary of someone coming to that conclusion on their own so quickly. My prayer for Maged was that he would continue to accept our teachings, and that we would continue to understand each other.

I prayed for Megan. We had only met with her a few times since Elder Fields had talked to her roommate on the street outside of Hooters, but she too seemed to accept everything so easily that it made me suspicious. She had read the entire Book of Mormon the first week we had given it to her. But she was in her twenties and single, and I worried she might be listening to us for the wrong reasons. She seemed to like Elder Fields a lot. But suspicion and worry were basically the opposite of faith. I prayed that Megan would continue to pray and receive answers, and that we would know how best to help her.

And finally, I prayed for Mary. Her apartment smelled of cigarette smoke and cat piss, with notes of burned coffee lingering around the edges. She seemed like she had the furthest to go before she could be baptized. I was always half-expecting her to start bombing us, but so far she had continued taking our calls.* I prayed that she would continue to be humble as we taught her the Word of Wisdom and the law of chastity, principles I anticipated her struggling with.

We closed in the name of Jesus Christ and slowly stood up. I don't know if Sister Lopez received the answer she wanted.

* Bombing meant missing an appointment. The current term that one would use instead of bombing would be ghosting.

I don't know if any of us did. But I think we felt heard. Like in the vast celestial bureaucracy, our concerns had landed on the right desk. They would be taken seriously. That was something.

If the city of Barrie wanted to give homeless people a place to warm up in the cold, they built the library in the perfect location, two blocks away from City Hall. There were often rough-looking men sleeping at the carrels, but they didn't cause any trouble. It was just a block away from our apartment. A house would have been more conducive to the Spirit, or at least more private, but the library was quiet, and so many books together in one place felt reverent.

I had met Glenn the night before while I was on an exchange with my zone leader, Elder Wiggins. While Elder Fields worked with Elder Wiggins's companion in their area, I took Elder Wiggins around to meet some of our investigators. I saw Glenn crossing the street in front of our apartment at the end of the night and decided to get one last testimony in. His wife, or maybe it was his ex-wife, was Mormon, he said. He was interested in a visit, but he was living in a shelter. We decided to meet Glenn at the library, but we hadn't picked a specific spot, either inside or outside. It was spring but the snow was reluctant to leave the ground. What remained on the streets now was sharp and dirty. It lay in big piles in parking lots and at the end of driveways. But the weather was doing its part. It was warm enough to be outside in only our suit jackets. Windy, but nothing two Albertans couldn't handle. We walked around the building, looking for our guy.

"Hey!" someone across the street on their porch yelled to us.

We answered.

"Were you guys walking downtown a few days ago?" he asked.

I looked at Elder Fields as if he'd know. "Probably," he said. "We're here a lot. We're sharing a true message about our Heavenly Father's plan. If you have a few minutes, we'd love to share it with you."

cliclick!

"Oh no, I'm not interested." He held up the beer that was in his hand, a cigarette between the fingers of the other. "But you guys shouted 'God loves you' at me and I thought, hey, they're right. God does love me. Anyway, it was nice. Thanks."

"No problem!" I shouted back. "And He does!"

We walked a few steps further and were at the front doors of the library. I looked at my watch. We were still a few minutes early. "What do you think, wait outside here?"

"Is that him?" Elder Fields asked, pointing at a man sitting on a concrete bench near the parking lot. I nodded.

Glenn had long, unwashed hair and a big strawberry nose. He wore jeans and a denim jacket over a blue flannel shirt, pretty much a uniform in that neighbourhood. He read our name tags as he shook our hands. He told us he actually couldn't stay long because he had to meet his son at school soon and walk him home. He had found a place to live—it wasn't much more than a room, but at least his son could start living with him.

We didn't get to say much, which sometimes happened with people who hadn't had anyone pay attention to them in a long time. Glenn wanted to talk.

"I've been having a rough go of it lately though, eh," he said. "That's why I said I'd meet with yous. I figured maybe it was a sign. Because I could use some kind of sign. Just because I don't know. It's been hard lately."

He started crying.

"And I'm usually a lone wolf. I don't talk to no one and keep to myself. But it's hard. It's hard when no one wants to talk to you. So I been alone for a long time. And I get used to it. It's who I am. But it's hard and I don't know why life is so hard for some people," he said.

The tears threw me off. Normally, this was a softball question. Q: why does bad stuff happen? A: God gave us free agency so we can choose right from wrong. Unfortunately, in this life, a lot of people choose wrong. But talking about Heavenly Father testing our faith seemed grotesque in front of naked pain.

Glenn was proud of his son, he said. Mason was fifteen and he was starting to write raps like Eminem, and he was really good at it. Glenn didn't love rap music, but he never knew his son to be so dedicated to anything before. "But I don't know how I'm going to pay for him," he said. "I don't know what life he's going to have sharing a room with his dad. But what else can I do?" At least he wasn't on the streets anymore. The question of Mason's mother never came up.

Falling back on bearing my testimony felt nearly as cheap as sermonizing, but it was all I knew how to do. I wasn't a social worker, or a lawyer. I couldn't even give him money. "It sounds like you're going through some things," I said. "But I know that the message we share can help with all your problems. I don't mean they'll go away, but our message will help in other ways. I know that."

He agreed to meet with us again and he gave us his address. Elder Fields closed with a prayer. We couldn't really count it as a discussion since we hadn't done any teaching, but it felt important that we had come.

"I always think it's funny when people say things like how they're a lone wolf, but then they open up immediately to a couple of strangers," I said after Glenn had walked away.

"Sounds like he's not a lone wolf by choice," Elder Fields said. "Imagine breaking down like that in front of Barrie's library. Talk about a broken heart and a contrite spirit."

We walked the block home in silence and then ate a quick lunch at our apartment.

Like all missionary apartments, ours was spartan, decorated like a CIA crash house with maps on the wall covered with pins and stickers of various colours. We lived in a two-bedroom apartment, but the second bedroom was strictly a place to hang our clothes and iron our shirts. There was no other furniture. Our desks were in the living room, facing each other. There was a small couch, but we hardly used it. On the wall were pictures of prophets from the scriptures, mostly from the Book of Mormon, all painted by an artist named Arnold Friberg. There was a small kitchen, though we rarely cooked anything more complicated than macaroni and cheese.

For a missionary, as for someone in a big family, the bathroom was a refuge.

The list of places where a missionary could safely be alone was short. It started and ended with the bathroom. You could maybe steal a few moments of alone time at your desk if your companion happened to be resting or whatever in the bedroom. But that was pretty much it. The solitude the bathroom brought was nice because it gave to each companion equally.

I was taking my morning shower, thinking about Maged's and Megan's baptisms. The assistants had been there. Barrie wasn't all that far from Brampton, where they lived, and sometimes they liked to attend baptisms to make sure the converts went through with them. It's not that they'd be able to do much if an investigator decided not to show up or anything; the assistants were more like good luck charms. And it was nice when they showed up because you knew that they'd probably talk about the baptism with President Sybrowsky later that evening.

Only the assistants didn't even wait for evening to come to talk to the president after Maged and Megan were baptized. One of them, Elder Tingle, called him right after the meeting. After speaking with the president briefly outside, Elder Tingle came back in and walked up to me.

"I'm on a special mission from President Sybrowsky," he said. "He wanted me to let Elder Hudson know he was doing great work and to keep it up."

Did that mean we were living up to our potential? Our companionship was specifically called of God; we were the product of revelation in real time. Elder Hudson and Elder Fields in Barrie. And yet two was hardly an explosion of baptisms. If I were really doing great work, they wouldn't have to say anything because it would be self-evident. As nice as it was to be recognized, wouldn't it be even better to be the kind of quietly dependable missionary that a president appreciated because he could forget about him? Trust? Those were the kind of missionaries that ultimately became assistants, probably.

Elder Fields banged on the door. "Elder Hudson, we gotta go!"

I turned off the water and grabbed a towel. "What's up?" I looked at my watch. Barely 6:30 a.m.

"It's Maged. Maged called. He's going back to Egypt."

"When?" I asked.

"Uh, right now, I think."

"How right now? Does he have a ride to Egypt?"

"He called from the bus station. I told him that we were on our way."

"He doesn't have the Holy Ghost yet." I scrambled out of the bathroom wrapped in a towel.

"I know that!" Elder Fields said.

"Call Elder Wiggins, see what he says." Elder Wiggins was our zone leader.

People are supposed to get confirmed—receive the gift of the Holy Ghost—the Sunday after their baptism. Sometimes you have the baptism on Saturday so that they get the Holy Ghost the very next day. Maged's and Megan's baptisms were on Sunday. That left a whole week where anything could happen and they wouldn't have the benefit of the gift of the Holy Ghost to help them make good decisions in their lives. A whole week where you might get deported back to the Middle East. There wasn't a big LDS presence in Egypt. If Maged was to have any hope of retaining the lessons we taught him, he'd need the Spirit.

Plus, the baptism wouldn't count if there wasn't a confirmation.

"Elder Wiggins says we just need to confirm him somehow. But he said we should probably call the bishop first and ask his permission."

"Maybe they have a room we could use at the bus station," I said, while I dialled the phone. A confirmation wasn't a big to-do. Priesthood holders place their hands on the new member's head and say a prayer.

I explained the situation to Bishop Stevens. He seemed tickled by being a part of some behind-the-scenes missionary work.

"Bishop is cool if we confirm him before he goes to Egypt," I said.

Elder Fields was already waiting at the door.

The bus station in Barrie wasn't large, but it was busy. We didn't know what bus Maged would be taking or even where he was going. Other than Egypt. We knew he was ultimately going to Egypt.

The place was loud. People were speaking to be heard over the other people speaking to be heard. Some might have been yelling just for the fun of it, or yelling because their brains were broken and exhausted. Announcements would cut through the din, but only barely. Over some invisible speakers, I heard a song I recognized from my life before I only listened to hymns. It was someone singing about a series of bizarre events. I thought it was fitting.

How bizarre. How bizarre.

Then Elder Fields saw Maged coming out of a bathroom and called out to him. We all embraced. Elder Fields and I walked Maged outside the station and explained what needed to happen. I tried not to be troubled by the fact that he hadn't remembered.

"So we need to find a place to give you a blessing," Elder Fields said.

"What about there?" I asked, pointing at the knife-winged metal spirit catcher across the street. "We're giving the Spirit, it's a spirit catcher. It works."

Elder Fields reached out his hand to feel for rain. The air was wet and foggy, but there were no raindrops. We walked across the street, closer to the lake. We stopped on the concrete base of the statue. Elder Fields laid his coat down over the wet cement and Maged knelt on it. I put my hands on his head and, by the authority of the priesthood, gave him the Holy Ghost. Then, with our hands still resting weightlessly on Maged's head, I blessed him that he would be a light unto his family and friends in Egypt, and I prophesied that one day he'd return to Canada and enjoy full membership in the Church. Then, as always, I closed in the name of Jesus Christ, amen.

We walked back to the bus station with the newest official member of the Church of Jesus Christ of Latter-day Saints.

Insofar as we were able to, Elder Fields and I followed the news of the world by reading the headlines in newspaper boxes we passed on the sidewalk. "Read only books, magazines, and other material authorized by the Church and your mission president," said the missionary handbook. So the papers stayed safely in their mysterious metal vending machines. That was how we had followed the SARS outbreak as it moved through Toronto, sixty-three kilometres away. And that was how we learned that the United States, along with a handful of its close friends, had invaded Iraq. Canada was conspicuously absent from America's coalition force, which Elder Fields and I felt good about.

On a warm spring evening, we had a dinner appointment with the Desjardins family. I wasn't certain, but I didn't think we had met them. We weren't familiar with everyone in the ward yet. But the Lake Simcoe Ward took care of their missionaries. We usually had at least four or five dinner appointments a week.

Dinner appointments were one great benefit of going to a boring North American middle-class mission instead of some far-off land. My brother Sam and sister Gill may have been fed every now and then during their missions in France and Russia, but they didn't have a free home-cooked meal nearly every day of the week. So there.

We pulled up to the Desjardins home, a two-storey house that looked like all the other two-storey houses in that neighbourhood, and in the city actually. In Barrie, it seemed there were either century homes made of ancient red bricks, built when Barrie was new, or subdivisions carved out in the 1990s, where houses aspired to look exactly the same as one another. The Desjardins had a few more trees on their property than their neighbours.

"What's your bet: spaghetti or frozen lasagna?" I asked.

"I'm going with spaghetti," Elder Fields said after a moment.

"I'm betting that it's going to be frozen lasagna, but they'll make some joke about not making spaghetti," I said.

"'We know you elders are probably sick of spaghetti, so we decided to be a little different. Hope you like lasagna.'"

"'We know you're sick of noodles and tomato sauce, so we decided to give you noodles and tomato sauce, *but in layers*,'" I said. I didn't know how it happened, whether some elder in our mission complained and word spread, or if people came home from their missions complaining about it, but the word was out in the Lake Simcoe Ward and beyond that missionaries got fed spaghetti too often. It was easy to understand why—it was fast and cheap and existed on a sliding scale of cooking ability. Now when people served us something different they made a little show of it, like they were in the know. The truth was I longed for some spaghetti.

"I'm still grateful for the food," Elder Fields said. He grinned at me like a camp counselor.

"Of course," I said. "Will you offer a prayer before we go in?"

"Dear Heavenly Father. We're thankful for our many blessings. We are thankful for this day that we have been given. We're grateful for the opportunity we have to serve the people of Barrie. And we're grateful for the Desjardins' hospitality. And we pray that whatever we end up having—probably some kind of pasta—will be delicious to our taste and nourish and strengthen our bodies. We ask for Thy Spirit to be with us so that we can help the Desjardins share Thy gospel.

"And we say these things in the name of Jesus Christ, amen."

"Amen," I answered. "Dibs out on giving the spiritual thought."

"It's probably my turn anyhow," Elder Fields said.

Brother Desjardins let us in, and I was able to confirm my suspicion that I had in fact never seen him before. I definitely had never seen Sister Desjardins. I would have remembered, since she would have been the only Black woman in the ward.

We were directed to make ourselves comfortable in the living room while Brother and Sister Desjardins finished making dinner. If they had had young children or even teens, this would be when we'd entertain them. Sometimes willingly, sometimes less so. The photos on the mantle seemed to indicate that this was not Brother Desjardins' first marriage.

"How do you like your burgers, Elders?" Brother Desjardins asked.

"Cooked," I said. When I was a restaurant server, we weren't allowed to offer hamburgers cooked any other way than well done. Consequently, the thought of a pink hamburger turned my stomach a little. "I'm just kidding. Well done is good."

"Oh, if you're offering, I'd love to have mine rare," Elder Fields said.

"A man after my own heart," Brother Desjardins said. He was a big man with grey hair that was tastefully long, in the manner of jet-setting multi-millionaires. He was carrying discs of pink meat piled on a tray. "I keep mine on the grill just long enough for it to stop mooing."

"Something like that," Elder Fields said.

Before taking a seat on their couch, I circled the room like it was an art gallery, seeing what I could talk to the Desjardins about over dinner. I looked more closely at the pictures on the mantle.

"Uh, Brother Desjardins, are these your kids?" I asked.

"Sure are."

"Huh . . . I think I went to high school with your daughter," I said. "Like, I definitely did."

"Where are you from, again?"

"We're both from Alberta. Raymond," I pointed at Elder Fields. "I'm from Edmonton."

"Well, then it's possible."

"Is her name Nicole?"

"That's her. Isn't that a small world. Would she know you?"

"I think so," I said.

"Well, this ought to be fun. I get to check up on you. What is your first name, if you don't mind me asking."

"Greg," I said. Hearing it come out of my mouth felt strange. It felt like a secret. I even signed my letters home "Elder Hudson."

He wrote my name down on a pad by the door.

"We'll just see about you, Elder Hudson." He went outside to light the grill.

Nicole was a year older than me. I never would have guessed that she was Mormon. Mormons weren't supposed to date until they were sixteen—a point made very clear in the pamphlet *For the Strength of Youth*. But in grade eight, Nicole dated Jamie, a handsome thirteen-year-old whose voice had already changed. They used to make out in the hallways.

"Uh oh," Elder Fields whispered to me. "Is anything going to come up in his background check?"

"I should be fine," I said. Every now and then, in moments like this, I'd get a reminder of how close to home my mission was.

When Brother Desjardins came back from the grill, he seemed quieter. Once we were seated around the table, he asked if I would offer the blessing on the food.

"Well, I called Nicole," Brother Desjardins said after we had all said our amens.

"Did she remember him?" Elder Fields asked.

"She certainly did." He paused dramatically. "And do you know what she said?"

"I can't imagine," I said.

"She had nothing but nice things to say about you. She said that everyone knew you were Mormon and you never broke the rules and you were always nice to everyone. She said you were a really good guy."

"Well, shucks," I said. Elder Fields patted me on the shoulder.

With that out of the way, Brother Desjardins changed the subject to the invasion of Iraq. "What do you boys think about it?" he asked.

"We don't know much about it, honestly," Elder Fields said. "We're not allowed to read the newspaper or watch the news. We heard about it, but I don't really know enough to have an opinion."

President Sybrowsky had made the rule clear to us. We weren't to talk politics with members, especially about Iraq. The Church had no official position on the invasion, so neither did we. Same went for gay marriage, which was starting to become legal in the provinces.

"You're probably not allowed to give your real opinion," Brother Desjardins said. Elder Fields and I shrugged our shoulders.

"Probably not," I said.

"Well, I think it's just horrible. It's a disgrace."

This, I assumed, was how most Canadians felt about the whole thing. Indeed, this was the only ethical response. War was pretty clearly unchristlike. Except when it was a commandment or in self-defence. I'd have to check to be positive, but I was pretty sure that in the Book of Mormon, the Nephites were never the first to attack the Lamanites. It was usually the other way around. But even though I agreed with Brother Desjardins, I wasn't going to say anything.

"Mhmm," I said, while Elder Fields made a similarly noncommittal noise.

"I mean, when your friend gets into a fight, you back your friend up. It's cowardly and disgraceful that Chrétien is refusing to help. It's not like the US even needs our help. You think they need Britain and Poland? But it's the principle of the thing."

"France, too. Or is France opposed to it. I can't remember," Sister Desjardins said.

"We shouldn't even need to be asked," Brother Desjardins continued. "Our big brother needs us? How many men do they need? We help out in Afghanistan, but with Iraq it's no thanks? I guess we're okay with dictators now?"

"They already said they can't talk about it," Sister Desjardins said. There was a hint of the Caribbean in her voice.

"I know, I know. But I don't see what's wrong with missionaries having political opinions," he said. "After all, there are two subjects that people say are off limits. Do you know what those subjects are, Elder Fields?"

"Politics and religion. Or was it death and taxes?" Elder Fields said, winking at me. Elder Fields often blushed a little when he tried to be witty or suave, like the joke was a silly hat he had to wear without knowing how everyone felt about headwear.

"Politics and religion, exactly. Death and taxes are the only two things you can count on."

"And close only counts in horseshoes and hand grenades," I said.

"I'm just saying that you already break one of the rules, why not the other, too? What about your parents? I bet they agree with me."

"Could be. My parents are, what's the word, when a person only cares about one thing?" said Elder Fields.

"Single-issue voters," Brother Desjardins said.

"That's it. My parents are pretty much single-issue voters. They'll vote for whoever promises to take care of farmers."

"What about you, Elder Hudson?"

"Oh, my parents are lefties. My dad always votes Liberal, my mom votes NDP."

"Liberal Mormons in Alberta? They must be pretty lonely," Brother Desjardins said.

"Yeah. There aren't many of them."

"Well, you know what they say, if you're a conservative in your twenties, you have no heart. But if you're a liberal in your forties, you don't have a brain."

"That's a good one," Elder Fields said. "I'll have to remember that one."

Missionaries didn't always keep their politics to themselves. I often thought about one of my early memories of missionaries. I was maybe seven. The missionaries came over for dinner at our house in Edmonton. There was a big one and a smaller one who could do a backflip on our trampoline. His name was Elder Bartholomew. His companion called him Elder Bart, like on *The Simpsons.* I was naturally drawn to the bigger one, though. I was always being told I'd grow up to be big, too.

While we ate dinner outside on our deck, the talk was at first biographical. Elder Bart was from Utah. The big elder was from California. They each had a number of siblings, and they'd each been on their mission for about a year. Then, somehow, the talk turned more serious. The big elder was suddenly at odds with something my mom was saying. He didn't seem to agree with what my sister Erin was saying, either. His voice was loud, and his accent made him sound holy, because all missionaries, and General Authorities, seemed to have the same humble, consonant-swallowing drawl.

Then he was talking about Black people. My teacher at the time, Madame Valerie, was Black.

"Call it prejudice, but you tell me they aren't lazy, let me show you the porch monkeys where I come from. Won't lift a finger unless it's to collect welfare," the big elder said. He paused then, as if waiting for laughter or nods of agreement. None came.

"That's not true, actually," he corrected himself. "They'll lift a finger to rob you, too."

"How often have your neighbours robbed you?" my dad asked the big elder. He was calm, even when he was angry.

"Not us, no. Even they know better than to try something like that. We got a sign, says 'Trespassers will be shot on sight.'" The big elder turned to Elder Bart, who was looking down at the scriptures in his lap. Then he told us that his cousin had crossed out the word "trespassers" and written the N-word above it. The elder deemed this hilarious.

Elder Bart nodded.

"Gross," my sister Erin said. "That's disgusting and racist."

"So it's okay to take someone's life if they happen to step over your property line. How Christlike," Gill said.

"No, it's okay to take someone's life if they are putting my family in danger."

"But you wouldn't know if your family was in danger," Erin said.

"Oh, so I should wait until they're attacking my daughter?"

Erin disagreed with his point. Sam and Gill got up and left.

The missionary kept talking, and Erin kept disagreeing. Soon, I got up and went to play Nintendo downstairs.

I knew that the word he used for Black people was a really bad swear word, which didn't seem right coming from a missionary.

The following Sunday the big elder sat down in the pew in front of me before church started. He had his scriptures open. "Hey, you think you can remember something? Can you remember Alma 43:47? Repeat it, Alma 43:47."

"Alma 43:47." I knew that was a scripture from the Book of Mormon, but it wasn't a famous one. He told me to repeat it again, so I did.

"Here, take a look." It was highlighted in red in his scriptures. He pointed at it, then read it out loud, helpfully jabbing a finger at each word as he went. "'And again, the Lord has said that: Ye shall defend your families even unto bloodshed.'" He mumbled quickly over the boring, irrelevant bit in the middle of the verse and picked it back up at "'to defend themselves, and their families, and their lands, their country, and their rights, and their religion.' What was the scripture again?"

"The whole thing?"

"No, just the reference. Alma . . ."

"Alma 43:47."

"I want you to tell your sister to look up that scripture. She can cry all she wants, but that's what the Book of Mormon says. 'Even unto bloodshed.'"

I nodded. He tapped my arm, thanked me, and called me bud.

But I didn't pass along his message. And I didn't like the way I felt when he talked to me.

I don't know what shocked me more, his racist views or the lengths he went to in arguing them. Now that I was a missionary, I didn't ever want to say anything that would imply disagreement with members. Let them sound off on whatever they liked, I was there to talk about the gospel.

And eat burgers, which we did.

We didn't have anything planned for after dinner, so we decided to go back to our apartment to figure something out. It was getting dark. In the summertime, we could tract past nine o'clock. People tended to gauge how to feel about someone calling by the position of the sun. So long as the sun was out, people answered their doors. With the sun being where it was, tracting would be fruitless.

Street contacting might not be, though. Downtown Barrie had people walking around. Spring was in the air. You couldn't look anywhere without seeing snow, but the night felt temperate.

"Where are we at for testimonies?" I asked.

"Seventeen."

"Elder Fields, would you like to do some testifying?"

"Oh, you know I would."

We decided to walk down the street to the library before turning toward the lake, then turning south on Dunlop Street, which was Barrie's main street. Walking south, we'd have at least a block of downtown before the street traffic became more sparse and angry.

At the library, someone leaving the building shouted to get our attention. "Elders! Elders!"

We turned.

"That's Denise, right?" I whispered as possible-Denise approached.

"You're the one that's good with names," Elder Fields whispered back.

I was pretty sure her name was Denise. She was a member of the Church, but less active. The sisters were working to bring her back. Although we had definitely talked about her at any number of district meetings, I couldn't remember if she had a real concern about the gospel, or if something always just seemed to come up on Sundays to prevent her from attending services. It was a good bet that if someone were less active it was because they had trouble living either the Word of Wisdom, the law of chastity, or the law of tithing. I couldn't remember which, if any, applied to Denise.

Last week, she had been feeling under the weather. Not wanting anything to prevent her from benefiting from at least part of the service, Sister Joy, who had replaced Sister Lopez, offered our services as priesthood holders to give her a blessing. The sisters were there when we got to her basement apartment. Elder Fields took out the vial of consecrated oil he kept on his keychain. He anointed Denise's head with a few drops, then we put our hands on her head and I gave her a blessing.

At this point in my mission, I was a poor judge of people's ages. I wasn't even twenty yet; everyone seemed older. I would have guessed Denise was in her early thirties, but I would probably have been wrong. She was dressed in an oversized sweatshirt and leggings, which gave away nothing.

"Elder Hudson, this is crazy that I'd run into you guys. I actually really wanted to ask you something," she said.

"Of course," I said.

"Okay, well, one of the things about the Church that I always loved is that we believe that Jesus is our brother. That's how I almost always refer to Him, that's like how I think about Him. He's our older brother."

"Totally," I said. "I like that, too. And I know that it's true."

I glanced over at Elder Fields to see if he was going to give me a click of the testimony counter. He shook his head. It was a fair call. She was already a member. We only counted testimonies to non-members.

"I wanted to ask. When you gave me the blessing last week you ended it 'in the name of your older brother, Jesus Christ, amen.'"

"Huh," I said.

"Is that something you always say?" she asked.

I told her that it wasn't. I had just felt like that was the way to end her blessing that particular day.

"Well. I thought that was pretty cool."

"Totally," I said again. We walked her to her car. Walking back toward downtown, we saw a figure leaning against a wall, just outside an alleyway.

"Well, what do we have here?" She was wearing what would be bright leggings if it were daytime, and an older-looking fur coat. Her hair was pulled back, with an eruption of curls coming out of a scrunchie. She looked safe, but only barely. She was interested in talking. "Who are you two?"

"We're missionaries for the Church of Jesus Christ of Latter-day Saints. We're . . ." I started.

"Are you Christian?" she asked.

"We are," I said. "It's right there in our name. Church of Jesus Christ. I'm Elder Hudson. This is Elder Fields."

"Okay, okay. And do you have a book?" she asked, like she was running through a checklist.

"In fact, we do," Elder Fields said. "It's a true book about Jesus Christ."

cliclick!

Elder Fields was quickly writing something in his pros copy—likely our phone number and a little testimony.*

"How did you know we'd have a book?" I asked.

"Everyone always has a book. I always read everyone's books." She took the pros copy from Elder Fields. "I'm hungry to know about all religions. Because all religions say they are the right one, but I don't know which one actually is, yet."

These were words missionaries loved to hear. The more the investigator's experience mirrored Joseph Smith's, the better. "How do you think you'll know?" I asked.

"By their fruits, ye shall know them," she said.

"We say the same thing," Elder Fields said. "That book is our fruit. If it's true, then our whole message is true."

"And what's your message?" she asked.

---

* Pros copy is short for a proselytizing copy of the Book of Mormon; it's what we called the floppy navy-coloured Books of Mormon with gold script the Church gave out for free. If you find a copy of the Book of Mormon in a second-hand store, it's likely a proselytizing copy.

"Our message is that you can ask God whether something is true or not. He knows everything, He probably knows which Church is right. We give people this book and ask them to pray about it to find out from God whether it's true," I said.

"Of course, I always ask God to let me know things. That's how I knew the Jehovah's Witnesses weren't right. I read their book and prayed and it wasn't true," she said.

"We'd love to come by and talk to you more about the Book of Mormon and how it can bless your life," Elder Fields offered. She was wary.

"I have to finish the book first. Your number is in it? I can call you when I'm done."

"The whole book?" I acted incredulous. "When you bite into an apple, how many bites do you have to take before you know it's an apple? Do you have to eat the whole thing?"

She took my point and allowed us to set up an appointment with her. She said her name was Chantini. We assured her that we really felt like we were supposed to run into her. She nodded vigorously. Definitely, she said. Then as we were walking away, she shouted, "We'll see!"

"Wants to know what Church is true, and asked us for a book? That's got to be one of the most golden people I've met on my mission," Elder Fields said. I liked Elder Fields's faith.

We walked the rest of the way to Dunlop. We talked to a few people also walking along the still-wintry street, bore our testimony seven more times, but didn't find anyone as interested as Chantini had been. It was a little early, but we decided to call it a night and walked back to our apartment to check our messages and plan the next day.

On our machine, there was a message from a woman we had never met. She asked us to call her back: it was about Miles Gotch.

"This ought to be good," Elder Fields said while I dialled the number she'd left for us. I sat down at my desk and rested the telephone on my shoulder.

"What do we think about Miles? Accountable or no?"

"He was baptized," Elder Fields said. "Someone thought he was accountable."

"Yeah . . . still."

Miles Gotch was a less-active member on our ward list. We had dropped by his place unannounced a few weeks ago and, with some convincing, he let us in. His first-floor apartment was hot, but clean. He sat in a La-Z-Boy in the centre of his living room in front of a TV that was surrounded by video cassettes.

"Looks like you like movies," I said to Miles. I scanned his collection. It wasn't in any particular order, but it was tidy. He favoured action movies, it seemed. But lodged in between the *Rocky*s and the *Rambo*s was a *Playboy Video Playmate Calendar*. The smiling face of Playboy Playmate of the Year Heather Kozar on the side of the videotape would be staring at me for the whole visit. I had to pretend I wasn't tempted to stare back. "What kind of movies do you like?"

"Oh, I like all kinds of movies."

"You don't have a kind of movie you like just a bit better than the others?" I asked. I did most of the talking at the beginning of visits. BRTing: building relationships of trust. My problem was knowing when to end the BRT portion and move on to the serious, salvation-granting stuff.

"I like Steven Seagal movies the best, probably," Miles said. He had a wide face that seemed unfinished. Like he had been in a hurry when he shoved it on his head. He had a lazy eye.

"Why do you like Steven Seagal movies?" asked Elder Fields.

"I like him because he's always out for justice. He gets justice. He's avenging his brother, or his wife, or his girlfriend, or else someone is kidnapped and he has to rescue them."

"I don't think I've ever seen a Steven Seagal movie," I said, more to Elder Fields than Miles. "I was more of a Van Damme guy."

"Oh, oh, oh, you like him! He's a pretty boy." Miles said it like he knew he was being naughty. "And he's a show-off. Steven Seagal is cool. And doesn't show off."

I was pulling *Finding Faith in Christ* out of my bag. "Actually, Miles, we happen to have a movie with us right now. We wondered if you wanted to watch it with us."

"It's okay. No thank you."

"Are you sure? It's about twenty minutes—that's shorter than a sitcom. And it's about Jesus. I think you'll actually like it. He has long hair like Steven Seagal," I said.

"It's okay."

"Yeah? Okay. Then how about I leave it here with you. You can keep it. And watch it whenever. Is that okay?"

"Yeah, that's okay."

I put the video cassette face out in front of the *Playboy Video Playmate Calendar*, blocking Heather from view.

"Because watching movies is great. I used to love watching movies. But there are good movies and there are bad movies. Some movies bring us closer to Heavenly Father, and some move us away from him. I think most movies are probably somewhere in between. But I know we have to be careful. Because we might like watching movies that don't bring us closer to our Father in Heaven, right?"

"I know. I saw where you put your movie. You want to take away my adult videos," Miles replied.

"We don't want to take anything from you, Miles," Elder Fields said, calmly. He hadn't clocked the *Playboy* video. But he was right. We weren't about to take it. Hide it from him was more likely.

"Missionaries always take away my adult magazines and adult videos. And these aren't cheap. These are beautiful women, and they are smart, and charming, and sophisticated. They took them all away. And I had to get more, and they aren't cheap," Miles said.

"We don't want to take anything. We just want to leave this video. Will you watch it after we leave?"

"Yes, I will watch it after you leave."

"One last thing, could we say a prayer with you before we go?"

"Yes, you can."

I asked Miles if he wanted to say the prayer, but he demurred. Then, with the slightest bit of encouragement, he changed his mind. I could see how Miles ended up getting baptized. He basically did anything we told him, so long as we encouraged him past his initial automatic no. In his prayer, Miles thanked Heavenly Father for us visiting him, and prayed that we would come back soon and talk more about the gospel.

Since that visit we had called once or twice to set up an appointment, but we hadn't had any luck reaching him.

The woman who had left the message picked up after the second ring. I introduced myself and she thanked me for calling.

"Miles wanted me to tell you that he doesn't want you to come by anymore," she said.

"Oh," I said. "Anymore? We've only visited him once."

"Be that as it may, he has asked that you not try to contact him again."

It felt like we were in trouble. Had he accused us of something inappropriate? "Oh, we just left a movie with him. We wanted to see if he had a chance to watch it."

"Uh huh."

"I don't think we said anything offensive or anything," I continued. Sensing my confusion, the woman on the other end decided to tell me a little more.

"I guess he felt that you guys were going to take some of his videos away. Miles likes his videos."

"That's why we left him one," I said.

"Makes sense," she said. "I could get the video back to you, if you'd like. We could arrange that."

"I'm just confused. We prayed with him before we left, and in his prayer he made it seem pretty clear he wanted us to come back. I'm just confused about when he changed his mind."

"Miles is very impressionable. He might have been saying what he thought was the right thing to say. But I am sorry."

"No, no, it's fine. We won't try to contact him again. It's all good."

She thanked us and hung up. "That was Miles's case worker, or something, I guess. We are not allowed to contact him anymore."

I was still a little torn on the "is he or isn't he accountable" question. In the end, it didn't matter. Heavenly Father would be the one to judge him, and He would know everything, including whether Miles Gotch had the cognitive abilities of an eight-year-old.

It obviously made sense to err on the side of accountability. There was no harm in baptizing someone who technically wasn't capable of sinning. It's not as though baptizing them made them more accountable if they weren't accountable to begin with. And it's not like we were about to administer IQ tests or anything. What would the threshold be? But, at the same time, baptizing someone on the edge of accountability felt a little like cheating. Low-hanging fruit.

For Miles, the question seemed to turn on the problem of those sophisticated Playboy Playmates. According to the Church the age of accountability is eight. Are seven-year-olds interested in *Playboy Video Playmate Calendars*? Clearly Miles had adult interests, but just because his body was that of a man, with adult urges, didn't necessarily mean he was wiser or more capable of making good decisions than a child. He obviously had some kind of helper or case worker. Should that have given us some indication?

"My money is on less accountable," I said.

A week or so later—this was in May, 2003—I was transferred to Kitchener to be the zone leader's companion. More so than in other companionships, I would now be responsible for baptizing lots of people in our area. You didn't just send anybody to be a zone leader's companion.

Zone leaders needed credibility in order to lead. They needed a history of baptismal success, and they needed ongoing baptisms in their area so that the missionaries over whom they presided would trust them. And because the zone leader's focus needed to be on the entire zone, it was the zone leader's companion's job to ensure that their area baptized regularly. If the zone leader's area didn't baptize, what credibility would the zone leader have? How would he teach and inspire the zone to baptize if he himself didn't baptize? And with no one to lead, guide, and walk beside its missionaries, the zone would fall into sin and rebellion and be lost.

There was a lot of pressure on the zone leader's companion. The success of the entire zone rested on his young shoulders.

But my first month in Kitchener was entirely fruitless. I worried I was constantly disappointing my companion, Elder Henry. Not that he'd ever show it—he was too kind for that—but it would have been a reasonable response.

Elder Henry was small. He wore glasses and smiled easily. In his previous life, he was a gymnast and ran track, but, like most missionaries, he had become soft of body serving the Lord. Too much frozen lasagna and spaghetti at members' houses. By the time I got to Kitchener, Elder Henry had been there for six months.

At that point, our best shot at a baptism had been Enid. We bumped into her while tracting one afternoon in a cluster of townhouses that looked well-maintained and not inexpensive, though we're not talking luxury condos or anything.

That was an unfortunate Catch-22 of tracting: according to the missionary handbook, we had a "special responsibility to seek out families, the eternal unit of the gospel." Since finding an eager nuclear family was pretty rare, you at least wanted to baptize singles with stability, with a job, a home, a healthy social life, and a willingness to get involved! But those kinds of people tended not to be home during the day, owing to them having jobs. And because their lives were in order, those people tended not to want to hear the Lord's message.

But there were neighbourhoods in Kitchener, and in every city, where you might find it more likely to be let in, where you might find people brought low by unemployment or disability who were thus probably more ready to hear the Word.

I guessed that Enid's neighbourhood was full of financially secure retirees and empty nesters. But that wasn't Enid.

Enid was probably about the same age as my mother, somewhere in her mid-fifties. She seemed professional, like if she worked in a hospital, she'd be an administrator and not a nurse. She was tall and had good posture. She wore fashionable glasses and her hair was short and intentionally silver. Her wardrobe probably consisted of a great many chunky sweaters.

"Mennonites, right? No thank you," she said after opening the door. Kitchener-Waterloo was in Mennonite country, if such a thing existed. Road signs alerted you to their presence along the sides of highways: the outline of a buggy in a yellow diamond.

I would see them dressed in their pioneer best, driving their horses and buggies on the shoulder of highways and thoroughfares. We Mormons were mistaken for Mennonites more than any other denomination.

"Not Mennonites," Elder Henry said, as if he were her kindergarten teacher. "Want to try again? No peeking at our name tags."

"Oh, Mormons," she said.

"Ding ding ding," Elder Henry said, somehow managing not to sound condescending.

"They're basically the same thing, aren't they?" she said.

"Well, they both start with the letter 'M,'" I said. "Mennonites don't believe in using modern technology. Whereas we Mormons are all about it. In fact, we have a new DVD about the Saviour that we'd love to share with you. I know it can bless your life."

"Still no, thank you. The only thing I like about Mormons is their family values. I respect that. But everything else—" She shook her head meaningfully. That was as good an opening as any missionary could hope for. It was just a matter of building on common beliefs. Yes, families were important!

"Wait, what don't you like about us?" I asked.

"Like I said, just everything else."

"Why do you think we have such strong family values?" Elder Henry asked, taking the smarter approach.

"I imagine, well, I don't know. I know why family values are important to me. I wouldn't be able to say why you have them."

"And why are they important to you?" Elder Henry asked.

"They are the bedrock of society. You can see how the world is getting, and that's because family isn't as important as it used to be."

"I totally agree," I said. "I know that the family is essential to our Heavenly Father's plan. So, as we strengthen families, we serve God, and that's kind of one of the purposes of life, right?"

"Right," Enid responded.

"The fact that we believe in strong families is also fruit. And I know that Christ promised that there would be false prophets, but he also promised that by their fruit we shall know them. Our defence of strong family values is one way you can judge us. Would you have a few minutes to hear about God's plan?"

"You make a good point. But, no, no thank you. I know there's something about Mormons."

"Another fruit we share with people is called the Book of Mormon," I said.

"That's what it was! That's what it was. You believe in a new book of scripture, instead of the Bible. I could never believe in that."

"Right, and that's why we don't try to convince you that the Book of Mormon is true. We share it with people and then we ask them to find out for themselves," I corrected her.

"I already know. It's false. There's no new Bible. The Bible says so."

That old chestnut.

Revelation 22:18. *For I testify unto every man that heareth the words of the prophecy of this book, If any man shall add unto these things, God shall add unto him the plagues that are written in this book.*

Sounds damning, especially since it's one of the very last verses in the New Testament, but it's an easily resolvable concern.

"Where does it say that?" I asked Enid, sounding genuinely curious.

"I don't know where, but I know it's in there. And it's very clear. No adding more to this book, or something."

Elder Henry tagged in. "We believe that throughout history, God has called prophets to teach His children—us—His truths. Because you believe in the Bible, I know you believe that, too. Because that's what the Bible is. It's the writings of God's prophets in ancient times, right?"

"Right." This was turning into a classic "doorstep first," as in a first discussion taught on a doorstep. An interaction counted as a discussion if it covered at least four principles—core truths—from any of the discussions. Elder Henry had just taught the principle that God chooses prophets. "Prophets and apostles," she said.

"Right. Exactly. People called and given authority by God to speak and act in His name." Elder Henry was going to skip past the Joseph Smith principle and go straight to the Book of Mormon one. I was ready to jump in if he wanted me to. "And one of the things we share is that God loves all His children equally, and so we believe that while the Bible was happening over there, there were people living on this side of the world.

And because God loved them too, He called prophets among them, too. Because why would He intentionally leave people in the dark?"

"I've always wondered that, too," she said.

"And that's all the Book of Mormon is. It's the records of God's prophets over here, in this hemisphere." Elder Henry paused just long enough for me to understand he was passing me the baton.

"And like I said before, we don't ask anyone to take our word for it. There's a scripture in the Bible that I really love, it's in James, chapter one, verse five. It says that if anyone lacks wisdom they can ask God, who giveth to everyone equally. To me, that says that if we want to know something, we should ask God. That's how I know the Book of Mormon is scripture, because I've prayed about it, and I know God answers prayers," I said.

"Oh, I certainly believe that, too."

"I bet we believe in a lot of the same things," I said. I thought Elder Henry was going to jump back in with the Holy Ghost principle, since that's how God answers, after all, but instead he offered a proposition. Because he knew Enid hadn't been expecting company, he suggested that we leave her with a copy of the Book of Mormon, just so she could actually read it before making a verdict. "We can call you and set up a better time to come and talk to you about it."

Enid supposed that would be alright. She gave us her number and we jotted it down on the blue weekly planners we kept folded in our breast pockets. I handed her the pros copy I had been carrying. "Enid, I don't usually tell people this, but—" Elder Henry paused to add weight to whatever he was going to say next. "I really felt like we were meant to run into you today."

But over the next couple of weeks, Enid had proven impossible to get hold of. The few times we were able to speak on the phone, she sounded harried and impatient. No time was good to stop by. It's not as though the doorstep first we had with her was miraculous—Elder Henry and I had both had better—but it felt important to set up another meeting. Elder Henry felt the same way.

One day when we were home for lunch, I tried Enid's number and she picked up. She still hadn't cracked the spine of her Book of Mormon, she told me. As a result, she had not prayed about it, either. Enid was still wary. It felt like she wanted to learn more, but she knew that that was how we'd get her. "I still keep coming back to the scripture in the Bible: don't add to or take anything away from the Bible."

"Right," I said. "You don't happen to have your Bible nearby, do you?"

"I could get it."

"No, no, it's fine. You'll just have to trust me that I'm reading from the book of Revelation. That's where the scripture is."

"Wait, where is the scripture?"

"It's in book of Revelation, 22:18. The New Testament."

"Could you read it for me?"

"Of course," I said, and began to read. Something was happening.

"Hold on. When it says 'this book' does it mean the whole Bible, or just the book of Revelation?"

I pumped my fists. The Spirit was teaching her! All I had to do was bear witness to it. "That's exactly right, Enid. When John talks about the words of this book, he means the book of Revelation."

"Huh."

"And we know that's true for a couple of reasons. One, the word Bible literally means books, plural. And two, we know that the book of Revelation wasn't the last book written in the New Testament. The people putting together the Bible put it back there because it seemed fitting."

"But obviously we added to the Bible because we added books that had been written after Revelations," Enid said.

"Exactly," I said.

"Okay. Okay. Now I'm open. Now I'm ready."

A few days later, we were in Enid's small kitchen laying out the serpentine plan of salvation on her dinner table. I thought back to Wendy, the lady in Sarnia who had been referred to the missionaries by Randy Bachman. However well I had hoped the plan of salvation lesson would go with Wendy, it went better with Enid. As we used our visual aids to lay out the stages of human existence, from premortal life to the celestial kingdom, it was like feeding someone who was starving, almost like we were reminding her of truths she had already known. Which is what we were doing, in a way.

"This all just makes so much sense! I always thought there must be something like this," she said, pointing at the circles representing the three degrees of glory. "The Bible even says that my Father's house has many mansions."

"And what I love about that part of the plan," I said, "is that the lowest kingdom, the telestial kingdom, that's where bad people go. The kind of people other religions might condemn to hell. In God's true plan, they still get a degree of glory that is better than earth."

"No, exactly. I've always had trouble with a loving God that also throws people into hell for all eternity," Enid responded.

"We call this whole process eternal progression," Elder Henry said. "We're always learning and growing. We were learning when we lived with Heavenly Father before we were born and, so, just like when you're here"—Elder Henry pointed at the circle that's split down the middle, paradise on one side, prison on the other, the kind of purgatorial state between one's death and eventual judgement—"in spiritual prison or paradise, you can still learn and accept the gospel. And that's why even if you end up in a lower kingdom, if you remain faithful you can move up to a higher kingdom," Elder Henry added.

This was a popular bit of false doctrine that I had been taught before, but I knew it was a heresy. I wasn't about to correct him mid-discussion though. The truth was that eternal progression does have an end point for everyone, unless you make it into the celestial kingdom. But we didn't talk to investigators about what lay beyond the celestial kingdom for the faithful.*

"And when you're here, in the premortal life, do you know what your mortal life will be like before you're born?" Enid asked, pointing to one of the cards on the table.

"I don't know how much we actually know for sure," I started. "But I believe that we're given the broad strokes of our mortal life."

"I think of it like going to college," Elder Henry said. "Before you go, you know what you'll be studying, and you know the

---

* We would talk around this by describing it as "becoming more like our Heavenly Father." We didn't say that we meant it literally. The actual end goal of the plan of salvation was for God's children to become gods themselves. A prophet once summed it up like this: "As man is, God once was; and as God is, man may become." But that was only if you made it to the celestial kingdom. For those who landed in the terrestrial or telestial kingdoms, that was where the eternal journey ended.

end goal, you probably understand that it's going to be more difficult than high school was, but you won't know the specifics of college life until you actually go."

"Of course. Of course. I know exactly what you mean," Enid said.

We left Enid's house quickly after that, not wanting to say anything that might spoil the Spirit that was there. But first, we set up a time to come back to teach her another discussion. She was going to be baptized.

Before our next appointment, Enid left a message on our answering machine. She thanked us for our time, told us we were very nice boys, but she had spoken with her sister and there was something off about Mormonism. She asked that we not contact her again.

"We need to go over there," Elder Henry said. We were both standing before our answering machine, looking down at it like it was fresh roadkill.

"She asked for no contact," I said.

"But she doesn't know we checked our messages. We pretend that we're just dropping by on our way home from somewhere," Elder Henry said.

Using guile to preach the gospel probably wasn't the most effective way, but was it really guile if the end goal was Enid's salvation?

"That's pretty believable," I said. I liked the idea if for no other reason than we'd get to hear what her sister had told Enid that made her change her mind so resolutely. There were a few possibilities:

a) Polygamy and related sexual perversions allegedly perpetrated by Joseph Smith. The Church was quiet about Joseph Smith practising plural marriage. As a result, it was hard to know what was true and what wasn't about Joseph's marital history. I knew he had more than one wife, but had no idea how many, or how old each one was.
b) Joseph Smith's involvement with both the Freemasons and the occult. In the minds of many, it was an equation wherein one plus one equals Satanism. Joseph was a Mason, but so were George Washington, Franklin D. Roosevelt, and Lyndon Johnson (to name a few). I knew that a lot of the Mormon temple ceremony was borrowed from Freemason rituals. But that was a topic that was easy to avoid since we didn't talk about what happened in the temple outside of the temple.
c) Separate but related: that the Church of Jesus Christ of Latter-day Saints was, in fact, a cult.
d) That because we didn't believe in salvation by grace alone we were not real Christians.
e) The Church's history of racial discrimination could be a possibility, too.

None of them were impossible to counter, though some were easier to refute than others. Like some of the stuff about Joseph Smith was probably just lies. People lie. That was the lesson I had taken from Dianna. Some people lie for no discernible reason. And while the polygamy stuff wasn't a lie, plural marriage happened in the Bible, so it wasn't unheard of—David and Solomon, two very popular biblical kings, had scads of wives and concubines, for instance. And the cult and occult stuff sounded shrill and alarmist, clearly anti-Mormon propaganda.

Enid was home when we stopped by. She let us in to talk. As it turned out, her concern was a predictable mélange of us being a cult, and not even a Christian one. Enid was pretty sure we had been duped. And also, what was the deal with how we treated Black people? We didn't let Black people get baptized?

Strictly speaking, this wasn't true. I assured her. "In fact, one of the reasons that Mormons were unpopular in the early days was because they were against slavery. We've never had any restrictions on who could be members of the Church."

"Do you still have that Book of Mormon we gave you handy?" Elder Henry asked.

"Oh, yes. I was going to give it back to you since I won't be needing it."

"Before that, would you read a scripture from the Book of Mormon with us? It's in 2 Nephi. Chapter 26, verse 33," Elder Henry said.

"Did you want me to read it out loud?" Enid asked. Elder Henry nodded, his eyes as encouraging as a new father.

"'For none of these iniquities come of the Lord; for he doeth that which is good among the children of men; and he doeth nothing save it be plain unto the children of men; and he inviteth them all to come unto him and partake of his goodness . . ."

"This next part especially," Elder Henry broke in.

"'And he denieth none that come unto him, black and white, bond and free, male and female; and he remembereth the heathen; and all are alike unto God, both Jew and Gentile.'"

Enid read the passage again silently, making sure it said what it seemed like it said.

"We call the Book of Mormon the keystone of our religion," I said, "like in an archway, how the centre stone at the top is what holds the whole thing together. If you take out the keystone, everything else falls."

"Which means this scripture is at the core of what we are, too. It's because of the Book of Mormon that we know that our Heavenly Father doesn't care about race, sex, or economic status, right?"

"Right," Enid said. Then, "Are you sure? My sister was adamant. And she's not one to tell tales. She usually knows what she's talking about."

Elder Henry looked at me. He was deciding how much we should say, too. "I don't think your sister was lying to you or anything," he said slowly. "I think she just got a detail wrong."

"The Church never denied anyone who wanted to be baptized, but for a while the Church didn't let Black men hold the priesthood," I said. We hadn't talked about the priesthood yet. That was usually covered on a later visit. That meant that Enid wouldn't really know what the priesthood was, which was handy at the moment.

In reality, not being able to hold the priesthood was pretty serious. It meant that Black people couldn't go to the temple to get their endowments, which meant they couldn't learn all the necessary signs and tokens, or be sealed (married) to their spouse for time and all eternity. Ultimately, that meant that Black people couldn't qualify for the celestial kingdom. Up until 1978, when the rule was changed, the best a faithful Black person could hope for was to be a ministering angel to the folks who had made it into the celestial kingdom. They could be like heavenly butlers.

But we didn't have to get into all that. Especially since things had in fact changed.

"And what does that mean?" Enid asked.

"It meant they couldn't do things like go on missions. But that was a long time ago," I said. In 1978, five whole years before I was born, the Official Declaration announced that the Church would start allowing all worthy men to hold the priesthood, regardless of race. Anything that happened before I was born felt impossibly far away. It had been nearly a quarter of a century. And because I had never known the Church when it discriminated against Black people—and, to be clear, it was only Black people; all other races were fine—I never had to wrestle with that doctrine. The Church I knew didn't carry the blight of racial discrimination.

"We don't really know why the Lord didn't let some people hold the priesthood," Elder Henry said. He sounded almost chastened. "But if we look at the scriptures, it's a pattern that He repeats throughout time. It wasn't until the book of Acts that the Lord allowed the gospel to be preached to non-Jews, right?"

"It always kind of bothered my mom that women couldn't hold the priesthood," I said. "But she knew that it wasn't because women are less worthy. For whatever reason it's just a part of God's plan."

"I'll admit, I'm a little relieved by your answers . . . or, that you have answers. But this still feels like racism. And I don't care what you say, that is not the way God works."

We told her that we agreed with her fully. But it was hard for two white boys to sound convincing on the topic of what was and wasn't racist.

We tried to remind her of the Spirit she had felt in our last discussion, emphasizing that if the plan of salvation was true, that meant that our whole message was true, even if there were parts that weren't easy to understand.

It was past nine-thirty when we finally left. We were late getting back to our apartment, but we both felt it was justified. We weren't able to get Enid back to where she had been at the end of our previous appointment, but she said that she would be willing to have us come back. Immediate disaster had been averted. As long as we were around her, Enid felt the Spirit, and recognized that we couldn't be as evil as her sister claimed. We knew she would be baptized, but it wouldn't be before Elder Henry left.

Transfer night wasn't stressful since we knew nothing major was going to happen. We knew that Elder Henry was going home to Utah. Our mission president could take this as an opportunity to reboot the area with a double transfer, but that didn't seem very likely.

Elder Hafoka replaced Elder Henry. He came from Sudbury. I had never worked with anyone who had spent time in the northern part of our mission, which I imagined to be like the tundra even though it wasn't any further north than my hometown. "I've met him once or twice," Elder Henry said. "We served in the same zone for a while. He always seemed like a really good dude. You'll like him."

Elder Hafoka was from California, but his roots were firmly planted in Samoa. He had that word tattooed on his forearm. But for a Samoan, at least the Samoans I'd seen in the NFL and the WWE, Elder Hafoka was a runt. He was shorter than I was, generally smaller, too, though much more fit. He had pectoral muscles.

But Elder Henry had been right. Almost immediately, I loved Elder Hafoka with the quiet fervour of a younger brother.

The tattoo—tattoos, actually; he had another one on his other arm, closer to the shoulder, that I never really got to see, since it was under his garments—gave Elder Hafoka a frisson of mystery. They weren't the kind of traditional tattoos you sometimes saw covering the arms and backs of New Zealanders. Tattoos like that would be culturally explainable. These were stick-and-poke ones, the kind of tattoos you gave yourself in prison with a needle, some string, and ink from a Bic pen.

The current prophet, President Hinckley, hadn't distinguished between DIY and machine-powered tattoos when he counselled against getting any. The prophet—many prophets, in fact—had admonished us to avoid getting tattoos. Our bodies were temples, and tattoos were like vandalism. But it couldn't have been that serious because you could have a tattoo and still be a temple-worthy member, in good standing in the Church.

I couldn't picture Elder Hafoka willfully disobeying the prophet. And yet the proof that he had was forever on his skin. What other bad things had pre-mission Elder Hafoka gotten up to? He wasn't the only missionary that had a tattoo. I just had a hard time imagining Elder Hafoka ever going through a rebellious phase. He was soft-spoken, but charming. Like how I imagined the Saviour was.

He told me that he had repented of his tattoo. He regretted doing it, confessed it, and forsook it. But that's all he would say about it, not that I was about to pry. Elder Hafoka was paying for the tattoo, though. He tried to get it removed with lasers before coming on his mission, but because he had given it to himself, the ink was distributed inconsistently. In some places it was close enough to the skin's surface for the lasers to blast it away, but in others he had poked the ink out of reach. Samoa wasn't going anywhere. That meant that, even in the summer, which seemed particularly sweaty in Kitchener, Elder Hafoka couldn't roll up his sleeves.

In the spring of 2003, President Sybrowsky gave the word that missionaries were allowed to forgo their suit jackets while working, except on Sundays (obviously). Starting after the May long weekend, instead of a league of mid-twentieth-century door-to-door salesmen, we looked like an army of science teachers in our ties and short-sleeved shirts, missionary handbooks tucked into our breast pockets like the protectors worn by Hollywood nerds.

Elder Hafoka aside, I wondered about tattoos. My questions were inconsequential, doctrinally speaking, so there was no one to ask, but I was curious: Elder Henry and I once knocked on the door of a big, messy, shopping-mall-Santa-Claus of a man. Based exclusively on his appearance, I assumed that he was, or had been, a biker. His white beard was yellowed from tobacco and his body was simultaneously solid and soft. An essential part of his aesthetic were the tattoos that covered his tree-trunk arms. In the same way that your brain picks out the sound of your name when someone says it in a noisy, crowded room, I saw that naked, wanton women were crawling up and down his arms. They all posed independently from the others, but their organization demonstrated forethought.

The woman on his forearm was leaning back against an invisible chair. She was wearing a dress, or had been before being immortalized in tattoo ink, and now it was pulled down, releasing her impressive breasts, and pulled up, to give the world a peek at what was between her legs. Beside her head was a woman on her hands and knees, smiling over her shoulder lasciviously.

Would it have been wonderful had the man with the tattoos accepted the gospel? Obviously. We invite all to come unto

Christ and be perfected in Him.* But it also might have raised some issues. No baptismal waters would wash off the pornography etched onto his skin. It wouldn't be that bad on a day-to-day basis; he could just wear long-sleeved shirts. But what about when he went to the temple? I imagined he wouldn't be allowed to bring that smut into the Lord's house, whether it was on his arms or not. He could maybe cover them up with bandages, but it would still mean bringing filth into one of God's most perfect places on earth.

But at the same time, not allowing that man into the temple just because of something he did to his body when he was younger seemed to limit God's capacity to forgive. Compared to the doctrinal dilemma that the man with the tattoos represented, Elder Hafoka's tattoos were nothing.

"You know what he could do?" Elder Hafoka asked after I told him the story of the man with the dirty tattoos. His tone was such that I didn't know if I was expected to answer him. He paused a little longer. "He could tattoo some clothes on them."

"Just make them a bunch of sister missionaries," I said.

"They're just praying . . ." he said.

"Man, I should have thought of that."

We parked around the corner from Enid's village of townhomes. We didn't have an appointment, but I was eager to have Elder Hafoka pick up where Elder Henry had left off. Parking in front of her house would be presumptuous. Better to keep it casual—*we were just in the neighbourhood!*

I recognized that Enid had been avoiding us. Despite our innocent appearance, missionaries were none of us too naive

---

* Moroni 10:32.

not to understand the behaviour of someone who didn't care to see us. But until we were explicitly told to stop dropping by, we would give people as many chances as possible.

"What's this woman's story again? She was anti-ed bad?" Elder Hafoka asked.

"Pretty much. By her sister," I said.

"And the main concern was Black people and the priesthood?"

"Yeah. So, uh, I'm not suggesting you lie, or, like, pretend to be Black. But maybe don't bring up your ethnic background."

"I see," Elder Hafoka said. He nodded his head solemnly—or ironically. I couldn't tell. "I got you, Elder Hudson." He offered to say the prayer before we got out of the car.

Elder Hafoka could have been a spokesperson for ethnic ambiguity. Like the answer to a prayer, he could be interpreted in many different ways. He had cream-in-coffee skin, and while his black hair was more wavy than curly, he kept it cut so short it didn't matter. It's not that he didn't look like he was Samoan, it's that he also looked Cuban or Dominican, or biracial. And if the Lord didn't want us to take advantage of that, then why have us meet Enid right before transferring him in to be zone leader? If she happened to confuse a Samoan for an African American, that wasn't our fault. Some amount of guile was acceptable in missionary work, right?

It's not that the Lord condoned lying, exactly. And anyway, there's lying and then there's not correcting an assumption. They weren't the same thing.

Enid seemed a little flustered as she answered the door, but she still smiled when she recognized who we were. "I don't really have much time today, boys." She swung the door open and waved us inside.

"That's okay. I know we didn't have an appointment. I was just showing my new companion around and since we were in the area, I figured I'd bring him by. This is Elder Hafoka."

"Oh, what happened to Elder Henry?"

"He went home. Can you believe it? His two years were up," I said. Naturally, we had told her this was going to happen the last time we saw her, but I forgave her for forgetting.

"And where was home for him again? I know you've told me."

"Utah," I said.

"Ah yes, the motherland. Is that where you're from, Elder Hafoka?" She pronounced it HAY-foka.

"I'm from California," he said.

She leaned against the wall across from a closet bursting with winter coats and clothes, Clintonian pantsuits, and pastel sweaters from Northern Reflections. It was also bleeding old shoeboxes. There were more boxes scattered along the hallway behind her. "And are there a lot of Mormons where you grew up?"

"There's a bit. More than there are here in Kitchener, but nothing like Utah."

"What's with the boxes?" I asked.

"Oh, that's right. I'm moving," she said. I knew that she had lost her job semi-recently—it was but one of the reasons she seemed to be a golden investigator—though I wouldn't have been able to tell you what that job had been.

"Where are you headed?" I asked, sounding entirely casual and not at all disappointed that our only investigator was disappearing.

"I'll be staying with my sister in Guelph for a little while, until I figure some things out."

"They have missionaries in Guelph," I offered. "Elder Hafoka, do you know who's serving in Guelph these days?"

"Yeah, right. As if my sister would be okay with that," she said.

"Your sister isn't very religious?" Elder Hafoka asked.

"Well, we were raised Lutheran, so—" Enid said, as if that would explain it all. Elder Hafoka neither smiled nor nodded. It was as if he were waiting for her to say more. And so she did. "And, well, like I was telling Elder Hudson and Elder Henry the last time they were here, she, uh, pointed out some things about Mormonism that I hadn't known."

It was like she couldn't find the outrage in front of Elder Hafoka. What did she know about being Black and in the Church? How could she, a white lady, reject the gospel because of how it treated Black people when there was a Black person in her home who wasn't offended by it at all? Who was her sister defending? This is what I imagined she was thinking.

"Oh?" Elder Hafoka said.

"When Elder Hudson and Elder Henry began stopping by, I hadn't been aware that the Mormon Church, well, that it had a history of how it treated Black people."

"Okay." Elder Hafoka finally nodded his head. Enid looked relieved. She waited for Elder Hafoka to go on, but he didn't. She looked less relieved.

"Which I'm sure you knew . . . know about. I'm not telling you anything you don't know," Enid said, tossing in a chuckle at the end. Elder Hafoka smiled and nodded now.

"Probably not," he said.

"And it doesn't bother you?" she asked. "I mean, I guess, obviously it doesn't. Or else you wouldn't be here."

"I've never once felt discriminated against in the Church," he said. "And though no one in the Church is perfect—except for maybe Elder Hudson—I've never felt anyone be racist toward me, personally. You know, for me, what it all came down to was whether I received an answer to my prayers. Growing up, I didn't really go to church. But as I got older, I started thinking about going on a mission. I realized I had to find out if it was all true. And so what I did was pray. I know it's not a very dramatic story, but one day I decided I needed to know and so I really prayed, as sincerely as I could. And I know I received an answer that day. I felt the Spirit confirm to me that this Church was true. And once I knew I had been answered, I guess I kind of refused to listen to doubts I might have."

"Well, that's interesting I suppose," Enid said.

"It looks like you're pretty swamped right now. I don't know about you, but I hate moving," Elder Hafoka said. "We'll let you get back to it. But I wondered if we could pray with you before we left?"

"Of course."

"Elder Hudson, would you mind saying a prayer for us?"

"Of course," I said. This was likely the last time we'd see Enid. She had to feel the Spirit so strongly in this prayer that she wouldn't be able to wait until she was settled in Guelph before looking up the missionaries and inviting them over. What a gift to the Guelph elders.

I thanked Heavenly Father for letting us find and get to know Enid, and thanked Him for Enid's spirit and humility. Her willingness to have us over to hear Heavenly Father's message. Then I asked Him to please help Enid remember the feelings that she had felt when we spoke before, and asked Him to please watch over and protect her as she moved. But more importantly, I asked Him to bless her with the spirit of comfort and peace during this difficult time. And I asked Heavenly Father to help Enid know how much she was loved. "In the name of Jesus Christ, amen."

"And hey," I said after opening my eyes and unfolding my arms, "we'd love to help you move. It's one of our favourite things to do."

"Really? Why?" she asked.

"We just get asked to do it a lot. I think I've probably helped someone move at least once a month since I've been out."

Elder Hafoka just nodded.

"I think that went well," Elder Hafoka said once we were back in the car. "We planted a very healthy seed."

"Yeah," I said. "Planting seeds."

That night I came into our room to go to bed. *Missionaries are to sleep in the same bedroom, but not the same bed.* If I had to pick a favourite line from the missionary handbook, that was it. I liked it because it was clearly a rule that was implemented in reaction to something, and the direction seemed obvious. It said more than it meant to.

Elder Hafoka was already saying his nightly personal prayer. His head was resting on his hands, which rested on the bed in the classic nighttime prayer position. I knelt down by my bed on the other side of the small room to begin my prayers.

It wasn't a contest, obviously. It's not as though long prayers were necessarily a sign of righteousness. No one was timing us, including and especially Heavenly Father, who, it must be remembered, already knew the contents of my heart. Even before I knelt down, Heavenly Father knew what I was going to say. Moreover, He knew not only what I was going to say, but what I wasn't saying, knew when I was trying to gloss over some less-than-perfect behaviour or put some righteous spin on the events of the day. Prayer was like a child covered in felt marker, coming to their parent to confess.

I couldn't hear what Elder Hafoka was saying in his prayer. I could guess the main subject matter, though. He was probably trying to exercise enough faith for the both of us. But I didn't really understand how that translated into a longer prayer. Did coming up with different ways of asking for the same thing show faith? How did people like Elder Hafoka think of all that much to say?

The truth was that praying next to another person was like urinating next to someone in a public bathroom. It mattered when you started and it mattered when you stopped. There was meaning in that, even if no one could articulate it exactly. People noticed. It seemed that righteous people had more to talk about with their Heavenly Father. Prayer duration was probably indicative of the quality of one's relationship with God.

I said a typical prayer. It was more personal and purposeful than the nightly prayers I said back home as a child, but it didn't change much from day to day. I added and removed names depending on the day's events, but since I wanted the same thing every day—mercy (on His part), patience (on mine), someone to baptize, and for everyone at home in Alberta to be alright—every day my personal prayers had a similar run time. I climbed into bed, conscious that Elder Hafoka was still on his knees. I didn't hear him crawl into his bed before I drifted off to sleep.

A few hours later, I woke up from a nightmare. In it, I was done my mission. I was back home in Calgary, preparing my homecoming talk. And I was struggling because I didn't have any miraculous stories to share. Why had my mission been so short? Why was I already home, with only three areas to report on? How did I skip the last year of my mission? I hadn't become the man I had expected to become, neither a baptizing missionary nor an assistant. And there was no going back on a mission. No do-over.

It didn't take long upon waking to realize that it had been a dream: I was still barely a year in the field, and still had a whole year left to go. I still had time to become a great missionary. In the dark of our room, I felt like Scrooge on Christmas morning. The time I had left was a gift, one I wouldn't take for granted. I said a quick prayer to make it official, and to thank Him for a view into my wasted possible future.

I looked over at Elder Hafoka's bed. He was still in the same position, on his knees, head resting against his mattress. I checked my small alarm clock. It was three in the morning. I was briefly in awe that Elder Hafoka had been petitioning the Lord for more than four hours. Then I heard his slow, childlike breath in and out. He was fully and completely asleep. I doubted even he knew when it happened.

Show me a missionary who has never fallen asleep during a prayer and I'll show you a missionary who doesn't either work or pray hard enough.

I pictured Heavenly Father tapping an angel on the shoulder, bemused. He asked them if they could keep an eye on this elder here, just until he woke up. Our Father in Heaven listens to each one of our prayers, but He's not about to wait on hold if we doze off.

And then it came to pass that we were given a third companion. We were a threesome. Or rather, we were in a threesome. We weren't *having* a threesome. We knew the sexual connotation of the word threesome. But that definition didn't seem real. We were a threesome because, with the addition of Elder Randall, there were three of us. The benefit of a threesome was that Elder Hafoka could travel the zone shadowing other companionships more easily in his role as zone leader. He wouldn't need to worry about our area at all, since Elder Randall and I would be there. Instead, he could focus on all the other companionships in the Kitchener zone. But despite the strategic advantage of having a third companion, we knew that wasn't why Elder Randall had been sent to us.

We were babysitting. Elder Randall suffered from an ill-defined condition that seemed sometimes like IBS and other times like chronic fatigue syndrome. It was unpredictable, but never affected him on preparation day. He was too sick to work most days, so we didn't leave the apartment. The condition made Elder Randall feel put upon and misunderstood. This manifested as negativity, which felt like the opposite of faith. That didn't help the work.

The summer of 2003 was filled with the electric whine of cicadas waking up and looking for sex. The hum started low, before rising in crescendo like an engine before switching gears. It sounded nearby and faraway at the same time. I imagined that this sound was the result of the heat affecting electrical lines—something to do with expanding and contracting. I had no reason to think this. It was just the only explanation I could come up with since I didn't know cicadas existed.

I had never sweated so persistently as I did that July. Growing up on the Prairies I'd lived through hot days, but I'd never experienced that kind of Ontario humidity. Every day the city was like a bathroom after a shower. Wearing a white button-up shirt and dress pants didn't help—God bless Elder Hafoka and his long sleeves—but miraculously most of the sweat leaked from my head and neck. Thanks in no small part to my garments, I rarely sweated through a shirt. I used a folded pass-along card as a squeegee for my forehead.* Unfolded, it didn't have the structural integrity to push the sweat away properly.

As we were making our way to a new neighbourhood to tract, Elder Randall warned me of their approach, but still I looked. He was very good at pointing out "fiery darts," so it was his job to let us know when any were nearby so that we could avoid looking at them. No one asked him to do this service.

I guessed these girls were fifteen years old, though they might also have been twelve. How old did teenagers look these days? They were either skipping class or walking home from school—how long was school these days?—since they were all dressed in variations of the same uniform. Most wore unflattering slacks and navy polos meant to curb bullying. But two were wearing skirts, which they had rolled up at the waist to make them shorter. They were wearing spaghetti-strap tank tops that showed their midriffs and their belts of rolled-up skirt.

The term fiery dart was from the New Testament. Paul is encouraging the Ephesians to put on the whole armour of God. After describing various pieces of armour—the breastplate of righteousness, shoes made from the preparation of the gospel of peace—he commands, "Above all, taking the shield of faith, wherewith ye shall be able to quench all the fiery darts of the wicked."** The lesson: it's only through faith that one can withstand temptation. I didn't know how sturdy Elder Randall's shield was.

* Pass-along cards are small trading card–sized tracts that offer a free copy of the Book of Mormon or *Finding Faith in Christ*, or the answers to life's questions, which could be found on the Church's website.

** Ephesians 6:13–17.

I wasn't about to teach this group. Not that they didn't deserve to hear the gospel, but I didn't think I was the appropriate messenger. Elder Randall was unpredictable. He might stop to have fun with them, chat them up, feel a little bit like a celebrity, as though to prove he could recognize and point out a fiery dart, but was impervious to their menace. He said that treating girls like they were a temptation to be avoided, like they were pornography come to life, only made them more tempting.

The girls settled into a clump on a small rise of grass at the outskirts of a schoolyard. Unless we changed course, we were going to walk right in front of them.

For me, it was about the image you presented as a missionary. Did it look right, two twenty-year-olds talking to a group of young girls? Or did it seem creepy? Inappropriate. *Avoid even the appearance of evil.*

"Matthew 9:12–13," Elder Randall whispered to me.* I didn't know the reference off the top of my head.

"Bingo," I said.

"Are you guys Jehovahs?" one of the girls yelled when we were still a ways off. "Hey, are you Jehovahs?" The other girls giggled at their friend's audacity.

"Did you know there was some survey done on *Oprah* or something that said the second most sexy uniforms are Mormon missionaries, according to women?" Elder Randall said to me.

"What was number one?" I asked, then regretted encouraging him. We were almost in front of the girls.

"Mailmen," Elder Randall said. "Missionaries were second though."

---

* "But when Jesus heard that, he said unto them, They that be whole need not a physician, but they that are sick . . . For I am not come to call the righteous, but sinners to repentance."

"Mailmen and Mormon missionaries? Not like a Marine?" I said. "That's a lot of Ms."

"Elder, girls think we're hot. It's because they want to corrupt us," he said.

Elder Randall might have had a point there, but I didn't acknowledge it. We were within earshot of the girls.

"Are you Jehovahs?" the same girl asked, not yelling anymore. One of the girls in a skirt told her to shut up. Two of the girls were whispering to each other as a way of hiding their embarrassment. The other fiery dart had her back to us, but was looking up at us like she didn't know how to turn around, so she was tilting her head straight up, seeing us upside down. She waited like that for an answer. I didn't like that Elder Randall stood closest to her. She was wearing a pushup bra that was working very hard without much material. "What, I'm just asking a question. They like when people ask them questions," the first girl said.

"You mean, are we Jehovah's Witnesses? Uh, no, we're not," Elder Randall said. "Jehovah's Witnesses don't dress so fly. They're usually old and only go out on Saturdays."

The girls all laughed. He continued, "But what's funny is Jehovah is actually another name for God. So, you were basically asking us if we were gods."

"And you were like YES!" the girl said. She was wearing slacks and a baggy polo with her school insignia on it.

"No, but we're sharing a true message about God, actually," I said. No reason not to get a testimony or two in while we were there.

"I'm Christian," one of the girls pretending not to listen said.

"Me too," said her friend.

"That's cool. So are we," I said. I wondered: if Elder Hafoka were here, would he say anything to this gaggle of girls, or would he keep his mouth shut and quietly disapprove? That was what Elder Hafoka did when Elder Randall spoke of home, or the darts that he left burning in previous wards he had served in. Elder Hafoka tried to memorize a scripture every day and when Elder Randall got unfocused, he'd pull out the cue card upon which was written that day's scripture and start repeating it. I wanted to ignore Elder Randall, too, but my inherent need to make others feel comfortable made that very difficult. I would try to show disinterest—avoid eye contact, keep my enthusiasm low, answer only after a pause—while still acknowledging that something had been said. Elder Hafoka might talk to these girls if he were here. But he'd stand a lot further away than Elder Randall was.

"So, what are you guys?" one of the Christians asked.

"They're Mormons, right?" a girl said.

I pointed my finger at her like a game show host. "Ding ding ding!"

"Why're you guys different?" the other Christian said.

"You guys don't believe in drinking and smoking, right?" the girl who knew we were Mormon said.

"That's true. But the question is *why* don't we drink or smoke, or do drugs, or . . ." Elder Randall trailed off.

"Murder people," I added.

"Or murder people—good point, Elder Hudson."

"Why are you both called Elder?" the girl looking up at Elder Randall said, finally turning around to face him.

"It's a title. Like captain or officer."

"Is it your name?" a girl said.

"He just said it was a title, dumbass," the first Christian said.

"I didn't hear. Because I was going to be, like, what are the chances that two guys would both have the name Elder?" This was the first fiery dart.

"Elder Randall, why don't we drink or smoke or do drugs?" I said.

"Good question, Elder Hudson. We don't drink because God told us not to. He told us through a prophet. Do you know what a prophet is?"

"It's the newspaper in *Harry Potter*," one of the girls who had been ignoring us said, giggling.

"A prophet is someone who talks with God and lets everyone know what He said. So, like if you imagine your principal to be God, then your teacher would be like a prophet. Your principal doesn't speak to every student individually, he talks to your teacher, and your teacher tells you," Elder Randall said.

"So you guys are prophets?"

"No, but God told a prophet that drinking, smoking, doing drugs, and all that fun stuff was against His rules. And it's cool to follow God's rules," Elder Randall said. This made the girls laugh.

"Mackenzie isn't cool then," said one of the girls to another; I didn't know which one.

"Shut the fuck up," said the one apparently called Mackenzie. "As if you guys are cool either." She made a drinking motion with her hand as a bottle and her thumb as a spout.

"Jesus drank wine," said the girl nearest to Mackenzie, which prompted a lot of agreement and head-nodding from the rest of the group.

"But that was mostly grape juice. It was barely fermented," Elder Randall said.

I didn't trust that explanation of Christ's drinking. Those days, I liked to keep the explanation for the Word of Wisdom simple: obedience. Heavenly Father told Joseph Smith no drinking, so there's no drinking. But that was a hard concept to teach to teenagers.

"He wouldn't drink it if He were around today though," I said. We could have an unfocused Q&A with these girls for the rest of the afternoon. We had nowhere else to be, but there were certainly more productive ways we could be using our time. "If you're ever interested in learning more, here . . ." I gave Mackenzie a pass-along card with a picture of the Salt Lake Temple, shining at night, on one side, and www.mormon.org on the other.

"I want one, I want one!" the other girls joined in. Elder Randall passed each one their own card.

"Why are you guys all wearing those bracelets?" Elder Randall said. They all had a stack of rubber bracelets in different colours around each wrist. These weren't the first girls I had seen wearing them. "Are you in a gang?"

Giggles. A chorus of "no"s.

"Each colour is, uh, each colour represents something. I'll just say that," Mackenzie said. The girls around her giggled.

"What do they represent?" Elder Randall asked.

"Well," one of the Christian girls started, "each colour is like a different sex thing. I mean, that's technically what they mean, but I just wear them because I like how they look."

Everyone seemed to agree with this.

"It's supposed to be like what you've done, or like what you're willing to do," Mackenzie said. "So, like, blue is blow job."

More giggles. Mackenzie's face got a shade redder, but she didn't laugh like the rest of her friends, even though she had just acknowledged the existence of oral sex to a couple of older guys.

"I thought blue was doing it underwater?" someone said.

"That's aqua, I'm talking about dark blue. And red is kissing. No, red is French kissing, and pink is kissing. And black is that you've gone all the way."

"Wow," Elder Randall said. We were both looking at all the colours on their wrists. These were some very experienced girls.

"Yeah. Wow," I repeated. The array of colours was staggering. If I tried, I wouldn't be able to think of a corresponding sex act for all of them. What was purple? Or silver?

"But it's not real," Mackenzie said.

"Some people's are. Amanda's are all real."

This set off another round of giggling.

"What grade are you girls in?" Elder Randall asked.

"Nine," they all answered.

As we walked away, Elder Randall seemed annoyed.

"We could have at least taught them a first discussion," he said.

"They were fourteen," I said.

"So what?" said Elder Randall.

"I think it would have been a waste of time," I replied.

"I guess my problem," continued Elder Randall, "is that I thought we were trying to hit our goals. But we haven't yet, so why start now, I guess. Right?"

"We hit our goals," I said. We set goals every month: how many testimonies we'd share, how many investigators we'd bring to church, and how many baptisms we would have. And since we were a zone leader companionship, our goals had to be healthy, whether I fully believed we could hit them or not. At the beginning of each month we'd ask God what our goals should be. We wrote down what we thought His answers were.

"We hit our testimonies goal, but we didn't hit the most important one. How many people did we commit to baptizing this month? Two? How's that going?" Elder Randall asked.

"I know, right?" There was no point arguing with Elder Randall. It was hard to see how we would be able to find, teach, and baptize two people in three weeks. They would need to go to church at least once, too. I told myself that miracles could and do happen, but I lacked faith.

"I just think it's funny that we basically stop believing in free agency when we do our monthly planning. 'This is how many people we'll baptize, whether they like it or not.'"

"Yeah. You just got to do all you can, I guess. Faith," I said.

"And that's what I'm saying. That's why we should have taught those young women a discussion," Elder Randall said.

"They were fourteen."

"It's funny when you look through Elder Strafford's photos," he went on. "The man baptized, but it's like page after page of Elder Strafford and a fiery dart in white, Elder Strafford and a fiery dart in a white jumpsuit, Elder Strafford and, what's this, another fiery dart standing next to him in a white jumpsuit. He baptized a lot of girls."

Everyone's mission photo albums were fair game for other missionaries. And everyone had at least one documenting their life on their mission. Usually they had one of people from home, too, but those weren't as interesting. If a missionary was in your apartment, sitting at your desk, it was pretty normal for them to flip through your photos.

"You think some of them maybe had a crush on him?" I asked. Elder Strafford was a handsome man.

"Oh, most definitely. It's just funny that he's called to be an assistant because of his numbers, but no one is looking at what those numbers mean. He can flirt to convert, but that's not exactly something you can teach."

"You're a pretty good-looking guy," I said. "You ever flirt to convert?"

"If any of the girls I've baptized had a crush on me, it wasn't because I was flirting. I can't help who people like and don't like," he said.

"Does President"—as we referred to President Sybrowsky—"really only call the highest-baptizing missionaries to be assistants?" I asked.

"Pretty much. You better start baptizing, son. You're not going to make it."

"Whoever said I wanted to be an assistant?" I asked.

"Whatever you say," he said.

I had been doing well—not spectacularly, but I had baptized the equivalent of one person every other month. Three people in Sarnia, another three in Barrie, four if I counted the young woman Elder Fields baptized after I had been transferred to Kitchener. To baptize someone monthly was the goal for every missionary. It shouldn't have been impossible to find twenty-four people to teach and baptize in two years. But my progress stopped when I came to Kitchener. I couldn't blame Elder Randall for that.

We did end up having one baptism. It felt like it shouldn't have counted, but of course it did. Probably a result of Elder Hafoka's faith.

Harris was a fifteen-year-old boy contending with puberty. He had the prickly defensiveness of the perpetually bullied. He wore glasses and he needed a haircut, which made his head look exceptionally large. He had been through the discussions a year or two earlier, with a couple of missionaries from the zone who had gone on to be assistants. Harris had wanted them to baptize him, but back then his stepfather wouldn't give him permission. Something had changed with the stepfather, though; I wasn't quite clear on the details. Either way, stepdad was momentarily out of the picture, and so the kid wanted to be baptized as quickly as possible. Some kids rebel with a tattoo, a piercing, a particularly insufferable haircut. This kid wanted to be baptized.

A baptism done in rebellion was still a checkmark on the celestial to-do list. Everyone needed to be baptized. Maybe Harris's desire to be baptized at that moment wasn't a hunger for righteousness, but presumably that had inspired his initial request.

In one day we ran through all six discussions with him. Harris remembered enough to understand the whys and whats and hows of his decision. And then he had his baptismal interview with our district leader. The questions in a baptismal interview: do you believe in Heavenly Father, His Son Jesus Christ, and the Holy Ghost? That Joseph Smith was a prophet? That the current president of the Church of Jesus Christ of Latter-day Saints, Gordon B. Hinckley, was also a prophet? Were they willing to live the law of chastity and the Word of Wisdom, and pay tithing, meaning ten percent of their income, to the Church? Had they ever had, or helped someone else have, an abortion? Had they ever been in a homosexual relationship? Answering in the affirmative to either of those last questions would put a pause on your baptism, until President Sybrowsky could perform his own more in-depth interview.

To my secret surprise, Harris passed. Not that I thought he'd paid for an abortion while in middle school or anything. I was just always surprised when people remembered what missionaries taught them. We were so steeped in the gospel that I worried we sometimes forgot our audience and spoke in our own language.

The way I looked at it was that Elder Randall, Elder Hafoka, and I had harvested what other missionaries had planted a year or two ago and cultivated and watered and fed. It meant our zone got one soul closer to hitting our monthly goal.

The fall came and so did transfer night. We were all pretty sure I would be leaving Kitchener and that Elder Randall would get transferred back to the Brampton zone so he could be closer to President Sybrowsky. We also thought Elder Hafoka would stay and finish his mission in Kitchener.

Of course, this was all conjecture. I had received no revelation concerning my own transfer. But I had been in Kitchener for three transfers, which was how long I had been in Sarnia and Barrie when I was transferred out.

Elder Randall changed into sweatpants after he got his call from the assistants. He sat on the rust-coloured couch by the window and watched Elder Hafoka and I finish making a battle plan for the next day. He was still wearing his white shirt and name tag, but no tie. He was listening to something on a Discman.

"Hey, Elder, want to join us for planning?" Elder Hafoka asked, even though there wasn't anything left to plan. Because of transfers, the next day would be preparation day. We'd do the regular preparation day things: laundry, letters home, grocery shopping. Then we'd probably meet up with other elders to play soccer or something at the church. Sports always perked Elder Randall up.

"I'm good, thanks. I'm just here to watch the show," he said, and put his headphones back on. "So, you still think you'll be getting a call?"

I looked at the clock on the wall above the phone. It was past ten. I understood that Elder Randall wasn't really asking if I thought I was going to get a call from the president. He was asking if I thought I deserved a call from the president.

"I don't know. Who knows?" I said. I hadn't even considered the possibility that I'd stay in Kitchener. "Did Elder McIntyre tell you anything?"

"Naw. He just told me I'm off to Brampton." Elder Randall spoke louder than he needed to. "I don't know, Hudson, it's getting kind of late. What's going to happen if you stay in Kitchener?"

"Then I stay in Kitchener," I said.

"Why not keep the winning streak going, right?" Elder Randall said.

"Exactly."

"It's too bad you already got the one freebie. How many times you think that can happen in one area?"

"I know, right?" I said.

The phone rang.

Elder Hafoka was closest. "You've reached the missionaries for the Church of Jesus Christ of Latter-day Saints. This is Elder Hafoka . . . Hello, President . . . Really good. He's been doing really good . . . That's true."

Elder Randall whisper-shouted that he bet Elder Hafoka was being called as an assistant.

"Thank you, President," Elder Hafoka said. Then he looked at me, finally. "He's right here . . . We love you, too. Please give Sister Sybrowsky our love as well . . . Okay."

He handed me the phone.

"This is Elder Hudson," I said.

"Elder Hudson, and how are you?" Mostly President Sybrowsky didn't actually sound much like the nerdy voice we all gave him. But it was closer to that voice when he made small talk.

"I'm doing well, President. Busy night?"

"It hasn't been too bad. We're getting to the last of the calls now," he said. "Elder Hudson, you are going to London. The London zone lost their zone leader this transfer, so you'll be going to London to do that. Will you go and baptize in London, Elder Hudson?"

"Yes, President," I said. "Are you sure you trust me to do that?"

"Well, the Lord trusts you. I'm just being obedient," he said. Then he told me that he and Sister Sybrowsky loved me and told me to be good and then he said goodbye.

"Well?" Elder Hafoka asked. Elder Randall had taken off his headphones. He was leaning on his knees, adorably cradling his head in his palms, like this was a slumber party and it was my turn to dish.

"I'm getting transferred to London. I'm going to be zone leader." I tried not to smile. A smile might make it look like I was bragging. Any look other than stoic acceptance could be seen as prideful. I nodded my head in a way that was meant to demonstrate stunned humility. "Crazy," I said.

Elder Randall sat up, suddenly less interested in my immediate future. "Look at Mr. Humble over there. He's doing the math in his head, trying to figure out when he'll be an assistant. Trying so hard to play it cool."

"You've been out for a year, right?" Elder Hafoka asked. I nodded. "That is pretty quick to be called as a zone leader."

"Yeah. Not the youngest, though. Elder Simonson must be being called as an assistant. We came out together," I said.

"But Elder Simonson is a baptizing missionary. He's like Michael Jordan going into baseball because he did all he could do in basketball. And that means you're getting traded to the Chicago Bulls. Good luck following that," Elder Randall said. I knew Elder Simonson from the MTC. I wasn't surprised that he had become a baptizing machine. He didn't know all the answers in the MTC, but he seemed very focused on learning. Then he was trained by Elder McIntyre, who was a living legend in the mission.

"The London zone" was all Elder Hafoka said.

"How are you feeling, though?" Elder Randall asked. "Because I'd be freaking out if I were you. London is like the most important zone, aside from Brampton. Like, London zone has to baptize. That's going to be so fun for you. It's not like President won't notice when the baptisms suddenly fall off."

I nodded my head. The Brampton, London, and Hamilton zones were the biggest in the mission. They had the most missionaries, and the most members. They needed to be drivers of baptisms. Those zones were like the A league. The rest of the zones in the mission were squarely in the B league.

The nice thing about Elder Randall being mean was that it was uncomplicated. His motivation was never secret. He was bitter about everything, all the time. He had become the kind of missionary who was suspicious of mission leadership—the rebel truth-teller who alone was clear-eyed enough to see the shades of hypocrisy all the assistants and zone leaders, except maybe Elder Hafoka, swam in. But like most eager missionaries—and I was sure there had been a time when Elder Randall was eager—he had probably had dreams of leadership when he was young. He was acting out of jealousy; his opinion was skewed by envy. I knew that, but that didn't mean his opinions were necessarily wrong.

I knew it wasn't Elder Hafoka's style to get involved when Elder Randall was being controversial. Elder Hafoka let his silence serve as the rebuke. But now his silence felt like agreement. I imagined that Elder Hafoka shared Elder Randall's skepticism, but was too kind to say anything.

"It's just funny, because how are you going to teach other missionaries to baptize when you don't know how to do it?" Elder Randall said.

"Totally," I said. Then I walked to the bathroom to start my nightly soak in cold water. We didn't have air conditioning in the apartment, and my bath routine helped me cool down before bed. I stayed in the bath until I figured my companions had fallen asleep. I didn't want to pray in the room because I didn't want to be heard. I got out of the bath and, wearing only my garments, walked quietly to the living room. I knelt against the couch. Mostly I prayed to know why I was being called as a zone leader now. If this had happened directly after Barrie, maybe I would have felt more capable, but I had just worked through nearly five months of nothing in Kitchener. And despite my failure, I apologized to Heavenly Father in my prayer for my vanity and pride, because obviously I had wanted leadership positions, and that was wrong of me. "I know that he granted unto men according to their desire," Alma wrote in the Book of Mormon, "whether it be unto death or unto life."* That's the Lord basically saying be careful what you wish for.

I felt rebuked and low. I knew it was impossible for me to have tricked the Lord, or President Sybrowsky for that matter, but I still felt dishonest. I prayed for forgiveness and understanding.

Heavenly Father answered my prayer when two thoughts came to me. The first: I remembered the scripture I had been reading in church that past Sunday. It was from Joshua, in the Old Testament: "And the Lord said unto Joshua, 'This day will I begin to magnify thee in the sight of all Israel, that they may know that as I was with Moses, so I will be with thee.'"

I allowed myself to marvel at the Lord's timing. Unbeknownst to me, He had led me to that scripture in preparation for this moment. He knew that I was about to be called as a zone leader, and knew that I'd be following Elder Simonson, and He knew I'd need this scripture at the ready.

The second thought was about when I got the part of Tevye in *Fiddler on the Roof* back in high school. There had been a few other young men in the running for the part, and most people assumed Daryl would get it. He was a singer, whereas I was an actor who sometimes had to sing. And though he was a year younger than I was, he was tall and could therefore pass for a Russian Jewish patriarch. Well, a patriarch anyway. Both of us looked about as Jewish as a Connecticut yacht club. For the whole time I had the role, I felt like I was being watched

* Alma 29:4.

by the rest of the cast, judged. Most of the time I felt like they found my singing lacking. It felt safe to be hard on myself. I couldn't think of a worse situation than to be bad at something you thought you were good at. If I always secretly thought I wasn't very good, then when I found out that was the case I wouldn't be shocked. It would hurt less.

But in the end, I hadn't failed. I might have missed some notes, but I had done well. If Heavenly Father could help me sing a few Broadway hits, of course he'd help with something that actually mattered, like inspiring missionaries to baptize in London.

I just needed to have faith.

In London, I tried to remember that whom the Lord calls, He qualifies. That was the maxim. And it was true, only I also thought about how being qualified doesn't immediately translate into success. Being called was like getting accepted to a university. Attendance alone didn't get you a degree.

In the end, Elder Randall was probably right. After three transfers, just under five months, and only two baptisms in London, it felt like a demotion when I was transferred to Niagara Falls. After all, the London zone had struggled while I was its leader, never reaching the numbers of baptisms that it had under my predecessors. I had been called up to the A league and I had flamed out. I knew whoever was coming in after me would probably baptize like crazy. That's what happened after I left Kitchener. Elder Hafoka and his new companion, Elder Rigley, didn't seem to have the same difficulty finding, teaching, and baptizing as I had. It made sense to send me off to the farm team. I was still a zone leader, but the Peninsula zone had fewer missionaries than London. It seemed to breed fewer legendary missionaries, too. But I was looking forward to feeling less pressure. The Lord's expectations wouldn't be different, but I'd be on a smaller stage.

The Peninsula zone was comprised of Niagara Falls (my area), St. Catharines (covered by two sets of missionaries, one set of whom were women), Welland (same), Simcoe (one companionship), and Fort Erie (also one companionship). And we had Spanish missionaries who were mostly in St. Catharines, but also went wherever the Spanish-speaking people were.

There was a drawing that was popular among missionaries and those who would one day answer the call. It was a comic of sorts, drawn in the style of a Disney cartoon. It showed two missionaries, one barrel-chested and broad-shouldered, the other small and skinny. Both are smiling and happy, marching in lockstep to spread the gospel. Unbeknownst to them, there is a group of angels in matching white robes hovering around them, each as big and muscle-bound as a professional wrestler. One of the angels is squeezing a little devil angrily. Another is catching a dollop of bird poop that would have otherwise landed on the short skinny elder. One is holding a sheet in front of a pretty maiden so that the elders won't see her. The elders are about to fall into a mysterious hole in the ground, only there are four angelic hands for them to step across. Missionaries are watched over, was the point of the drawing. But that was a very popular way of depicting missionaries: one big and hunky, the other snack-sized.

Up until Niagara Falls, most of my companions were roughly the same size as me. My second companion, Elder Grey, was at least four inches taller than me, but he walked with an unconscious stoop so he didn't make me look too small. When I first got to Kitchener and was paired with Elder Henry, I was the burly one. But my companion in the Falls, Elder Clark, made me look like a pipsqueak. He was a power forward, or he would be when he finished his mission. A college back home in Arizona was saving a spot for him.

Elder Clark had been in Niagara Falls for three months and he was very happy to get a new companion. It wasn't that he hadn't gotten along with my predecessor, Elder Braugher. It's that Elder Braugher had gotten trunky. He was ready to be home. It was a fairly common condition among missionaries in the last month or so of their mission. The fire they had been maintaining in their bellies since the MTC finally goes out. A trunky missionary will still work, can still baptize, but the sense of urgency is gone. That could make working with a trunky elder feel like pedalling a tandem bike alone.

What was worse for Elder Clark was that apparently, in his deep trunkiness, Elder Braugher had developed a little infatuation with a righteous young woman in the ward named Lisa. There had been no serious infraction, but it hadn't been entirely appropriate, either. They talked on the phone at night, and Elder Braugher always came up with a reason to stop by Lisa's home. The courtship, such as it was, had been condoned, if not encouraged, by the girl's parents. It was like their daughter had caught the eye of a celebrity, a captain in Heavenly Father's army who could bring their daughter back to Zion (Utah), where the Church was real.

Early in my time in Niagara, Elder Clark and I were about to have dinner with Lisa's family, the Coxes, and were planning our spiritual thought in the car. "She flew down to visit him last week," Elder Clark said. "I don't know if she's back yet or not.

It's weird to be back here. We used to stop by their house pretty much every night on our way back to the apartment."

"Why?" I asked.

"Because Elder Braugher and Lisa liked each other."

"No, no, I get that. But did you have a pretend reason to stop by so often? Or did everyone just know what was happening?"

"Lisa apparently had a friend she wanted to invite to church or something. So we were helping her with that. But we all knew what was really happening."

"And so, are they going to get married now?"

"I don't know," Elder Clark said, sounding annoyed. "Lisa was thinking of transferring to a school in Utah or something. I think that's the excuse she used to make the trip. Even though everyone knows it's to see Elder Braugher."

When we got inside, Sister Cox was excited to show Elder Clark the pictures her daughter had emailed from Utah. There was Elder Braugher, his arm around Lisa, in front of Temple Square. There they were, embracing and looking at the camera as if to say "Can you believe what we're doing?" Elder Clark seemed to take the photos personally, like they were tormenting him. The last picture in the email was of the two of them kissing. It was an exaggerated, showy kiss, but their lips were definitely touching. Elder Clark worked hard to smile, but it was the sportsmanlike smile of someone trying hard to show they are in on a joke that's at their expense.

I didn't recognize Elder Braugher. I didn't think I had ever heard his name before. He had obviously been at zone councils, the once-per-transfer meetings in Brampton that President Sybrowsky held with just the zone leaders, but he hadn't made an impression on me, I guess. It was a good reminder of how inconsequential the Peninsula zone leader was.

"So they're dating now?" Elder Clark asked. "I mean, officially."

"They weren't dating when he was here," Sister Cox clarified, looking at me. I nodded. "But he did finally apologize for the oats story, apparently."

"The oats story?" I wasn't familiar.

"It was stupid," Elder Clark said.

"It was offensive, is what it was," Sister Cox said, again looking at me.

"Fair enough," I said.

"It was a story about horses. These horses when they were away from their farm, they would start to eat barley—was it barley or oats?"

"Oats," Elder Clark said.

"Right. Horses are supposed to eat hay. Or something. While the horses were away from their ranch or whatever, they started eating oats, let's say. And even though the oats weren't as good for them as the hay, they got used to them. Then they got hooked. And when they got back to the ranch, they would only eat oats. They should have eaten hay since it was better for them, but they were hooked on oats. Or something."

"Oh, okay," I said, but I didn't get it. I assumed something had been lost in the retelling.

"Elder Braugher said girls at home were the hay, and girls on the mission were the oats."

"Oh, I get it. Gross," I said.

"You've never heard that story, Elder Hudson? Trevor said all missionaries talked about it."

"Trevor is Elder Braugher," Elder Clark said. "Trevor Braugher."

"No, never heard it. I try not to think too much about girls. I still have a long way to go before I need to start worrying about that," I said.

"He apologized when he was here," Elder Clark said.

"Do you have a girlfriend back home in Alberta?" Sister Cox asked. I told her that I didn't.

"So, they are dating?" Elder Clark asked again.

"We'll see," Sister Cox said. She clicked out of her email and put the computer to sleep. "Let's eat. The lasagna has cooled by now."

After dinner and dessert—because heaven forbid members feed missionaries without also giving them dessert—we drove to a neighbourhood where a less-active church member lived and pulled over. Our plan was to tract up and down the street and hopefully run into the member, like it was a miracle.

People like to hear they were the reason for some heavenly intervention.

"You know, I complain about always having to eat dessert at members' houses," I started, "but then on the rare occasion when they don't serve dessert, I'm always a little offended. Like, what, we don't deserve ice cream all of a sudden? You think just because I'm diabetic I don't want some ice cream?" Elder Clark didn't respond to my bit. "You alright, Elder? You want to say a prayer?"

"He's kissing her as much as he wants," Elder Clark said. "They're probably making out right now."

"Who is?"

"*Trevor*," he said, as if first names were something to be ashamed of. "I should have done more stuff before my mission. That's the problem," Elder Clark concluded. He made a noise that was equal parts growl and harumph. Like the Hulk. "Before my mission, I didn't do anything with girls. I never had a girlfriend. I kissed one girl, but after she just wanted to be friends. One girl."

"That's not that crazy," I said. I would have thought that Elder Clark—a good-looking basketball player—would have had a few girlfriends in high school. But you never can tell.

"But if I had done stuff before my mission maybe I wouldn't be so obsessed with girls and stuff now. It's bad. It's freaking bad," he confessed, then seemed to think better of it. "It's not something I should really talk about."

"Fair enough," I said.

"It's like all I can think about. I try to think pure thoughts. I try to sing hymns when bad thoughts pop into my head. But it's useless. Then I see pictures of Elder Braugher and a girl that is all over him. And it's so dumb."

"Maybe you should talk to President, or something," I said. In London, one of the missionaries in the zone had confessed to me that he struggled with masturbation. He was a popular missionary who could do a flawless Homer Simpson impression, but his transgression, his inability to quit self-pleasuring, was dragging him down spiritually and emotionally. But it wasn't really my place to say anything, not to him then, nor to Elder Clark now as he struggled with his own self-control. It wasn't my place to know about someone else's sins, past or present.

"Of course I've talked to President. A bunch of times. I've tried everything. I even bought handcuffs," Elder Clark said.

"Handcuffs?"

"I figured if I handcuffed myself to the bed, I wouldn't be able to do it anymore."

"It didn't work?" I asked. I struggled to picture it. Somehow it seemed like handcuffs would be counterproductive.

"It didn't work. Nothing works," he said.

We sat without saying anything, listening to the heater battle the February cold outside.

"I know it probably won't fix anything, but this kind of reminds me of one of my favourite scriptures," I said. All scriptures were one of my favourites. That's just what you said before having someone read a verse or two. "Mind if we read it, real quick?"

Elder Clark rolled his eyes and nodded.

"It's in 2 Nephi. 2 Nephi 4:17—though the whole chapter is really good. Want to read it? I mean, you probably know it. It's not like it's an obscure scripture or anything. But."

"Sure. 2 Nephi 4:17." He began: "'Nevertheless, notwithstanding the great goodness of the Lord, in showing me his great and marvelous works, my heart exclaimeth: O wretched man that I am! Yea, my heart sorroweth because of my flesh; my soul grieveth because of mine iniquities.'"

"Maybe read until verse 20," I encouraged him.

"'I am encompassed about, because of the temptations and the sins which do so easily beset me. And when I desire to rejoice, my heart groaneth because of my sins; nevertheless, I know in whom I have trusted.' And verse 20?" Elder Clark asked.

"Actually, skip to verse 28," I said.

"'Awake, my soul! No longer droop in sin. Rejoice, O my heart, and give place no more for the enemy of my soul,'" he read.

"I guess I like it because it's relatable. Nephi is like the personification of faith and obedience, and yet even he gets depressed because of his sins. You're in good company is all I'm saying."

"Yeah, thanks," he said.

We tracted the neighbourhood but didn't run into the less-active member. And no one else let us in when we came calling. But enough people came to the door that we were able to hit our daily goal for testimonies. So it wasn't a complete waste.

That night, after all our planning and prayers, I lay in bed and wondered about Elder Clark's confession. When was he doing it? Did he leave the room after I fell asleep, or did he touch himself with me in the room? In the handful (ha!) of times I had fallen prey to that particular sin before my mission, masturbation had been the salt to pornography's pepper. They went together, like breaking and entering. I didn't know which part of the sin was worse, the porn or the touching, but I suspected it was the porn. At least that's what I would confess to when I did it. I assumed my bishop understood that masturbation had been a part of it, too. If I had just confessed to touching myself, I would have felt like I'd been trying to get off (ha ha!) easy by not mentioning the naked ladies. After all, the Church authorities always talked about the evil of pornography. There was only one major pamphlet about masturbation—*To Young Men Only*—and it was from the 70s or 80s. It talked about the little factory we have, and how if we increase production at the factory, it will be harder to then slow production down. It was an interesting way to talk about ejaculate. I read it as a kind of penance on occasions when I had abused myself. It mentioned pornography briefly, though it implied that the reason porn was dangerous was because it could turn straight boys gay, which seemed very counterintuitive.

I didn't think Elder Clark had any inappropriate reading materials stashed in the apartment. His problem didn't seem to need inspiration. Some elders got so worried about being tempted by dirty thoughts that they stapled the Song of Solomon shut. That's a spicy book in the Old Testament that compares the Lord and His people to lovers. Even scripture can be porn when it talks about breasts.

Elder Clark woke me up around midnight. He thought he might need to go to the hospital. But before that, he wanted a blessing.

"What's up?" I said, sitting up. The lights were off. He was already in his missionary attire. He stood up to turn on the light.

"I think I'm allergic to something?" His face wasn't entirely red and swollen, but broad swaths of it were. He looked like he had been punched in the face several times by someone who is paid to punch people in the face. I sat up, still unsure what was happening. When I finally looked over at Elder Clark, I reflected his pain back at him. "Where are my keys?" I said, trying to sound awake and eager to help.

"I know, it looks bad," he said apologetically. "But what I'm actually concerned about is my throat. I feel like whatever is happening to my face is also happening to my throat."

"Can you breathe?"

"I can."

"Obviously. Sorry. Alright, let me get dressed and we'll head out," I said.

"Would you mind giving me a blessing before we go?"

"Right, of course. Obviously," I said. Dressing never took long. I put on a short-sleeved shirt that was clean and the suit

I had worn yesterday. My keys were on my desk. I kept my little silver vial of consecrated olive oil attached to them.

Elder Clark sat in his chair and I stood behind him. Normally, one priesthood holder anointed the person with a few drops of oil and said a prescribed prayer, and then another priesthood holder gave the actual blessing. But one person could do both. I prayed that Elder Clark would be well again, and that the doctors would help him. I asked that we have a safe drive to the hospital and I closed in the name of Jesus Christ, amen.

"I feel like my face is still growing," Elder Clark said once we were in the car. "My arms are itchy, too."

"What happened? Did you eat something?" I asked.

"I don't know. I ate what you ate. Lasagna at the Coxes'."

His arms were blotchy and red. I couldn't tell whether his hands were swollen or if they were just always that massive. I remembered how when we first shook hands, I nearly laughed at how completely my hand disappeared into his. It was like a grizzly bear shaking hands with a poodle, albeit a pretty tall poodle, thank you very much.

Owing either to Elder Clark's appearance or to the fact that it was Tuesday at 1:00 a.m., we hardly waited in the emergency room after we reported to the triage nurse. I followed Elder Clark through the swinging doors that separated all the medical treatments from the anxious people waiting for them. I left him when he was in the examining room with a doctor. I sat in a small waiting area in the corner. I wasn't about to go back to the main waiting area; that would have been too far away from my companion. The missionary handbook was very clear that missionaries were never to be alone.

In our rush to get to the hospital, I neglected to bring my scriptures. I had nothing to read but what was in my shirt pocket, hiding behind my name tag: my blue weekly schedule, my white missionary handbook, and a small stack of pass-along cards. I closed my eyes and, without hope, tried to sleep.

Before too long a woman in scrubs called me into Elder Clark's room. At some point he had changed out of his missionary clothes and into a flimsy blue hospital gown. He hardly fit in his bed. Floating above him was an IV bag of antibiotics. He was asleep.

"He's fine," the nurse told me. "But we'll need to keep him here for a while, just to make sure. You can probably go home and get some sleep, if you'd like. He'll be fine."

"How long is a while?" I asked.

"Doctor said four more hours. You're free to wait here, too, of course."

"I'll do that. Do you know what happened?" I asked.

"He had an allergic reaction to something. He has to finish this course of antibiotics."

"No idea what he was allergic to?" I asked.

"Sorry," she said.

She gave a friendly shrug and motioned to the waiting area where I would not be sleeping for the next four hours. There was a TV hanging from the ceiling in the corner and a scattering of magazines on the side table beside me. Not much entertainment news penetrated my missionary bubble. Like the missionary handbook counselled, I only read, watched, and listened to things that were mission president approved. Who was Hilary Duff? What was *The O.C.*? Pop culture didn't seem real anymore. It wasn't tethered to anything I was familiar with. I still recognized some of the faces on the magazines, of course, but I had no clue what movie or gossip had put them on that particular cover. The infomercial playing on TV was selling a chair that would give its user rock-hard abs. This was highlighted by an animation clip that clearly indicated where the abs were on the human body, and that they were engaged by this chair. Newly skinny people raved about the effectiveness of the chair. According to the small print on the screen, their results weren't typical, but that didn't mean they weren't possible!

It was not a busy night at the hospital. I was the only one in the waiting area and there wasn't a lot of movement among the staff. I checked my watch. I had been there a little over an hour.

At some point the infomercial changed. What came on the screen was from a world I wasn't prepared for. I watched it for half a second and immediately knew that I wanted no part in what it was selling. Up to this point, the billboard for Buffalo Jeans near our Niagara Falls apartment represented the most considerable temptation I faced in the chastity department. It bore a picture of a young woman lying on her back. She was wearing a white shirt and jeans, but her jeans were open enough to see that she was also wearing white underwear. The look she was giving the camera made it clear that this wasn't an oversight. Her legs were open, too. It was the definition of suggestive imagery. But no one would call it pornography.

I didn't think I could make that same distinction with this infomercial, though. Technically, obviously, it wasn't porn—it was on TV in a public place. Yes, it was the middle of the night, so standards were more lax, but weren't there still rules? Pornography or not, the infomercial offended the Spirit. The program was loud even with the sound off.

It was selling a series of DVDs called *Girls Gone Wild*. The premise of the program, and presumably the videos it was pushing, was that the *Girls Gone Wild* camera crews would visit American nightclubs—especially in university towns—and film women dancing. When these women saw they were bathed in the camera's glaring spotlight, oftentimes they would lift their shirts, eager to bare their breasts. And the crowd dancing around them would cheer. Some of the young women would also be interviewed in the *Girls Gone Wild* bus. Here, instead of just flashing their breasts, these women removed their clothes slowly, all while speaking to whoever was holding the camera. It looked like after they had stripped down, they were given a trucker hat, tank top, or thong as payment.

The footage was heavily censored, of course. Whenever the girls lifted up their shirts, their breasts were covered by star-shaped *Girls Gone Wild* logos of various sizes. Inch for inch, there had probably been more skin shown during the Ab-lounger infomercial. But context mattered.

To me, at that moment, *Girls Gone Wild* was so wicked it felt like satire. As if a society could revel in such wantonness and still escape the calamities foretold by ancient and modern prophets. The arrogance was nearly as bad as the sexual immorality. Nearly. I felt the familiar roiling in the pit of my stomach. I always felt sick to my stomach in the face of temptation like this. My hands, legs, and chest began to shake. Temptation always spiked my adrenaline. But only the kind that involved looking at breasts. The prospect of seeing even a portion of a naked breast made me feel like I was walking through a haunted house. I looked away from the TV, toward what I decided was the nurses' station. No one was there. I looked at my shoes, at a chart hanging on the wall that meant nothing to me. I looked back at Elder Clark's room, his door just barely ajar. But then my eyes would return to the TV screen.

I stood up, skilfully sweeping my erection up so it was held against my body by the waistband of my garments: a skill every teenage boy masters or dies. If I'd had my scriptures with me I would have held them like a textbook in front of my crotch for added security. Then again, if I had my scriptures with me, I wouldn't be in this predicament. I'd have had something to read instead of watching girls going wild.

I couldn't walk far. I wasn't supposed to let my companion out of my sight, which in this situation meant his room. But I could stand away from the cluster of chairs, with my back to the TV. I was halfway there. I just needed to turn around. But maybe the girl on the screen, who appeared to be leaving the club with her keys in her hands, maybe she would keep her clothes on. I owed it to her to see her safely to her car.

But soon she too was naked, rolling around on the grass and wearing only the chyron that the editor provided in post-production. It looked like she was getting ready to do more than just roll around on the ground. I really needed to look away. With my back turned to the TV I walked over to the magazines on the side table. In flagrant defiance of the stereotype, all the magazines in the waiting room seemed current. I pushed the *Cosmopolitan*s and *InStyle*s to the side, and considered maybe opening a *People* magazine. It would still be breaking mission rules, but it would offend the Spirit less.

But I knew this internal discussion was really moot, that I was going to turn around and keep watching the *Girls Gone Wild* infomercial. Some horny, sinful part of me swore I'd regret it if I didn't watch it. I needed to harvest some of those images. That part of me was convincing.

Then, screaming at me from the magazine table, in bold red letters: *Maxim Hot 100*. What kind of hospital was this? Porn on the television, and hidden among innocent fashion magazines this temptation.

The *Maxim Hot 100* was a slight twenty-five pages. It was a bonus insert that probably came free with the monthly issue of the magazine.

My mind went blank. I didn't even attempt a justification to myself. All that existed for me in that moment was this *Maxim Hot 100*. The editors of *Maxim* had done great work compiling and ranking these beautiful daughters of Heavenly Father. I wouldn't have been able to choose one over another, let alone decide on a number one.*

Some of the women were wearing bathing suits, some lingerie, some were in other various stages of undress: open Oxford shirts, Daisy Duke shorts, dresses with plunging necklines. Their skin was shiny, many of them had wet hair. It was all I could do to breathe. It had been so long since I'd allowed myself to look at anything sexy. I hadn't seen bare skin between a woman's neck and her knees in nearly two years, aside from the midriffs of young fiery darts, but they were easy to ignore. I mistakenly thought that after all the teaching and testifying, studying and praying I had done, all temptation would be similarly easy to dismiss. I assumed I was cured. That the devil no longer had any power to drag me down to the gulf of misery and endless woe.** But no, if anything it had become more difficult to look away. I remembered why looking at scantily clad women used to be so enjoyable. The shortness of breath I felt, the nerves jangling in my stomach, the legs shaking with nervous energy: they weren't unpleasant sensations.

I suddenly needed to get to the bathroom as quickly as possible. There was one attached to Elder Clark's room, and one

---

* That year, it was Jessica Simpson.

** Helaman 5:12.

down the hall in the opposite direction. Elder Clark's was closer, but there was no chance I was going to risk anything happening with my companion in the room. I threw the magazine into the nearest garbage can, lest it defile anyone else, and made my way to the bathroom down the hall. Jogging, even walking briskly, just made the problem worse.

Steps away from the bathroom it happened. With the limited control I had, I tried to walk normally, to tamp down and smooth out any spasm even as my brain short-circuited and I died a little death. The ground fell away and I came in my pants.

I went in the bathroom to catch my breath and to whisper one of what would be dozens, hundreds of prayers for forgiveness for what had just happened. Even if Heavenly Father couldn't forgive me at that moment, I prayed that He'd still show mercy. I prayed that I wouldn't be sent home from my mission. That I'd somehow be able to come back from this iniquity. I cleaned myself up a little and went back to the waiting area.

"You sure motored to the washroom there. Everything alright?" a nurse asked.

I nodded and smiled. "All good," I said. Whatever soupçon of excitement had been accompanying my nausea before had disappeared. Now I felt like I was going to throw up. I deserved to throw up. I felt sick to my stomach and I hated myself. I was suddenly very sleepy. I sat down in the same chair I had been in before and looked up at the TV. Someone had changed the channel to CNN.

It would be another hour until Elder Clark could be released. I spent that time leaning forward, elbows resting on my knees, my eyes closed in prayer and exhaustion.

I decided I would confess to President Sybrowsky at the next zone conference. I was pretty sure that what had happened—my insistence on looking at inappropriate images—and my owning up to it would disqualify me from ever being called as an assistant. I would probably be emergency transferred out of the zone and sent elsewhere so that someone more righteous and unsullied could lead the Peninsula zone to baptismal glory. These were harsh consequences, but I just wanted to be clean and forgiven. I didn't want to sully my mission with one act. I wanted to return home from my mission pure.

The question was, should I include the accidental orgasm in the confession? On the one hand (ha), I hadn't used either of mine. The orgasm came (ha) unprompted, at least physically. It had been completely uncalled for, an entirely unwanted physical response to visual stimuli. I was as responsible for it as I was for sneezing in the springtime. But on the other hand, the orgasm followed on the sin of looking at pornography, and made it impossible to downplay or forget it. If I hadn't ejaculated I probably would have walked away thinking I had dodged a bullet.

Was it the intent, the action, or the consequence that made something sinful? Surely there was some nuance. Was drinking alcohol the sin, or was it getting drunk? It wasn't a sin to want a drink, it was a temptation, and we were assured that it wasn't a sin to be tempted. That worked alright for something as cut and dried as the Word of Wisdom. Drinking was the sin, and getting drunk compounded it, like running a red light while escaping a bank heist.

Typically, when you confess to your bishop in the Mormon church, the meeting takes place in his office. It feels less like how confessions are depicted on TV and more like a performance review. But President didn't have an office at the church building we had our zone conference in, so I was going to have to speak with him in one of the empty classrooms. It was like talking to a teacher after class.

When I confessed to President—about the ogling, not the orgasm—he wasn't mad or disappointed. He didn't remind me of how grave my sin had been, or warn me against ever committing anything similar again. Although he couldn't absolve me like a Catholic priest, President Sybrowsky made it seem like less of a big deal than I had made it out to be in my head. But he said it was good that I had spoken with him. Then he asked about the performance of the zone. And then he told me to stick to the *Ensign* if I wanted to look at magazines.*

"Definitely," I said, as though I'd learned my lesson and would never take the car out again without asking first.

Six weeks into my time in the Falls, it was time for transfers. Elder Clark and I were pretty certain of what would happen. Elder Clark would be transferred somewhere new, and I'd get another companion whom I'd be with for two transfers, or roughly three months, since it was rare for a zone leader to be in an area for less than three transfers. After that, I hoped in my heart, it would be my turn to be transferred to Brampton, where I'd spend my last two transfers as an assistant.

* *Ensign* was the Church's official monthly magazine.

I would be an assistant like my brother had been. Even though it was unrighteous to hope for it, it's all I wanted. But I knew that wanting it so badly was risky. Pining for leadership positions was a good way to disqualify myself from them. But I couldn't help it.

It was also possible that I'd get the call to be an assistant that night. Why not? After nearly three years away from Utah, President Sybrowsky was down to his last transfer. A new mission president would replace him in a little over a month. It made sense to make me an assistant now so that I'd learn the ropes with President Sybrowsky for six weeks and be better prepared to help the new mission president with the transition. Why else had I been called as a zone leader so early in my mission? It was so I would be able to be the assistant for the presidential changeover.

So much time was spent thinking about transfers. Every forty-two days, life could change entirely. Every forty-two days you might have a new apartment, in a new city, with new roommates, and, hopefully, a new best friend. And we had no control over any of it. The Lord alone knew where we were supposed to be, and why.

But so far as we could be sure about such uncertain things, we were sure that Elder Clark would be getting a call. Both of my paths to being an assistant depended on that.

Only the call didn't come. After the district leaders had checked in, our phone didn't ring for the rest of that night.

I knew what that meant. By my calculations, that meant there was no longer a path for me to serve as an assistant. I wouldn't make it.

From our balcony I could see mist rising from the falls like smoke. It looked like something was always on fire in the distance. It reminded me of home.

In Edmonton, we lived close enough to an oil refinery that you could see a flame from one of the smokestacks from the bottom of the hill near our house, forever burning. When I was a kid, seeing the fire had inspired a nightmare about standing in front of a house on fire, watching as people passed by without seeming to care about the inferno. That was what had made it a nightmare. Not the fire, or the destruction it caused, but everyone's apathy toward it.

If God were to smite the people of Niagara Falls, He'd definitely start around the falls. To entertain the crowds of vacationers, there was an area of attractions that began across the street from the water. It was called Clifton Hill. There was a Ripley's Believe It or Not! museum there, shaped like the Chrysler Building collapsed onto its side, complete with a giant ape hanging from the radio tower. There was a haunted house next to a Burger King. On the roof the two establishments shared was a big green Frankenstein's monster holding a Whopper. Across the street was one of the city's many wax museums—this one an ode to contemporary celebrities. I recognized Britney Spears and Michael Jackson. I didn't know who the fancy pirate fellow was, but I assumed he was in a rock band because of the eyeliner. There were chain restaurants and candy stores and a statue of the world's tallest man that Mormon missionaries who served in the zone liked to take their picture beside. We called the area Clifton Hell. We thought we were very clever.

Victoria Avenue intersected with Clifton at the top of the hill. This street presented tourists with more traps, these ones markedly cheaper-looking. Here there were more souvenir and head shops mixed in with the overpriced breakfast places, the wax museum dedicated to criminals, and the smattering of ethnic food spots. There was no upscale dining in Clifton Hell. Likely because there was nothing upscale about Clifton Hell. One of the covenants everyone makes in the temple is to "avoid all loud laughter, light-mindedness and evil speaking of the Lord's anointed." Clifton Hill was loud laughter. There was nothing for us in that area.

In the summer of 2004, a new attraction opened. The Fallsview Casino Resort was going to employ the city and bring in the stars to perform in its state-of-the-art theatre. It would class up the Falls's tourist zone, which felt like it should be called downtown, but that was just because it was where all of Niagara Falls's tall buildings were. The actual downtown—the historic downtown—was a deserted street a few kilometres from the falls, with darkened shops and one Mr. Sub. It was like it had gotten out of the downtown game and was just trying to live a normal life as a regular street.

The further away from Clifton Hell you travelled, the more rundown the city got. It seemed like city money rarely made it out of the tourist centres. Tourism was the main industry in Niagara Falls, the favourite child that got all the attention. I guessed it was a shaky foundation upon which to build a city. We heard that the American Niagara Falls, across the river in New York, was worse off. Their side of the falls was smaller, less iconic, and they weren't getting a Fallsview Casino Resort.

Clifton Hell presented an illuminating juxtaposition. If one stood along the Niagara River Parkway looking southeast, to your left would be the falls. All breathtaking majesty, awesome and powerful. Loud and fast and immovable. The mist they threw up would catch the sunlight and send rainbows everywhere you looked.

And then, as if answering a challenge, on the other side of the parkway, a kingdom of gaudy consumerism, tinny music, and blinking lights. All the sounds blasting and barking at once, trying to drown out the roar of 230,000 cubic feet of water plummeting off a ledge and dropping 187 feet.

Behold, the beauty that God created, free for everyone, all are welcome. And lo, the hodgepodge of capitalism that man hath wrought, where nothing is free or beautiful. Every storefront trying to convince passersby that it offered the only means to enjoy the falls, the one true destination in the city.

At night, the mist from the falls was still visible from our balcony, but barely. It was muted and smoky against the night sky. But lest the falls become less enticing after sunset, the city shot giant spotlights at them, bathing the waterfall in green and blue and red. And every other night, a fireworks display would burst and twinkle above the rushing water. Usually the fireworks were from the Canadian side, except on the Fourth of July, when the two sides of the falls battled it out with celebratory light shows to see who loved America the most.

The Canadian side was the clear winner.

But after we'd seen the fireworks for months, they had lost their novelty. The distant booms became just one more sound of the city that I stopped noticing, like ambulances screaming about someone else's bad day or tricked-out Hondas burning down the highway near our apartment. We were on the top floor of a seven-storey building. Ours was the only balcony covered by a screen. Presumably, it was to keep out mosquitos, but I often joked that the mesh was there to prevent us from jumping.

Was that an appropriate joke for a missionary to make? Did other missionaries frequently think of jumping off their balconies? Did every zone leader who passed through this apartment feel the same about our balcony? That but for the screen it offered a sweet release from the zone's failure to rise out of the B league of zones? I believed that in the rare instances when missionaries died on their missions, they were guaranteed entrance to the highest level in the celestial kingdom—much like dying while saving someone else's life. But surely suicide complicated that. Not that I would have actually jumped if the mesh screen were not there. It was just something I thought about. In a lighthearted way.

Mostly what I did on the balcony was pray. There were so few places I could be alone and pray out loud. I would wait until Elder Clark was sleeping and quietly slide the door open. It was probably pretentious of me to go somewhere other than the side of my bed or my desk to pray. Did I want to feel cinematic? To seem profound? Did I think Heavenly Father would answer my prayers more clearly if I were outside and closer to heaven?

Or was it okay to find a special place to pray?

Being outside wasn't just about being alone and not waking my companion; it helped me visualize the magnitude of my responsibility as a missionary in Niagara Falls. I looked out over all the houses below and reminded myself that I was responsible for all of them. How would everyone learn about the restored gospel, the one true church, if not for my companion and me. We were the only missionaries in the city. For as long as we were in the area, we were the city's best and only hope.

That night, I prayed first for forgiveness. Without newspapers, television, or radio, we had no way of knowing what the weather was going to be like on any given day. Since we had a lot of tracting planned for the next day, I wanted to know what to expect. It wouldn't really make a difference, since we would walk regardless, but it seemed like reasonable information to have. And so I knocked on our neighbour's door to ask her.

But I couldn't lie to God any more than I could lie to myself. Yes, I wanted to know the weather, but though I told myself it was a convenient solution, I didn't really have to ask our neighbour to find out. The reason I did was because our neighbour was distractingly pretty. She had long raven hair, a belly button ring, and a butterfly tattoo on her lower back which was usually visible because her shirts rarely extended all the way to the top of her pants. And her pants were almost always skin-tight. She would smile at us when we passed in the hall. Her smile was bemused, with a hint of pity.

She answered the door wearing tight white pants and a tank top. Not an outfit she'd be able to wear if she wore garments. I asked her if she knew what the weather was going to be like the next day, and she answered me. Aside from some forgettable pleasantries, that was the extent of our conversation. From the outside, it was entirely innocuous. But I knew I wasn't innocent. I asked about the weather because I wanted the thrill of looking at her and the uncomplicated joy of talking to a pretty girl. And even though that was the extent of it—I wasn't going to run back to my apartment so I could masturbate or anything—it was still offensive to the Spirit. Because my intentions weren't entirely pure.

I had given up on being an assistant. The Lord wanted me in Niagara Falls, apparently. So this was where I'd finish my mission. In mission parlance, I'd die here.

But with a final leadership position off the table, I cast about for other signs and tokens that I had been, and was still, a good missionary. I wasn't anywhere near the highest-baptizing missionary. An Elder Reid had taken that title—he was closing in on sixty baptisms, from what I heard. I was aiming for a fraction of that. It would be impossible to catch up to him when I only had six weeks left. I just wanted to break twenty.

And then I asked Heavenly Father's forgiveness again for how poorly the work was going in my zone. A few months earlier, Peninsula zone had actually led the mission in baptisms, in no small part because Elder Clark and I had done four in one month. He was transferred to London soon after that. Two months later and Peninsula zone was back at the bottom, along with the zones in the north. I knew the decline had to have been my fault, though I didn't know what I should have done differently.

I was failing all those people living in the houses and apartment buildings spread out below me. And I was failing Heavenly Father, too. Before I closed my prayer I did my best to be grateful for all that I still had. Then I wiped my tears away, got up, and went back to bed.

I wasn't yet bitter. The disappointment and feeling of powerlessness hadn't fully broken my spirit. I liked to think that I was a long way from being bitter. But I was starting to understand how bitterness could creep up on a missionary. Not bitterness from not being called as an assistant, but rather a bitterness toward the world. For some missionaries a certain misanthropy settled in during their time in the field, a distinct lack of grace toward non-missionaries.

Every day we waded into a sea of humanity. From some angles, when the light hit it right, humanity could be breathtaking. Up close, though, the water was dirty and smelled like dead fish, a yellowish foam at its edges. But focusing on the ugliness of the world wouldn't help me baptize.

IF WE FAIL THIS MONTH, WE FAIL OUR WHOLE MISSIONS

That became my mantra, my motto. Was it harsh? Maybe a little, but it was also unavoidably accurate. If an athlete chokes in the final quarter or inning, it doesn't matter how strong they were in the first half. If they fail at the end, they fail the whole game. Besides, what would it mean if I couldn't make a miracle baptism happen after twenty-three months in the field? Had I learned nothing? Did I even know how to follow the Spirit?

IF WE FAIL THIS MONTH, WE FAIL OUR WHOLE MISSIONS

I wrote that message on Post-it notes and stuck them around the apartment, along with some other words of encouragement.

Heavenly Father's love was complicated. It was a sign of how much He loved us that He had such high expectations of us.

We were tracting in a nice, middle-class neighbourhood. The houses were all new and neat, the postage-stamp yards trimmed and clear of residential detritus. It looked like a neighbourhood that had been built on a movie studio's backlot. Middle-class neighbourhoods were unpredictable. This was where I imagined all the young families in the ward were, with parents still open-minded enough to be searching for a church.

This neighbourhood was friendly. A lot of the people we talked to belonged to the same church, a non-denominational church with a generic, forgettable name. Church of Christ, or something. I wondered if the church members recruited all their neighbours, or if the community all moved together with the church. How culty was this place?

"This must be what it's like being a missionary in Utah," Elder Arcann said.

"This must be what it's like being a Jehovah's Witness in Utah," Elder Allen corrected him.

These were my new companions. Elder Clark was finally transferred to the London zone to be a district leader. For reasons none of us understood, the Lord decided to put together three missionaries who were all going home at the end of the transfer. Three dead elders walking.

Only Elder Allen couldn't do much walking. He was suffering with a herniated disc in his back, so he was going home a transfer early. He had been the Windsor zone leader before he was emergency transferred to Niagara Falls for unknown reasons. I liked him fine. At twenty-seven, he was impossibly old. Most twenty-seven-year-olds in the Church were married with a kid or two already. For Elder Allen, getting sent to Niagara Falls was a miracle. As it turned out, the previous bishop of the ward, Brother Armstrong, was a chiropractor. He happily offered his daily service to Elder Allen for free.

The Lord knew where Elder Allen needed to be.

As for Elder Arcann, we came out together from the MTC in Utah. He hadn't changed much since then. He was still quiet and humble. A peacemaker. But in the interim he'd become a confident teacher.

"At least everyone is still nice here," I said. "Elder Clark and I once tracted in a neighbourhood where everyone seemed to go to a really Anti church. Let me tell you, it was very difficult not to just prosturbate with them all afternoon."

I had recently coined that term: a witty portmanteau of proselytize and masturbate, I felt. To me it highlighted how ineffectual getting into doctrinal debates with people was, even as it was incredibly pleasurable. Bible-bashing, as it was sometimes called (or just bashing), served no purpose except self-gratification.

"It feels so good sometimes," Elder Allen said. "I have definitely been a dirty prosturbator in the past."

"Oh, me too. And yet it's strange. In all my battles, not once has my opponent bowed to my superior scriptural knowledge and lightning-quick reasoning," I said.

"If you can convince someone to join the Church, anyone can convince them out of the Church," Elder Arcann said.

"You can't bash someone into baptism," Elder Allen said.

"Elder Connor in Fort Erie will sometimes call in at night and be like, 'Elder Hudson, I need to confess. I prosturbated hard today.' He's like, 'We were on that dude's doorstep for an hour.'"

"Time flies when you're really going at it," Elder Allen said.

"I never think it's very fair," Elder Arcann said. "Mostly people don't know what they are getting into. They don't know we study every day."

"A Jedi never starts a fight. But he always finishes it," Elder Allen said.

"Man, what is it with missionaries and *Star Wars*?" Elder Arcann asked.

"What do you mean? The comparison is apt," Elder Allen said. "They are basically warrior monks from outer space, same as us."

"Minus the warrior bit, and the outer space bit, and we're not exactly monks. But other than that, yeah. We are basically Jedis," I said.

The next door was mine. A man with white hair and a beard opened the door. He had an academic's hairline, receding at a leisurely pace in the front as it started to get a bit longer in the back. As if his entire head of hair was migrating toward his shoulders.

"Hi, I'm Elder Hudson, these are my friends Elder Allen and Elder Arcann. We're missionaries from the Church of Jesus Christ of Latter-day Saints."

"Aren't there usually only two of you?" the man interrupted.

"Usually, but today we're offering a three-for-two special. It comes with a true message about Jesus Christ. Do you believe in Jesus Christ?" I asked.

"Am I a Christian? I am, yes." The man seemed to be a practised smiler.

"That's awesome. So are we! Hey, a lot of people in this neighbourhood seem to be members of the what's-it-called church," I said.

"Redeemer Church?" Elder Arcann offered.

"In fact, I'm the pastor," the man said.

"You're like a celebrity on this street," I said.

"I wouldn't say that. But my wife and I started the church about twenty years ago. We've been able to see families come together in Christ. And now, we're starting to see those blessings continue in the next generation. It's very special."

"I think you, and your church, might be really interested in the message we share, especially about families," I said. Imagine baptizing an entire congregation. I was taught that kind of stuff had happened in the early days of the Church.

"Maybe. But I'm pretty familiar with your message, though I appreciate your desire. How old are you boys?"

"Twenty-one. Except Elder Allen. He's twenty-seven," I said.

"If you don't mind my asking, how did you become familiar with the Mormon Church?" Elder Arcann asked.

"Oh, I read quite a bit, here and there," the man replied. "I'm sure I have a copy of your book somewhere in here. I've read it. I've read the Qur'an, too. You know, when I first became a believer, I was incredibly hungry for truth. I went searching for it, and, just like you I'm sure, I felt like God was leading me in that search. But mine didn't end with the Book of Mormon."

"What was it about the Church you didn't like?" I asked.

"Oh, I'm sure I could quickly bone up on some of your doctrinal statements and we could have a grand old SYI session. Share your ignorance. But I'm willing to bet that neither of us is going to convince the other."

"So, what you're saying is you don't want to get baptized," I said.

"Nope," he grinned. "Not even when I'm dead."

He laughed, and we did, too.

"It was very nice talking to you," I said.

"And all your parishioners, or members, or whatever name you prefer, everyone on this street has been very kind," Elder Arcann broke in.

"There's no reason for them not to be, but thank you, that's wonderful to hear. Now, like I said, I appreciate your devotion. I hope you have a most unsuccessful day."

"And I hope everyone leaves your church!" I added and smiled.

"What a nice man," Elder Allen said as we were leaving the neighbourhood.

As we were walking past a one-storey motel, Elder Arcann broke away from our triad and went to speak with a blonde woman sitting outside room number seven. She had been sitting with a man, but he ducked inside when it became clear that Elder Arcann was heading toward them. She was smoking and shielding her eyes from the sun with her other hand. Elder Allen and I hung back. I was pretty certain she wasn't going to invite us in to meet the man she had been smoking with. I couldn't quite hear what Elder Arcann was saying, but after a short back-and-forth I saw him pull out his weekly planner from his shirt pocket. I watched him nod like a police officer taking a statement. Then he put the planner back in his pocket and came back to Elder Allen and me.

"Nice work, Elder," Elder Allen said.

"What did she say?" I asked.

"She wasn't interested," he said, trying to feign disappointment. "But she really wants us to meet and teach her son. He's apparently fourteen and she says she wants him to have some positive role models. She gave me her address and said we should drop by today."

"That's one," I said.

Young John never had a chance. Three grown men dropping by just to pay attention to him? Come on. He didn't have to prove himself to us or impress us to earn our attention. He came pre-accepted, which is one of the best feelings in the world, especially for a teenager. And thus he was a breeze to teach. John accepted everything we taught. Of course he did. Why wouldn't he believe his three new older brothers? More impressively, he kept his commitments, too. All the calls to action at the end of each meeting: he did them. He read a few key verses in the Book of Mormon and prayed on whether or not they were true.

He came to church. He promised to live the Word of Wisdom and the law of chastity, though we didn't get into any discussion about masturbation. If he had money, he said, he would pay tithing. He passed his baptismal interview. And then he followed the example of Jesus Christ and was baptized.

Shelly, his mom, was well pleased.

I hoped the elders who would eventually replace us would try to connect with John after we went home, that they'd become his older brothers, too. Because that was one way it could go. Young John could become a kind of mascot or constant sidekick to whoever the missionaries were in the area. If John could just stay active in the Church for five more years, he'd go on a mission and he'd be set for life. But I thought about how long the years between my fourteenth and nineteenth birthdays had been and didn't have much hope that John would stick to the plan. Still, I knew that on balance it was good he got baptized. It was good that he met us and felt loved. But deep down I didn't think it would stick.

Chances were slim that any of the people I baptized would stay active in the Church past a year. And I saw it over and over. I'd met so many less-active church members who spoke wistfully of the missionary that baptized them. They could remember when they were the miracle, but now wouldn't come to church. I knew the people I had baptized weren't going to be immune from this. Some had better chances than others. I probably had the least hope for John.

The week after John's baptism, my mission was over. The day before we left the Canada Toronto West Mission, all the returning elders went to the temple in Brampton together. I was exhausted and not in the right frame of mind to receive any new insights from the film we were shown or the different handshakes I performed. But I felt better after I had walked through the cloth veil into the celestial room. But for our green aprons and floppy crowns we looked like a room full of angels, milling about reverently at God's open house.

I found an empty seat in front of the giant floral centrepiece and under the crystalline waterfall chandelier. Like most of the other soon-to-be-released missionaries, I bowed my head to pray. Many moments could count as the end of my mission, narratively speaking. Bearing my final testimony as Elder Hudson, baptizing John, getting on the plane, or the moment I was actually released by the stake president. Each was like a checkpoint along a border. A place to cross over. But this visit to the temple felt different from that. This felt like I was submitting my passport. Like I was defending the thesis of my mission, only defending wasn't the right word at all. I was laying my offering on the altar, hoping it would please God, because I couldn't do anything different now.

I had spent the last few months in Niagara Falls feeling worse and worse while watching the zone carry out fewer and fewer baptisms. Not only had I not been called as an assistant—which felt petty now—but I wasn't sure I had even learned how to be a good missionary. Ultimately, my faith hadn't been strong enough. We spoke of faith like a resource, a commodity, but of course it was intangible. What would stronger faith feel like? I didn't know, but with stronger faith I'm sure I would have known the right words to say, and I would have had more courage to say them. I would have invited more people to be baptized. With more faith, I would have inspired my zones. They would have felt and taught with the Spirit, and would have been useful tools of our Heavenly Father. Mostly, with more faith I wouldn't have felt so useless and unworthy. I wouldn't have felt so sad, so often. Because I would have known . . . something more. I would have known the secrets that are only offered to the truly faithful. All the important ones.

My prayer was simple.

Dear Heavenly Father, did I do okay?

He answered not with a vision, but with a thought.

I had the thought of a parent rushing to me, bemused by my crying, chuckling sympathetically to show I was being more serious than I needed to be. I didn't have to be sad, or worry. I felt picked up and embraced. Smiled upon. *Did you do okay? Oh, Elder Hudson. Of course! Of course you did.* Like He assumed someone had told me already. Like it had been so obvious I didn't even have to ask. Spiritually, I collapsed into my Father's arms, spent.

It was the clearest answer to a prayer I had ever received. It felt too sacred to tell anyone about. Because maybe it was self-serving and predictable and as accurate as any self-diagnosis. But that thought was an answer, and it was real, and in that moment, I knew it.

I didn't feel ready for the rest of my life. After two years in the field, I would have nothing to do—no schedule, and no pressing reason to make one. I was going to be alone, which promised to be a mixed blessing. No one around to protect or judge me.

All the elders going home gathered at President's house for a final sleepover. It was the first time we had all been together as a district since our first night in Ontario. And now it was our last. We had been at the MTC together, and now look at us! We all looked like American presidents beginning their second term. We looked older, with baby bags settling below our eyes, the first wrinkles on our brows. Recently returned missionaries might be the oldest-looking twenty-one-year-olds who aren't in a war, or the porn industry.

We had a testimony meeting in the living room. The mood was reverent, bordering on morose. We were all excited to go home. We were all devastated we were leaving. Going around the room, we all found slightly different ways of describing how much we had loved being missionaries: the lives we saw changed and the (hopefully righteous) pride we took in serving our Saviour. And we all ended by affirming our faith—no, our knowledge—that the Church of Jesus Christ of Latter-day Saints was true. That Joseph Smith was a prophet, seer, and revelator. That the Book of Mormon was true. Oh! How very many experiences each of us now had of studying it and teaching it. And, obviously and especially, we each had a firm testimony of Christ's divine mission.

The senior missionary couple that worked in the mission office, the Shermans, were there. Having never served near the mission office in Brampton, I didn't recognize them. Elder Sherman heard all the sniffling and saw the room full of sad young missionary men (and two sisters). He stood and mounted his defence of civilian life. We would still have a life full of wonderful spiritual experiences and service, he said. Life was changing, not ending. Missionary work wouldn't suddenly stop. Opportunities to share the gospel would present themselves, he promised, and there would never be a shortage of ways to serve in the Church.

I pitied Elder Sherman. It's not that he was trying to placate us with comforting fiction. He was just wrong. If he thought we'd do something, anything, as meaningful as our missions, then he must not have gone on a mission. Or he had forgotten what it had been like.

That's one of the reasons I was blubbering. I was mourning the death of Elder Hudson. He was imperfect. His eye wandered sometimes, and he struggled with patience and charity, but boy did he want to be good.

The closing hymn was *O Canada*. I didn't try to sing it.

At dark-thirty the next morning, we all got up to go to the airport. I felt hungover, or how I assumed being hungover felt. My eyes were wrung out and my head ached. My stomach rebelled against the early hour, refusing to want food despite my being obviously hungry.

I wouldn't be able to sleep on the plane, so I used the time to catch up with my journalling, to recap all the final miracles I saw during the last two weeks of my mission, like John's baptism, lest I somehow lose the moments forever.

By the time we landed in Calgary, I had a cold sore on my lower lip, fully bloomed. It was a debutante, rosy and bright, full of potential.

My family met me at arrivals at the Calgary airport. Not my sisters Mary and Erin, since they lived in Utah and New York, respectively. But everyone who lived in town was there. They even had a couple of signs. Sam's wife, Karen, whom I was meeting for the first time, since they met and got married while I was away, had made them. I couldn't picture my family remembering to make signs. These signs—one a drawing of a house under the words "Welcome Home," and another that said they loved me—felt extra special because I honestly wasn't expecting anyone to be there at all. Not in a maudlin, woe-is-me-they-don't-even-care-that-I'm-home kind of way. But punctuality wasn't a strong Hudson trait. And, actually, neither was sentimentality. I pictured someone running into the airport after my flight had cleared out, apologizing for being late, and taking me home. I figured that's when I would see the rest of my family. But what I figured didn't matter, because there they all were.

We went from the airport to the stake centre, which was basically on the way to our house, so that I could be officially released as a missionary. If I wanted to move forward with my normal life, I had to get the missionary mantle removed by someone in the stake presidency. My family and I sat around a boardroom table. I would officially report my mission to the stake presidency later that week; for now, President Norris asked me a few questions about the areas I served in. Then he put his hand on my head. When he said that I was released there was the now-familiar dam burst. Tears are often associated with the Spirit. But these weren't that kind of tears. These were the heartbroken kind.

PRONE TO WANDER, LORD, I FEEL IT

(2004–2009)

SINCE IT WAS a normal September day for everyone else, after I got home from the airport my family went about the regular business of their day and I was left alone. For the first time in two years, I was alone.

I sat on the white leather couch in my parents' TV room, pulled a quilt around me, and watched the *Lord of the Rings* movies I had missed while I was thrusting in my sickle: *The Two Towers* and *The Return of the King*. The battle scenes shook me a bit. Reading about the many battles in the Book of Mormon hadn't prepared me for the violence and tragedy on the screen. But I had nothing else to do. No appointments. No job. The airline had misplaced my luggage, so I didn't even have anything I could unpack. I watched six hours of Middle Earth in one sitting.

I came away from the movies feeling dazed and spent. Despite the Christian parallels in the films, I still felt a little guilty that I had wasted so much time on such a trivial thing. If I could return to normal life so easily, I wondered if I had changed at all. I didn't know what I should have done instead. Read my scriptures, I suppose, maybe gone for a run.

My sister Mary, who had also gotten married while I was away, sent me a welcome-home package from Utah. It included a CD full of non-church songs she thought I should listen to: some Modest Mouse, the Killers, Justin Timberlake, Wilco, and the Yeah Yeah Yeahs. Along with the CD, she had made a little scrapbook with pictures of the pop culture stories I had missed out on: the death of John Ritter, the rise of Paris Hilton, Charlize Theron winning the Oscar for *Monster*.

As the days went by, the hardest part for me was accepting that nothing I was doing, nothing I had to do, was as important as the business of saving souls. It made putting together a resumé feel silly and superficial. Any job I applied for seemed inconsequential in the same way. How do you even put "Mormon missionary" on a resumé? Where do I put "Learned how to recognize and follow the Spirit, and point it out to others?" Would that be under special skills, or part of the missionary job description?

In the end, I went to Earls and got my old job back.

I gave my official homecoming address in my parents' ward on the first Sunday after I got back. Recently returned missionaries are usually good speakers, so it wasn't long before the bishop of a young single adult ward that met in the same building asked me to speak on an upcoming Sunday.

When that Sunday came, I sat up on the stand and waited for sacrament meeting to start. Given my age and general demeanour, any visiting member would be able to guess that I was a returned missionary. I looked scrubbed and eager and just a bit weighed down. When I was growing up, I always liked hearing returned missionaries talk about their missions. All missionaries looked so wise and holy and superpowered when they returned from the field. Having them remember their mission was like learning their secret identity, like Peter Parker talking about how cool it was to be Spider-Man. I scanned for familiar faces as people filed into the chapel.

The organist played "Called to Serve" and the sound spread over and through the people and pews, dampening the din of singles settling down. Normally it was a stirring march, but the organist was playing it slowly. It sounded like a haunted carnival.

From where I was sitting, I appreciated how similar this chapel in Calgary was to every Mormon chapel I saw in Ontario. Mormon chapels were as consistent globally as McDonald's or IKEA. They all shared the same aggressively inoffensive aesthetic, like houses of worship as imagined by Holiday Inn Express. This chapel was all dark brick and burlap. But for the organ, pulpit, and rows of pews, it felt a little like a basement rumpus room.

Back by the doors, two missionaries kept entering and exiting the chapel. I guessed that they were waiting with diminishing hope that an investigator they had been working with would show up. It had only been a couple of weeks since I'd been released, and I was shocked by how much they looked like children.

I didn't know Desiree was the bishop's daughter when I first saw her. And when I first saw Desiree is when I decided I was going to date her. Or I would try to date her. Obviously, she would have some say in the matter.

She sat in the middle of the chapel, which surely denoted an eagerness to be nourished by the good word of God.* Desiree was leaning back, her arm resting on the top of the pew. Someone behind her tapped Desiree on the shoulder and said something into her ear, and she laughed. Her smile was goodness. It twinkled. She seemed to be the epicentre of the pew, everyone wanting to be close to her. Or maybe that was me projecting. I didn't stare. I took note of her, and then focused on my talk, which I realized was a pretty good way to introduce myself.

The talk went fine. It was on prayer. It was premised on a quote I had written on a Post-it note and stuck in my scriptures on my mission. My scriptures were a testament to the many hours I had spent studying them over those two years. There were several Post-it notes scattered throughout, and the pages were full of highlighted verses and notes in the margins.

The quote I was speaking about was from Spencer W. Kimball, who had been the president of the Church when I was a baby. He bore a passing resemblance to Yoda. The quote: "God does notice us, He watches over us, but it is usually through another person that He meets our needs." I had a few anecdotes from my mission that proved the truthfulness of the quote.

Later, I ran into Desiree, whose name I still did not know, outside the Relief Society room. She was taller than she had looked sitting down. I noticed because my first love, one of the girls I dated in high school, had been short, and so I had assumed that I had a type.

---

* Moroni 6:4.

"Oh, hi there," I said and smiled broadly. "I'm Greg Hudson." I reached out to shake her hand. I realized that this was where, on my mission, I would have introduced my companion, but I no longer had one. A slight twinge of mission withdrawal. "What's your name?"

"Hello, Greg Hudson. My name is Desiree," she said. She was looking over my shoulder, but trying to be discreet about it.

"Desiree, or Deseret? Did you say?"*

"Desiree. But it is close to Deseret."

"Too bad. Did you know, interesting fact about Deseret, that's what they wanted to call Utah. But the federal government named it after the Ute Indians instead. You could have been named after a state," I said.

"Interesting," she said.

"You're friends with what's-her-bucket . . ."

"I'm sorry, what did you say? What's her bucket?" she interrupted.

"Yeah. I got that from one of my companions. He was German and so he'd be like, *Vhat's-hizz-bucket's name*? And, yes, my German accent is flawless."

"But who's what's-her-bucket?" she asked.

"You were sitting next to her in sacrament meeting. What's her name? She's got a sister who's close in age to my little sister. Her name sounds like a country singer? Like not Reba or Shania, but in that neighbourhood."

"Oh, I know who you're talking about. But I like watching you struggle."

"Raylene?" I guessed.

---

* Deseret is a word from the Book of Mormon meaning honeybees, which became a symbol for Utah because bees are industrious. Now, many Mormon things are named Deseret, including an LDS publishing company.

"Bingo. That's who I'm waiting for, in fact," Desiree said.

"Do you mind if I stand near you? I'm waiting for her too, actually."

"Really?" she asked.

"No," I said. "But since we're here. What's new? How are things? What are you doing with your life, Desiree?"

She was working two jobs, she said. Saving up for school—probably dental hygiene, she thought. As for the jobs: one was at a clothing store—she was the assistant manager—and some nights she was a server for a catering company.

Every bit of information I obtained had required its own question. Not a promising sign. Possibly she was just shy. I also knew that in trying to show interest and enthusiasm, I could come off glib and patronizing. But she was also in the service industry! Here was some common ground I could build a proper conversation on. She would see that I was being genuine with all these questions.

"I'm also a server!" I said. "We have so much in common."

Desiree laughed at my childlike excitement. Finally. And then she asked me where I worked.

This was engagement. It was impossible to deny my golly-gee shtick.

"I work at a little restaurant called Earls," I said. "You should come by sometime. I could get you free pop. As much Coke as you want."

She did not seem impressed. "Oh, I don't go there. Members aren't supposed to go there. You work there?"

I quickly searched her face for signs of irony; I did not find any.

"My whole family has worked at Earls over the years. It's a

Hudson family institution. Who said members aren't supposed to go there?"

"Well, missionaries aren't allowed to go there, so it's like, should anybody?" Desiree said.

"Why aren't missionaries allowed to go there?" I asked. It was like my parents were fighting.

"I guess a little while ago a missionary hooked up with a server there—like, *hooked up* with her—and had to be sent home," Desiree explained. "So they made a mission rule that missionaries weren't allowed to eat there anymore."

"At Earls, both men and women wear modest black button-up shirts, thank you very much," I said. "Unless you're a woman working on the lounge side. Then, yes, you dress in short skirts and shirts with plunging necklines. But there is no reason for a Mormon, let alone a missionary, to sit on the lounge side. Earls is a family establishment."

"Maybe your family," she said. She waved at Raylene. "I'm going to class now."

"Wait. Are you going to the fireside tonight?" Asking about the fireside, or devotional talk, showed that I was righteous, which I didn't expect I'd have to prove to Desiree. I had just given a very sincere, very spiritual talk after all. But I'd do better at the devotional. There would be refreshments afterward, served in the gym, while people took down and put away all the metal folding chairs. The whole thing would be really conducive to mingling and light repartee. Even better, the fireside that evening was going to be about Brigham Young, famed polygamist. Everything would go much better.

"No, I have a family dinner thing," she said.

"What? Not going?"

"Nope. Family thing."

"It's called priorities, Desiree. I mean, what's more important: your family, or the gospel?" I arched my eyebrows to convey that I wasn't being serious.

"Family first, I guess."

She might not have recognized that I was joking. "Well, will you pray about it at least?"

"I'm sorry?"

"Ask God whether you should come to the fireside tonight. I know you'll get an answer." If I'd had a golf swing counter, I would have clicked it.

"Okay?"

"Great! I'll see you tonight."

Admittedly, I'd hit a rough spot there with regard to my part-time employment, but I rescued it.

The hallway was emptying. I walked toward the stage, which was part of the cultural hall. Derek, a fellow in my ward that I liked, who was deciding whether he wanted to be more active in the Church or not, was waiting for me outside the library.

"Going after the bishop's daughter. Bold move," Derek said. You could tell he was semi-active because of how he was dressed. He had a tie on, which was good, but it didn't make up for the blueness of his shirt. "Living the dream."

"She's the bishop's daughter? Desiree Hooper?"

"Yeah, and plus I'm pretty sure she just sent her long-term boyfriend on a mission. I don't know if she's technically on the market."

Derek hadn't gone on a mission. Otherwise he would have known that as a returned missionary I didn't have to respect the dating status of a missionary out in the field. Young women sent boys out, then dated (and likely married) men as they returned home. That was just the way of it. If you had a girlfriend when you went on a mission, you knew there was a very good chance you wouldn't have that girlfriend by the time you got back. The Church encouraged young men not to have girlfriends waiting for them, as they could be distracting from the work. One more reason.

"Huh. That's too bad. But I bet her boyfriend needs to focus on the work anyway. I'll be doing him a favour, really."

"The Jews would call this a mitzvah," Derek said.

"Exactly," I said.

"But do you really want to date Bishop Hooper's daughter?" Derek asked.

I hadn't started on a good foot with Bishop Hooper. I had once inadvertently interrupted his night out with Sister Hooper when my date and I were seated next to them at a 70s-style steakhouse. To fit with the decor, the girl I was with and I dressed up as though it was 1978. I wore a yellow plaid blazer with massive lapels. My date's dress looked like it was from *Saturday Night Fever*. We thought we were a laugh riot. But it's possible Bishop Hooper saw me as deeply unserious. I hoped my talk had demonstrated that I was actually only superficially unserious.

"I'm likable. The bishop could like me," I said.

"Dating his daughter will help," Derek said.

In the weeks to come, I continued my efforts to talk to Desiree. At church, at institute class on Tuesday nights. I even stopped by her store to say hi while I was shopping at the mall. By that point I think her heart had softened. We would go on a date.

But the date was a formality. By then, I already knew she liked me. At the previous week's dance—young single adults' dances were essentially the same as church youth dances, only one could wear jeans—I had spent a good amount of time chatting with her.

After the dance, Desiree came along when a group of us went to Boston Pizza. These were mostly people Desiree had grown up around, but at the restaurant she sat beside me. While I waited for my barbecue chicken pizza to come, Desiree quietly took my hand and held it. Secret hand-holding was generally a move reserved for when two people were watching a movie on a couch and sharing a blanket. Your eyes stayed glued to the movie while your hand got busy with their hand. Doing this without the cover of a blanket was a risky move. The table shielded our hands from the others, but anyone beside Desiree would have been able to see what was going on.

But Desiree risked it. She chose me.

At the movies a week later, our hands made passionate love on the hard plastic armrest between our seats. Fingers caressing fingers, tracing the lines of each other's palms. Our hands were like flowers blooming and wilting in time-lapse. It was as though they had been apart for too long already. After the movie, which was a forgettable Pixar knock-off, we'd planned to meet up with a group of ward members who were gathered at someone's house to watch another movie.

Walking into the basement with Desiree was a statement in itself. In the eyes of everyone there, she had gone on a date with someone other than her missionary. Because I was just back from my mission, it was easy for me to imagine Desiree and me dating, but most of the other people in the dark basement had known Desiree as part of a pair. Maybe she realized that by bringing us here, she was volunteering to be the subject of gossip.

She didn't want to stay long. That was fine by me. Desiree drove me back to my place.

"You don't have to walk me to the door," I said when she pulled up by my house. "I can probably manage."

But Desiree got out anyway. I walked around to her side of the car. Standing with her door still open, she grabbed my belt and pulled me in close to her. Then she kissed me.

According to the stereotype, women have to be on the defensive against their dates' wandering hands. It's the man who will always want to take things further physically. But right from the start, that wasn't our dynamic. I wasn't used to playing defence. And, as it turned out, I wasn't that good at it. While we were kissing, Desiree's hands would search for my zipper, my belt, feel the front of my pants, checking for swelling and always finding it.

Saying no with a non-member would probably have been easier. They knew not what they did. But Desiree had received all the same lessons as I had. She knew the rules, and presumably believed in their sanctity. Correcting her and her handsiness would seem like I was being judgemental and self-righteous. Did I think I was better than her? Rebuffing her advances, I soon learned, was also a good way to hurt Desiree's feelings.

And obviously I hated hurting anyone's feelings. But I especially didn't like hurting Desiree's feelings when I knew our relationship was precarious to begin with. She was still technically waiting for her missionary, Elder Boswell, and still hanging out with his family on a weekly basis, presumably in preparation for when she would become one of them—and so I was in constant competition with him *in absentia*. I wanted to win. Possibly even more than I wanted to date Desiree, I wanted to win.

I reasoned that Desiree and her missionary, whom her family liked, had been entirely chaste, otherwise he wouldn't have been able to be a missionary. But if she had been virtuous with her last boyfriend, it meant that if we got too handsy it would have everything to do with me. I must be weaker than he had been, and I had been on my mission. Plus, as the man, I was the priesthood holder in our relationship. That meant that I was responsible for the spiritual well-being of our unit, just as it would be in a marriage. And because I had been to the temple, I had made some serious promises to Heavenly Father. If I had fornicated before I was endowed, it would have been serious but it wouldn't have put my membership in jeopardy. Now that I had covenanted in the temple to always obey the law of chastity, breaking that oath could've meant excommunication from the Church.

I was pretty sure, anyway.

As with everything, it came down to desire. God "granteth unto men according to their desire, whether it be unto death or unto life."* So why had this young lady come into my life? Clearly I desired it. I thought I desired righteousness, but after a few weeks of dating, when Desiree succeeded at opening my

---

* Alma 29:4.

fly, I obviously wanted something else. How should I know what I really desired when different parts of me clearly wanted different things? What did I really want? I wanted to be good. I wanted to repent.

But maybe I wanted to have sex more?

We still hadn't technically broken the law of chastity, but we were finding new ways to bend and test it. In that area alone, I was like a mob lawyer, carving out loopholes and finding hitherto unseen shades of guilt and innocence.

It was all bullshit and I knew it. Heavenly Father didn't split hairs. There was no caveat at the beginning of his law of chastity stipulating that so long as I didn't have an orgasm I didn't sin. Getting naked in bed with Desiree wasn't *good*, but if my penis remained outside of her vagina, and I didn't come, maybe it wasn't a serious sin. And if it wasn't a serious sin, I wouldn't have to talk to a bishop about it.

Like her dad.

The purpose of the sacrament was to give members the opportunity to renew the covenant they made when they were baptized. It's not a saving ordinance, but it's salvation-adjacent. When taken worthily, it can be a means of starting each new week with a clean slate.

By eating the bread and drinking the water, we promise to always keep Heavenly Father's commandments, and remember Jesus. In return we are promised the Spirit. It doesn't explicitly say that all our sins are forgiven when we take the sacrament, but it's implied. That's only when the sacrament is taken worthily, though.

After I started dating Desiree, I stopped taking the sacrament in church on Sundays. I always felt unworthy; I knew I wasn't living up to my commitment to Heavenly Father.

Desiree always took the sacrament, even when I didn't. It wasn't my place to suggest she do otherwise, but I was sometimes disappointed she didn't follow my example. I wanted to feel like we were both tortured by our weakness of the flesh, that it wasn't just me. Because if she didn't feel guilty about what we were doing, did she really have a testimony? These things were intrinsically connected. The more you believed in the rightness of the gospel, the more saddened you were about sin. Plus, what hope did we have of ever not sinning if she didn't care?

Desiree said she cared about remaining chaste. But then, next time I wanted to stop our makeout session, she'd get offended. And not just emotionally. Sometimes I would stop us mid-makeout, when we were pressing against each other, and she'd close her eyes and grimace tightly, then move away as if in great pain. She would be fine, she said, it was just that if a woman had to stop abruptly after she got aroused, it could be very painful. I had never heard that explanation before, but what did I know?

More and more, it seemed like marriage would be the only way out of sin, but I knew the Hoopers wouldn't accept anything but a temple marriage. And with how quickly things were progressing, that seemed impossible. One has to be living all the rules of the Church for at least a year to go to the temple, and neither of us was worthy. Having cupped her breasts once, how would I now stop? Now that we knew the bliss that was dry humping, there was no way to put that knowledge back in Pandora's box. We were heading down the road to fornication, and turning around would take superhuman willpower.

There was also the fact that I didn't know if I wanted to

marry Desiree. Which, of course, made everything worse. Without marriage, was I just going to sully and degrade Desiree and then, what, leave her?

From his seat on the stand, Bishop Hooper had an unobstructed view of Desiree on the Sunday she made the decision not to take the sacrament. I didn't take it either, of course. We were sitting together, so he also saw me not take it. Did he decide right then that he needed to speak with us that day? Did he feel prompted by the Spirit? Did he say a silent prayer to know what, if anything, he should do? Did he wrestle with his decision throughout sacrament meeting? If he had seen one of the other couples in the ward skip the sacrament, would he have talked to them that day? Did that occur to him? Was he thinking as a father, or as a bishop?

Bishop Hooper had Desiree pulled out of Relief Society, the last block of church. Meanwhile, his executive secretary informed me in priesthood class that the bishop would like to speak with me too.

"He's got a couple of interviews right after church," the secretary said. We were in a YSA ward, so the executive secretary was only a little older than me. I had started attending Desiree's ward, and I had been enough times to recognize that Bishop Hooper very clearly had favourites in the ward, mostly people who had grown up with his kids. The executive secretary was one of Bishop Hooper's favourites. "But you shouldn't have to wait long. Is that cool?"

I said that it was, though I immediately felt sick to my stomach. The executive secretary never knew why the bishop wanted to speak with people. Nor did he ask why people wanted to speak with the bishop when they called him to set up an appointment.

I met up with Desiree in the foyer after church. There were two foyers, one on either side of the chapel. They looked exactly the same, the same floral-print loveseat, the same velvet chairs. The only difference was the prints on the wall. One side had resurrected Jesus appearing to Mary Magdalene, the other had Jesus standing in a pillar of light with Heavenly Father, speaking to Joseph Smith. We were on that side since that was where Bishop Hooper's office was. Desiree had been crying.

"Did your dad talk to you?" I asked.

"It was fine. It was good," she said. "Have you?"

"I'm meeting with him now," I said. "As soon as he's done with a couple of appointments."

In between appointments, Bishop Hooper came out of his office and chatted with ward members. He always seemed chuffed to be talking to young adults. I imagined him not being very popular growing up, and relishing in the power his position brought him now. I didn't know if that was the case—maybe he was the life of every party when he was a young man, back when he hadn't yet joined the Church, but I couldn't picture it. He wasn't particularly funny, or sharp. Not that I observed when I was at his house, anyway, and I was there often. But now, look, see how many people—young, vibrant, happy people—wanted to speak with him. They teased and joked with him, buttering him up.

Watching Bishop Hooper operate, I thought about how one of the purposes of life, one not covered in the plan of salvation, must be to find some place where you feel important. And wasn't the Church great, because it offered that opportunity to people who might otherwise never feel that way? Being a bishop was like a second full-time job, and there was no payment of any kind, but it gave so many men the chance to be a little famous, to be celebrated. YSA bishops are usually called for three years. I pictured Bishop Hooper deflating once he was released in a year or two. When would he ever be this important again? The man was an accountant for a cardboard box company.

I didn't think to ask Desiree what she had told her dad. I assumed, because it was her dad, that she hadn't told him anything.

Desiree and I were standing by the glass doors.

"Did I ever tell you about what happened with these doors when I was six?"

Desiree shook her head. "What are you talking about?"

"These doors. Windows and doors. When I was six—I think it was even this same building, actually. We were in Calgary to see *Les Misérables* that night. But of course we still went to church before."

"Naturally."

"And I was excited to leave the building, so I went to run through the open doors. Only I didn't realize that the windows weren't doors. And that they weren't open. So I ran full speed into the glass. Got a bloody nose and a tiny scar on my forehead."

"Aw, you were like a bird."

"Seriously."

Bishop Hooper caught my eye then and nodded.

"Looks like it's my turn," I said. "Wish me luck!"

"It'll be fine," she said. I wondered if she believed that.

Above Bishop Hooper's desk was a picture of the Cardston Alberta Temple. On the wall facing the desk was an org chart of all the jobs in the ward, with a picture of whoever held each calling. But for the lack of red thread, it looked like someone's diagram of a conspiracy theory. We were all in on it, and it went straight to the top. I remembered when my photo was taken. It was my first Sunday in the YSA ward after my mission. I looked like I had just come from a rough day at the office. My tie was loosened and the top button of my white shirt was undone, but I can't deny that there was some brightness in my eyes in the photo. Zeal. I imagined I had lost that light now.

I sat down in one of the chairs directly across from the bishop's desk.

"Take a seat," he said, after I already had.

"This alright?"

"Wherever," he said.

What was the appropriate way to sit in such a moment? Should I try to project confidence and maturity, like this was a meeting between equals? Or would I try to show humility in my posture: not hunched exactly, but with rounded shoulders, hands clasped in front of me, almost as if I expected to be asked to pray. Without realizing it, I crossed my arms. I wanted to show contrition, but probably came off as belligerent. As he closed the door and returned to his side of the desk, Bishop Hooper started like a cop at a traffic stop.

"I suppose you know why I wanted to see you?" He sat down and leaned back in his leather chair. He looked small. There was a clear delineation in the Hooper family between which children looked like their mother and which had their father's features. Desiree was clearly her father's daughter. She had the height, the pale skin tone, everything but her eyes, which may or may not have come from her mother, but certainly didn't come from Bishop Hooper. His were small, nearly lupine. Or maybe they were just narrowed every time he looked at me.

"Probably," I said.

"I'd noticed over the past few months you haven't really taken the sacrament. I don't know if it's every week, but I know you skip it more than you take it. Is that fair to say?"

I nodded. There was nothing unfair about him saying that.

"And I thought many times that I should talk to you about it. Now, I realize those were promptings by the Spirit, and I ignored them. I ignored warnings that the Lord was trying to give me. That's my fault. I take responsibility for that failure."

He paused and I wondered if he was expecting me to say something. *Aw, don't beat yourself up about it?*

"I think I also assumed that you weren't taking the sacrament for the reason a lot of people skip the sacrament, because of inappropriate, uh, media, the pornography." I had tried to nod vigorously enough that Bishop Hooper would move on before saying the word pornography. It's an ugly, clunky word when anyone says it—porn is a much nicer, warmer word—but when Bishop Hooper said it, he always sounded like he was saying it for the first time. Like his mouth had trouble getting around it. I didn't know if we had the same definition of pornography. He was right, though. Even if I hadn't been sinning with Desiree, I would have been declining the sacrament because of my habit of looking at pictures from *Playboy*.

"I guess I decided it wasn't my business because I'm not technically your bishop," he went on. "I assumed you would talk to Bishop Kepler about it. You know, the Lord's hand is outstretched, but He can't pick you up. He stands at the door and knocks, but we still have to get off the couch and answer the door. If you were still struggling with pornography, you should have spoken with me about it, or Bishop Kepler."

He kept almost calling it fornography. I assumed this was because he was jumbling it together with fornication. The word fornication was on the tip of his tongue.

"But now I see that it isn't just your problem, is it?" Bishop Hooper said. "How do you think it feels to watch your own daughter deny herself the sacrament? How do you think that makes me look as a bishop, and a father?"

This was a detour I wasn't expecting.

"Why would anyone else notice?"

"Oh, people notice. The brother passing the sacrament notices, the speakers sitting on the stand notice. The chorister notices. Anyone sitting behind you guys will notice."

"Okay," I responded.

"But the point is, it's like an insult to me. It hurts me. To see her pass on the blessings of the sacrament, it hurts. And you've been on a mission. You should know how important the sacrament is."

That's why we didn't take it, I thought. But I didn't say that. Of course I knew how important it was: *For whoso eateth and drinketh my flesh and blood unworthily eateth and drinketh damnation to his soul; therefore if ye know that a man is unworthy to eat and drink of my flesh and blood ye shall forbid him.**

And it says the same thing in the Bible, too.**

"I wish you two had come to me earlier and on your own. It's so much easier to repent when it's your own idea. But I wish you had had the decency to speak to someone before you brought Desiree down, too." Another pause, to collect his thoughts.

---

* 3 Nephi 18:29.

** 1 Corinthians 11:28–29.

"Now I've spoken to Desiree, so I think I know the gist. But you need to tell me what we're talking about here."

I cleared my throat.

"Sir, what we're talking about is that on Friday night last, your daughter took my erect penis into her mouth and performed oral sex on it. But this already-grave sin was actually in addition to the several times she has brought me to orgasms by stroking my penis with her hand, both over and under my clothing, along with the many, many times we've rubbed our genitals together while wearing pants in a desperate simulacrum of intercourse. As you can imagine, though I've always felt horribly guilty afterward, I have been a willing participant in these activities. Touching your daughter's breasts, for instance, has been revelatory.

"Friday night was a little more complicated in that regard, though. It wasn't the first time Desiree had made it clear that she would like to perform fellatio on me, but I always said no and moved on. Which is what I did on Friday. I pushed her head away and said no. A few moments later, she attempted again and I declined. I didn't stop her the third time though. It was unlike anything else in the universe. She did not sin for very long, if you know what I mean.

"As you say, I'm sure your daughter has shared all this stuff with you already. But did she tell you how, afterward, she walked me inside my house? And then how, once inside, I broke down completely in her arms? The guilt and sorrow were immediate and sharp. I sobbed. She stroked my hair as I tried to gain control of myself. It was probably an odd time for it, but I asked her to please say a prayer. I wasn't worthy to address Heavenly Father, but I needed us to do something to start the impossibly slow process of repentance as soon as we could. I knew only Father in Heaven could help me feel any peace at that moment, even though I knew I wasn't worthy to ask for it, let alone receive it. I had just thrown away my salvation. My life.

"So I suggested that we not take the sacrament today. We had already sinned, and I didn't want to compound it by taking the sacrament unworthily, mocking the Atonement. I'm sorry I didn't once think about what that would mean for you. I was selfishly thinking about my own damnation."

What I actually said was, "I don't know if I feel comfortable talking about this with you?"

"What do you mean?"

"She's your daughter," I said.

"Therefore, what?" Bishop Hooper asked.

"She's your daughter," I repeated. "Why would you want to know?"

"It's not about wanting or not wanting to know," said Bishop Hooper. "It's about repentance. It's about not allowing my daughter to be unworthy of taking the sacrament."

"Right. We had already planned on talking to Bishop Kepler."

"Why would you need to speak with him? I'm Desiree's bishop," he said. "I think you'll find that the gospel is the same no matter what bishop or stake president you speak to. The consequences of sin are the same, no matter what. You can't shop around for the best deal."

"I understand that," I said. "But she's your daughter."

"Fine," he said finally. "But how will I know you've done it?"

"Done it?"

"Spoken to someone?" the bishop clarified.

"You can ask Desiree, I guess."

"Oh, believe me. I will," he said.

The meeting was wrapping up, but I felt like I couldn't just get up and walk out.

I nodded. "Thanks, Bishop," I said, because it felt appropriate.

When I got out of his office, the foyer had cleared. It was just Desiree chatting with the executive secretary. He hailed Bishop Hooper as soon as he followed me out of his office.

Later that week, I met with Bishop Kepler at his civilian office, in one of the many small conference rooms at the law firm where he worked. The room was white, with a glossy high top table and matching chairs. It was like a café in an Apple store, only with an impressive view of downtown Calgary. I didn't know what kind of law Bishop Kepler practised, but I was confident this room had heard secrets much more impressive than mine.

I told him the story I hadn't told Bishop Hooper. My efforts to dissuade Desiree from fellatio wouldn't absolve me, especially since I hadn't been resolute—I had not endured to the end. If I had shot someone and killed them, it wouldn't matter how many times I could have shot them and didn't. In the end, I had given in. Still, I thought it might at least speak to intent. The blow job wasn't premeditated. I allowed it to happen.

In the Robbie Williams song "Better Man," there is a line that has always resonated with me even though I was only a teenager when I first heard it. As the title suggests, it's a song about Robbie trying to be good, or at least better than he has been. When the song was recorded, the singer was battling addiction to substances and was likely having a lot of sex, too. In the second verse, Robbie begs the Lord to go easy on his conscience, because while he's been taught to take the blame for his mistakes, they weren't entirely his fault. And besides, as the chorus promises, he's doing all he can to be a better man.

Naturally, as a sixteen-year-old, I saw myself in those lyrics. I felt a kinship with the singer. We both knew vice, addiction. Robbie had alcohol and drugs. I looked at titillating pictures in non-pornographic magazines. But I liked the sentiment, and I wished it were true. I knew better though. Going easy on my conscience would be wrong. It would be dishonest. I had been taught to take the blame because it was entirely mine to take. That's what having free agency meant.

Bishop Kepler was younger than Bishop Hooper, probably not even fifty yet. He sat forward in his chair. He told me that typically oral sex is grounds for Church discipline. I wouldn't be excommunicated, but I could be disfellowshipped. That would mean I wouldn't be allowed to take the sacrament, pray or give talks in church, or have a calling, but I'd retain my membership and probably be put on a more concrete repentance plan. But, he said, being disfellowshipped would preclude me from certain leadership callings in the future.

"And I've seen your potential. I was there for your homecoming talk, remember?" Bishop Kepler said. I was crying at this point in our conversation, so he had adopted a more encouraging, fatherly tone. "And I think, with your potential, we don't want anything limiting you."

To avoid disfellowship, I had to do some things. I was about to move to Toronto for school. Desiree was staying in Calgary.

He didn't say I should break up with her, but we definitely couldn't do anything bad in the two weeks I had left in Alberta. Once I got to Toronto, I was to set up an appointment with a counselor at LDS Family Services; this person would help me with my addiction to pornography. I also had to get in touch with my new bishop in Toronto and see him the first Sunday I was there. I could still take the sacrament and have a calling, but I would have to give Bishop Kepler my temple recommend, which was like a licence to enter the Lord's house that worthy members keep in their wallet.

I nodded and cried some more, surprised yet again by Heavenly Father's mercy.

Sometime during my mission I had decided that I was going to be a journalist. I think I always wanted to be a writer, but I needed to go to school for something more practical. When I was on my mission, I noticed that people seemed comfortable opening up to me. I realized part of that was the magic of a twenty-year-old dressed like a supermarket manager. But mostly I think it was because I was an indiscriminate listener. If someone was willing to talk, I wasn't going to turn them down. I also enjoyed writing my weekly letters home.

I decided Ryerson University (now Toronto Metropolitan University) was the best journalism school in the country, since it was the only one I had heard of without doing any research. When I got accepted, it was confirmation that the Lord wanted me in Toronto. Maybe I'd meet a young lady I was more certain about marrying, and who wasn't still half in love with a missionary out in the field.

And I very nearly did. There was a handful of young adults in the ward in Toronto. A pair of sisters from Vancouver and their mom welcomed me into their little family, and I quickly fell in love with a girl from Calgary named Eva who had just finished getting divorced. Rounding out our group was a newly married couple who were also from Calgary. Calgary has a lot of Mormons. None of us knew each other before meeting in Toronto.

But as welcomed as I felt with this new group, I knew that I was harbouring a secret life of sin. It wasn't the stuff I had done with Desiree that made me feel set apart. It was the porn. As liberal as Eva and the Ashcroft sisters were, they'd be repulsed by my addiction to looking at naked women.

Because I was still technically in a long-distance relationship of some kind with Desiree—mostly out of guilt and fear of being alone—Eva was wary to get too involved with me. In response, I decided to more fully devote myself to Desiree. I decided to confess to her my struggle with pornography, promising the Lord that if she could somehow see past my weakness and still love me, I would definitely marry her.

When I got back from my first year of school in May, 2006, Desiree and I started up again as if no time had passed. While I was away in Toronto, she had moved into a basement apartment with her brother near the mall where she worked. Her brother, who had his own post-mission girlfriend, was rarely ever home. We didn't have to spend time worrying about being chaperoned in her father's basement. Instead, in our own domain, we were doing exciting work in the field of non-penetrative fooling around. It involved being naked in her bed—or shower—and moving together so that my male member knocked on the door, so to speak, but never walked in.

There were times when I was pretty sure I slipped inside Desiree, because how much better could actual sex have felt. But she always assured me that our virginity was safe because she had been "clenching." Even if my penis had entered her, it hadn't gotten past the foyer because the main doors were clenched shut.

I had never heard of vaginas having an anteroom. I knew that if someone had told me they were a virgin because of clenching, I would have pitied them for their ignorance and sin. But I chose to trust Desiree. I needed to, in order to preserve any hope that I could one day be redeemed. She told me I didn't have to worry.

I did though, obviously. I went with her to the doctor once. It seemed the adult thing to do somehow. Like we were already an old married couple living a life without boundaries. The doctor asked if we were sexually active. When Desiree said yes, I was as surprised as a kid learning the truth about Santa Claus. Disappointed, but not shocked. We never spoke of clenching again.

I kept thinking of a line I half-remembered from Shakespeare's *Richard III*, which I hadn't read since high school.* I couldn't recall the exact words, but the idea was that Richard, while trying to usurp the throne, had already covered himself in so much blood by murdering people that any more blood he took on would just land on blood that was already there. Like, what difference would one more sin make? That was how I started to feel with Desiree.

But ironically, even though according to the Book of Mormon, sexual sin was the sin closest to murder, I wasn't

---

* The lines are from *Richard III* 4.2: "But I am in/So far in blood that sin will pluck on sin."

feeling as bad about breaking the law of chastity with Desiree.* If we got married, then sex wouldn't be a sin at all. I still felt sick to my stomach if I really thought about how far I'd allowed myself to fall since my mission, but at least I saw a way out. I could imagine an end to the sin.

But I couldn't shake my *Playboy* addiction. It felt like there was no way out of that, and it made everything worse. I wasn't only breaking the law of chastity with Desiree, I was breaking it behind her back with pictures of naked women. Was my desire for sex really about deep feelings for Desiree, or did I just want to gratify myself?

I felt so stupid. Because I knew I could exist without seeing naked breasts. I could live a productive, morally clean life. Heck, I had done it for two whole years on my mission. It wasn't impossible, I was just weak.

Heavenly Father sent us, His spiritual children, to earth for two reasons: to get a physical body to house our spirit body (check!), and to be tested, "to see if they will do all things whatsoever the Lord their God shall command them."** Life was a test. And I was failing it. Badly.

If you were taking a test in school, and you were certain that failure was inevitable—would there be any reason to finish the test? It was just wasting time.

Except if I left a math test entirely blank, the worst I'd get would be a zero. But in life, I could score less than zero. If I stuck around, I'd just keep sinning, making it ever harder to repent and be forgiven. If I walked out on the test, I'd still fail, but at least I wouldn't continue making it worse.

---

* Alma 39:5.

** Abraham 3:25.

Quitting the test seemed to be the most rational thing to do.

I always thought Heavenly Father would be merciful with people who committed suicide. That was the Heavenly Father I described to investigators. Endlessly patient and loving. Desperate for any relationship with His children. Or like how Joseph Smith once described Him: "Our Heavenly Father is more liberal in His views, and boundless in His mercies and blessings, than we are ready to believe or receive."

But that didn't account for Bishop Hooper. He had been chosen by God to be a bishop. And he didn't like me very much. He would have liked me better if I were different, more like other returned missionaries: eager to get married, have babies, and join the workforce, preferably as an engineer, dentist, or salesman. But I wanted to be a writer, and to do that, I was going to a school in Toronto where there were hardly any other Mormons. I was choosing to be of the world, not just in it.

Bishop Hooper's respect was conditional. And that's how I started to see God's love. It was a notion that was easily backed up by scriptures, too. God loved the righteous, and hated the wicked.

When asked why He spent his time with prostitutes, tax collectors, and various other riff-raff, Jesus compared the gospel to healthcare: "They that be whole need not a physician, but they that are sick." When we taught about the importance of going to church every Sunday, I likened church to a hospital. We're all sick, so we all need to go to the hospital regularly.

Only now that I was sick, it felt like all the doctors in the hospital confused diagnosing an illness for treating it.

But I knew I was sick. And I knew I'd never be able to get better. There was only one thing I could do.

On a quiet night in August when I didn't have to work at the restaurant (I'd picked up some shifts back in Calgary over summer break), I started filling up the bathtub.

I couldn't decide how serious I was. Did I think about killing myself often? Of course, but who didn't? It seemed like the most viable solution to my problem of sin. If nothing was done, I'd just keep sinning, digging myself deeper and deeper.

I was a villain, and I had to be stopped.

So of course I thought about it. I had a sense of how I would do it. But it's not like I researched whether my idea would actually work. If I had been really serious, wouldn't I be more prepared? I didn't think I'd die. Not really. Humans are hard to kill sometimes. But if I did die, I was okay with that, too.

As the bathtub filled up, I opened a new document on my laptop and wrote: "I always thought I would write more."

I thought that was a particularly clever suicide note because it had two meanings: 1) I always thought I'd write more in a suicide note, but also 2) I wanted to be a writer, but, despite my plans, I never got around to writing much. I liked the brevity, too. No one needed to read a long melodramatic epistle.

But I worried about my potential audience. I didn't think about my parents, or my siblings, and how my suicide might make them feel. Instead, I pictured Bishop Hooper feeling vindicated. He had always known I was weak. He certainly wouldn't feel guilty. So at the bottom of the page I wrote, "This is nobody's fault. Though, if I'm being honest, Bishop Hooper didn't help."

Then I took five or six times the amount of insulin I was supposed to take at mealtime and I got into the bath. Low blood sugar was so unpleasant; I included the bath in the hope that I might pass out before I got too shaky. That fainting was more a side effect of having low blood *pressure* didn't occur to me. I waited for the insulin to steal every trace of sugar in my bloodstream. I closed my eyes and tried to relax.

The worst thing about low blood sugar wasn't the shaking, the sweating, or even the weepiness. It was the hopelessness.

People understand hunger, but hypoglycemia isn't the same. It's not just a worse version of being hungry. It's as though when your blood glucose level drops below where it's safe, a hole opens at your core. An emptiness. It's a vacuum that immediately needs and expands. And as it grows it becomes harder to stop. When it's small it's impatient, but as it grows, you shake. It grows and you're exhausted, sweaty, and then close to tears.

The Lord is pretty clear in the scriptures about what we need to do to have eternal life: "If you keep my commandments and endure to the end you shall have eternal life, which gift is the greatest of all the gifts of God." For the first twenty-two years of my life, I had tried very hard to do the first part: to keep the commandments. And not just the ten big ones. I was baptized, and received the gift of the Holy Ghost. I didn't date until I was sixteen. I went to church, lived the Word of Wisdom. I went to the temple, and I served a mission. But it was the next step I was failing at. I wasn't enduring to the end. I couldn't stay faithful.

And in the bath it was the same. I lacked the strength to endure to the end. Both in life and in death. Weak and shaky, I got out of the tub and made my way downstairs to the kitchen to drink juice.

I had a doctor's appointment a few days later. My mom had arranged it at the beginning of the summer, along with a dentist appointment. I was about to move back to Toronto, and it's not like I'd find a doctor there. It was with my dad's doctor, who was eager to check on my diabetes, too.

I imagined it would be like every other doctor's appointment I'd had since being diagnosed with diabetes when I was seventeen. Upon witnessing my nearly pathological apathy toward my condition, the doctor would employ various tactics to help me see the dangers of my ways. If I didn't smarten up and start testing my blood sugar levels, I would end up blind, footless, and impotent. The doctor would be both good cop and bad cop. This doctor, though, had some psychology in his CV. He asked different questions, possibly to get to the bottom of why I didn't seem to treat my disease with the respect it deserved. Did I ever think about suicide? Had I ever tried? I told him about trying to overdose on insulin, even though it felt irrelevant. Had I really been trying to off myself? I was just being silly.

Doctor Rogers was quiet. Then he said, "I'm afraid I have to tell someone in your family about this. I would be irresponsible if I didn't."

He didn't understand how unserious my "attempt" had been. But he was the same way with my diabetes. I was the only one who seemed to know how unserious my problems actually were. I just wasn't *that* diabetic, nor was I *that* suicidal.

"I mean, I didn't really think I would die," I told him. "And I barely had low blood sugar before I got out of the bath and ate a bunch of sugar."

"Fine, but that's not really a healthy thing to do. I mean mentally. Who would you like me to call?"

"I don't think you need to call my parents," I said. "My brother Sam, probably? Do I have to be here when you call?"

"No, no, I'll call when you leave."

I gave him Sam's number at work. "So, was I close though?" I asked.

"Close?"

"The amount of insulin I took. Was it close to a deadly dose?"

"I'm not going to tell you that," the doctor said.

"I suppose that makes sense. I was just curious."

"I know. That's the problem," Doctor Rogers replied.

I left with a prescription for antidepressants.

Sam didn't make a big deal out of it. He didn't call the rest of the family and organize an intervention. But when I met him at his office at the ad agency he worked at the next day, he broke down a little bit when he told me how devastated he would have been if I had actually killed myself. While I didn't love the prospect of only staying alive so other people wouldn't be sad, giving some thought to how others might feel about me gone seemed only fair.

On a sunny Saturday a couple of weeks later, the shift leaders at Earls were going on a scavenger hunt. There were two teams. Since I was working there over the summer, I was asked to drive one of the teams. I wasn't a leader, but, as a Mormon, I was a good choice. There would be drinking on this scavenger hunt and I didn't drink. Also, my parents had a van.

I drove my team across Calgary, stopping at various stores, restaurants, and libraries so they could run out and take photos of the items on the list. Then I brought them back to the restaurant. The other team was declared the winners. Not that winning mattered. This was a bonding exercise, after all.

With the activity portion finished, all of the twentysomethings crowded around the bar, ordering appetizers and drinks. With my Diet Coke, I observed.

Everyone was happy.

Latter-day Saints were always taught that there was a difference between pleasure and happiness. One was fleeting, momentary; the latter was lasting, deep. I was trained to look on drinking and its attendant goofiness with pity. Sure, they looked like they were having fun, but deep inside they must have known that this was all meaningless.

Next to me at the bar, a co-worker I had a bit of a crush on was making out with someone I didn't recognize.

I knew the gospel of Jesus Christ was the only way to find true happiness. I had borne that testimony thousands of times as a missionary.

Only now I wasn't sure I knew what it meant.

A lot of what people in the Church described as happiness in the gospel context sounded more like the absence of guilt and shame than the presence of some special contentedness and peace. And while I couldn't disagree that I felt happier when I didn't feel guilty, that seemed obvious and hollow.

I kept watching my co-workers laugh and play the way twentysomethings do. Basically every single one of them was doing things contrary to God's plan of happiness. And yet it didn't seem to be tearing them up inside. They weren't going to go home and think about ending things.

I was the one who knew the plan of happiness, the one who was supposed to know the difference between pleasure and joy, and yet I was the one who felt so badly about my sins that I wanted to die. If I had been born a non-member, my sins wouldn't be sins. They would be normal. Even healthy. I was twenty-three years old. It was normal to have sex.

I felt like shit not because I was doing and enjoying shitty things, but because the Church had defined certain things I was doing as shitty. The Church made living what any non-Mormon would see as a normal life sinful, something to be ashamed of. I wondered what it would be like to be able to just enjoy a normal non-member existence.

This kind of thinking was dangerously close to justifying sin. Was I looking for, and finding, an easier way of life? Wasn't this the path of apostates, sinners, and Jack Mormons? Then again, if I really believed that God loved His children as much as I said He did, then, sinner or not, did He like that I had toyed with suicide?

I remembered being on the balcony in Niagara Falls. Even on my mission, when I was the most obedient to God's rules I had ever been, or would ever be, I wasn't happy. I recognized that then, but, at the time, I also knew my unhappiness was earned somehow.

But damn, these kids at the bar seemed happy. I envied them. That wasn't the way it was supposed to be. But I couldn't deny it.

I wanted what they had.

Or maybe it's more accurate to say: I didn't want what they didn't have.

I needed to break up with the Church. For a time. I needed some space, a break from feeling guilty all the time. Maybe that was selfish of me—of course it was selfish—but maybe that wasn't so wrong. I knew we would probably end up together at some point down the road. But we weren't right for each other now.

Ironically, I was having a similar conversation with Desiree. It felt like she was pulling away from me. She was eager to try other things that were verboten in the Church. Specifically, she was ready to ditch the Word of Wisdom. She wanted to order cocktails with her meals. I wasn't in the same place. It caused fights. I knew I was a hypocrite for feeling hurt that she wanted to drink. I knew it made no rational sense to accept that premarital sex was somehow okay, but a beer wasn't. It didn't help that I couldn't explain it to her.

Part of it was simple: throwing away the Word of Wisdom felt like throwing everything away, and I didn't think I wanted to do that. The part that was harder to explain was that, in my mind, sex had weight and gravitas. Every time we had sex, we were flouting the eternal consequences for a moment of passion and connection. That was true love, wasn't it?

I was heading back to Toronto in a few weeks for my second year of school, and it just made sense to break up with Desiree. For a while, anyway. We both believed we'd ultimately end up with each other, down the road.

I broke up with the Church quietly. I stopped going like a dripping faucet. And though my parents knew I wasn't living the rules of the Church when I was in Toronto, I attended church with them when I was in town. When my sister Mary left the Church around the same time, she made noise about it on social media. And when my other sister Anne left a few years after that, when she was nineteen, it was after coming out, which was a risky thing for her to do while attending Brigham Young University. She could have been expelled if the school found out she had a girlfriend.

Compared to them, I left like a coward.

After graduating from Ryerson, I moved to Edmonton for a job at a magazine that covered the oil industry. I didn't mind the work, but I loved my apartment. The unit was one of two on the top floor of a mid-century walk-up. It was a one-bedroom with crown mouldings, real hardwood floors, and easy access to the rooftop balcony. The view wasn't great: just a parking lot and a back-alley intersection. But downtown lights were in the distance, reminding me that I lived in a city, near its centre.

The only problem with the place was that I couldn't really afford it. I didn't go hungry, but most of my paycheque went to rent. I didn't have enough money to furnish or decorate the place. The apartment was big enough that it looked nearly empty, like I was just waiting for the moving truck to come back so I could pack one final load. The couch floated like a kidney in front of the purely-for-show hearth and mantle. The bookcase stood alone on the far wall. Missionary apartments had more furniture than mine. And certainly they had more things on the wall. The apartment echoed.

It wasn't a short walk to work, but I liked walking.

And that's how I met the missionaries.

I spotted them as they walked toward me. Two children wearing suits, with sweaters of different colours underneath their jackets. They were delaying wearing coats. It was a crisp autumn evening, the sun still resolutely out, all the leaves fire-hydrant yellow. They stood out like two lost pallbearers, walking side by side without a casket. As they got closer, I wondered if the Spirit was going to prompt them to talk to me. They weren't stopping everyone that passed and one of them seemed to be stopping more people than the other, who would walk several steps ahead while his companion talked. I guessed that they didn't like each other all that much.

What would it mean if they did stop to talk to me? What if they did feel a prompting? What did it mean when I had felt prompted to talk to people? I still remembered what it had been like to be a missionary. There are times when the Spirit definitely does, in its still, small voice, scream into your mind's ear to knock on a specific door, or stop one person walking toward you but not another one. But lately I was having trouble accepting the idea that there even was one true church. I couldn't square that with a loving God. And I knew the Church had an answer for that—the spirits of the people who never had a chance to hear the gospel would be taught it in the spirit world after they died—but that seemed like an inefficient process. And it meant that Heavenly Father was totally cool with most of His children not knowing He existed. And I was having an especially hard time accepting that even if God did have a church He preferred, that that church would have been founded in a small town in Upstate New York in 1830.

I thought back to a radio show I had listened to a few weeks earlier, while I was driving back to Edmonton after eating Sunday dinner with my family in Calgary. I stumbled on the station late so I didn't really know what the show was about, but the guest was some kind of historian. And he was talking about a sex cult in the mid-1800s. They were all about free love more than a hundred years before it was cool. I shook my head at the historian's description of the crazy man who had been the leader of the cult, and thought poorly of the members who had been duped.

I did that a lot: frame other religions as almost too crazy to be believed. Every religion was so obviously kooky, except for mine. But now, possibly for the first time, I realized that how I saw other religions, especially those more on the fringe, was how the world saw Mormons. We were a curiosity, the answer to a trivia question. Had I not been born in the Church, I'd see Mormonism the exact same way. During my mission, it always felt like the Church was on the cusp of taking over the world. But I was realizing that Mormons weren't actually that important to anyone else.

And why, out of all men—presuming that He did indeed prefer men to be prophets—did God choose Joseph Smith to be the one who brought the Book of Mormon to light? Before he was called as a prophet, Joseph had gotten into some trouble with local authorities for claiming he could find buried treasure on people's properties. America was relatively new, and there were rumours that the surrounding land was peppered with buried treasure. It seemed remarkably short-sighted for a Deity to pick that fellow with a sketchy rep to dig up the long-buried gold plates. Why not call a prophet with a cleaner record, without a history of treasure-hunting?

But what do these questions even mean when you're talking about an omnipotent being? How do you put a probability on God? So, was it unlikely that Heavenly Father restored His ancient Church to the world starting in the Eastern United States? Of course. But also, who knows? On my mission, when people brought up some of the Church's more unusual beliefs, I'd talk about how we can't put God in a box. We can't say anything is impossible.

The Church was probably not what it said it was. But it was something. I had felt it.

I had settled on the idea that God accepted basically everyone into heaven, but he steered people toward the religions that would do them the most good on earth. As a theory, I'd grant you, it had a few holes. Considering the amount of violence that has been justified by differing faiths, one had to wonder if God was very good at sorting people. But it allowed me to believe that the Church was not entirely true while still providing a reason for me to have felt the Spirit so many times.

It was possible, too, that the fast-approaching missionaries could be prompted to talk to me for their own sakes. Maybe I was a lesson they had to learn. I couldn't think of what that lesson might be, but it was an option. I wasn't testing God to see if He'd inspire His two dorky servants to introduce themselves, but I was curious. What kind of vibe was I putting out? What kind of things was God saying about me?

I wanted the two elders to talk to me. If that counts for anything. I wanted them to ask me if I wanted to hear a true message about Jesus Christ. And I'd say yes! Yes, I would love that! I wanted it all to be true. I wanted to have all the answers again. I wanted to have God's power. I wanted it to be true and for Heavenly Father to prove it by guiding these missionaries to me. I wanted to have certainty. To know exactly who I was, even if it meant knowing I was falling short of my potential.

But the young men walked past me without so much as a nod.

As soon as they passed me, I turned to call them back. "Elders! Elders!" I was going to make it into their journals tonight. "You guys are Mormons, right?" I asked.

"Yes, sir," the talkative elder said. "Are you familiar with the Church of Jesus Christ of Latter-day Saints?"

ACKNOWLEDGEMENTS

I think it appropriate to offer my acknowledgements in the style of a Latter-day Saint bearing their testimony, something I haven't had cause to do in more than a decade:

I'd like to bear my testimony; I know this book is true. Even though it is only my name on the cover, I know that I could not have written this book without the help and support of many others. I'm reminded of a scripture in Alma, when a missionary named Ammon rejoiced in the miracles he witnessed on his mission, where he converted thousands:

"But Ammon said unto him: I do not boast in my own strength, nor in my own wisdom; but behold, my joy is full, yea, my heart is brim with joy, and I will rejoice in my God," he said. Then he continues in the next verse: "Yea, I know that

I am nothing; as to my strength I am weak; therefore I will not boast of myself, but I will boast of my God, for in his strength I can do all things."

And just as Ammon praised God, and acknowledged His hand in all things, I know that I too must acknowledge the many hands through which I could write this book.

I am so grateful to the Saints in Edmonton and Calgary who influenced me for good while I was growing up, as well as the Saints in Sarnia, Barrie, Kitchener, London, and Niagara Falls who opened their homes and hearts to me as a missionary. By that same token, I'm grateful to the fifteen young men who served as my companions while preaching the gospel to the folks in Southern Ontario. I hope that the ones I wrote about will forgive any mistakes I have made in writing about them.

I thank my Father in Heaven for Scott Sellers, my editor, who helped bring forth this record. And Rob Firing, who helped find it a home.

Brothers and Sisters, I would be remiss if I didn't thank Shaughnessy Bishop-Stall for the many times, through his optimism and faith, he made me think I could write this, or any, book.

Finally, and in all seriousness, I must acknowledge the sustaining love of my parents and siblings, who never asked to be written about, as well as the Kastoryano family, for their patience and integral support.

And of course, of course, of course, more than anyone else, I am grateful for my wife, Hannah, for I know beyond a shadow of a doubt that I would be nothing without her love and grace. Our kids aren't half bad either.

I am reminded of one final thought from the Book of Mormon. It's found on the title page: "And now, if there are faults they are the mistakes of men." Ain't that the truth.

I say these things in the name of Penguin Canada, my publisher, amen.

Greg Hudson
August 2025

GREG HUDSON is an award-winning journalist who has written for a number of publications, including *Toronto Life*, *Sharp*, and *Fashion*. He lives in Toronto.